THE
COMING
GLOBAL
BOOM

THE
COMING
GLOBAL
BOOM

How to Benefit Now from Tomorrow's Dynamic World Economy

Charles R. Morris

BANTAM BOOKS
NEW YORK • TORONTO • LONDON • SYDNEY • AUCKLAND

THE COMING GLOBAL BOOM

Bantam hardcover edition / June 1990
Bantam trade paperback edition / February 1991

ISBN 0-553-35311-X

Published simultaneously in the United States and Canada

---

*Bantam Books are published by Bantam Books, a division of Bantam
Doubleday Dell Publishing Group, Inc. Its trademark, consisting of the words
"Bantam Books" and the portrayal of a rooster, is Registered in U.S. Patent
and Trademark Office and in other countries. Marca Registrada. Bantam
Books, 666 Fifth Avenue, New York, New York 10103.*

PRINTED IN THE UNITED STATES OF AMERICA

FFG 0 9 8 7 6 5 4 3 2 1

ACKNOWLEDGMENTS

A special word of thanks to Andrew Kerr, my business partner at Devonshire Partners for a long list of helpful criticisms and suggestions. Feisel Nanji and John Tracey at Devonshire were also particularly helpful. Thanks also to Doug Love of Matrix Capital Management, Rita Hamilton at Comstock Partners, Sam Katz of the Blackstone Group, and Ricky Gukal of the Columbia School of Business; and thanks to my agents, Tim Seldes and Miriam Altschuler, and to Charles Michener, my editor at Bantam. A large number of people in a number of companies went out of their way to provide materials, make themselves available for interviews, or otherwise assist in the project. I thank them all.

Portions of this book appeared in substantially different form in *The New York Times Magazine* and *The Atlantic Monthly*. I benefited greatly from the superb editorial staffs at both publications. Finally, a special thanks to my wife Beverly, who makes these projects much easier than they probably ought to be.

CONTENTS

Introduction

A SUMMARY OF THE ARGUMENT

A Culture of Pessimism

Pessimism is the new cottage industry in America. Almost every day someone identifies a new impending catastrophe—the budget deficit, America's "international debt," the junk bond overhang, the savings and loan crisis, the loss of American competitiveness—the list goes on and on. Ravi Batra's books warning of a thunderous six-year depression to start just about now, have been runaway bestsellers. Batra says that the "theory of social cycles" developed by an obscure Indian historian named P. R. Sarkar proves that we are heading for a total collapse in commerce and prices, an arms-flailing free fall into the economic abyss. The best place for your money, according to Batra, is a safe-deposit box or a mattress. Paul Erdman, the Swiss banker turned novelist and prognosticator, warned us about "the Panic of '89" and counsels investors not to buy stocks until the Dow Jones hits 1200.

There is a ready audience for people like Batra and Erdman because economists more in the mainstream, such as

Stephen Marris and C. Fred Bergsten of the Institute for International Economics in Washington, D.C., have been preaching the same story of gloom and doom for years. Marris and Bergsten worry that Washington's persistent budget deficits are about to cause a worldwide recession. Unless America gets its economic house in order, they warn, the future holds only a choice of horrors. Budget deficits will fuel reckless consumerism that will ignite runaway inflation. To head off the inflation, the Federal Reserve will jack up interest rates so high that all the world's debtors, from countries to corporate conglomerates, will be driven to bankruptcy and collapse.

It is perhaps not fair to single out Batra and Erdman or Marris and Bergsten. These are the same arguments that most economists make. The predictions of collapse have been coming with clocklike regularity since at least 1984 and, year after year, have been just as regularly wrong. At times, the predictions take on an almost desperate air. Remember the glee among economists and economic writers after "Black Monday" in October 1987? At last the world crisis was here! All the predictions had been vindicated. And remember the surprise when, just a few months later, it slowly became obvious that nothing of very much importance had happened. The stock market ended the year higher than it had started. Growth in the fourth quarter of 1987 and the first quarter of 1988 was quite strong. The doomsayers slipped back into confusion.

The argument of this book is that, despite all the predictions of catastrophe, the world, and the United States, are on the threshold of a long-run economic boom. The boom will last well into the next century and will be marked by rising manufacturing output and productivity, steadily falling interest rates, and a broad distribution of economic benefits.

The argument is a complicated one that draws equally from developments in business and industry, from changes under way in population and demographics, and from important trends in politics and government finance. I will set it out in some detail in this introductory chapter to help the reader see how all the pieces fit together. Stating it in summary form also helps show the large number of different forces that are converging to create a positive momentum of almost overwhelming power.

How This Book Came to Be Written

Before summarizing the argument of the book, however, it might be helpful for the reader to understand how I came to write it. I am a writer who has written many articles for newspapers and magazines, and three books, primarily on economic and financial topics. But I am also a businessman. I am a partner in a small firm called Devonshire Partners. We perform business and industry analyses for our business clients and for large investment banks. We also have an active merger and acquisition advisory practice for mid-size and smaller companies.

For some years, many of our clients have been manufacturing companies, of all sizes. No one could spend time in manufacturing companies during the 1980s without realizing that fundamental changes were afoot. American manufacturing was dealt shattering blows by overseas competitors in the 1970s and early 1980s. As I shall show later, it still has not recovered from some of them. But the lessons were taken to heart. One hears the same story in almost any factory today. Everyone, from the workers to top management, talks about cutting costs, speeding design, and making products simpler, about how all customers now demand the highest quality, and about the need to outproduce competitors from all over the world. Sometimes the talk is mostly talk; not every company is successful. But the change is fundamental, and it is one that is measurable. The growth in American manufacturing productivity in the 1980s has been quite remarkable.

Gradually, I became convinced that the changes under way in American industry was one of the reasons—but as we will see, only *one* of the reasons—why the economy has stubbornly resisted sinking into the economic catastrophe everyone has predicted. As I began to frame the argument for my newspaper columns and for articles in *The New York Times Magazine* and *The Atlantic,* I discovered that there was indeed a small group of economists who had been arguing in the same vein for some time and had formulated a great body of data to counter the prevailing doom scenario.

The "optimists," as I'll call them, are gathering a growing

body of adherents—among economists, businesspersons, portfolio managers, and professional investors. But even today their voices are drowned out by the din of the mainstream consensus. Ed Yardeni, the chief economist of Prudential-Bache Securities, was one of the earliest of the optimists and among the most vocal. He has been a helpful data source, as has Steve Nagourney, the chief international strategist at Shearson Lehman Hutton. Both have been generous to me with their time and their research.

But Why Has It Taken So Long?

The puzzling question, of course, is why the arguments of Yardeni and others have been ignored for so long. The mainstream consensus, after all, has been predicting a major economic collapse for at least five years. Such a consistently poor track record, one might think, would prompt some reexamination of basic principles, or at least a touch of self-doubt. The fact that such a reexamination has not taken place says a great deal about the intellectual blinders habitually worn by most economists and economics writers. It is important that the reader understand what those blinders are, because the arguments in this book attempt to look beyond them, to step outside the self-imposed boundaries that so frequently cause us all to overlook the obvious.

John Maynard Keynes, who died in 1947, was a great economist, much greater than his followers, the so-called Keynesians and neo-Keynesians. Keynes was the father of "macroeconomics," or the radical notion that economists could study a nation's economy *as a whole*. Previously, economists had studied price or supply-and-demand movements for individual commodities or industries. As developed by his followers, Keynesian economics taught that if we kept in mind certain basic relations between consumption, investment, and government spending, we could steer the economy along almost any reasonable path the government wished.

Keynesian economists came into their own when John F. Kennedy moved them front and center in the policy-making apparatus of his "New Frontier." The dazzling economic successes in the first half of the 1960s persuaded almost everybody, Kennedy included, that recessions were a thing of the past. With the help of mathematical models that supposedly captured the interplay of the economic factors Keynes had identified, Kennedy's economists thought they could "fine-tune" the economy to a steady path of solid growth and full employment. That preconception still dominates most teaching and writing about economics, although for at least the last fifteen years, it has been proven obviously, painfully, untrue.

But there is another tradition, one that is associated with an economist named Joseph Schumpeter. He was an Austrian, but did much of his work in Great Britain and America. He died in 1950 after more than forty years of teaching and writing. Schumpeter did not scorn mathematical models, but he thought they captured only a very small part of economic reality. The factors that drove a modern economy, Schumpeter taught, were deep, instinctual, pre-rational forces. They might be a burst of innovative energy cutting across the entire economy or a suddenly coalescing set of technological developments, new principles of organization for large-scale enterprises or major changes in consumer tastes.

Because of the sporadic, essentially uncontrollable character of the basic economic forces, Schumpeter taught that in the normal case, economies progress in fitful starts and stops, interspersing long periods of economic dislocation with stretches of sustained growth and development. In Schumpeter's terms, the decade of economic turmoil that began in roughly 1973 was a period of "economic dislocation," a gathering of forces that has set the stage for a new industrial "golden age."

The argument of this book is expressly Schumpeterian. The forces driving the coming global boom are not the neat, easily quantifiable variables, such as marginal changes in government spending, that fit so conveniently into economists' mathematical models. That is why the mainstream predictions have been so consistently wide of the mark. As Yardeni puts it: "Most economists don't look much at the real economy. It's messy and doesn't translate well to models." As with the "body counts" that were so misleading in Vietnam, looking only at things that are easy to measure means overlooking almost everything that is important.

One more preliminary point. I am *not* claiming that there will never be recessions in the 1990s. As this is being written, the American economy has enjoyed almost eight years of uninterrupted growth. One must expect that, sooner or later, there will be a pause, a breathing space to work off production bottlenecks or cool overheating in one sector or another. There may well be a recession in the first part of 1990, in America at least, although the East Asian and European economies appear to be in relatively good shape. But recessions in the 1990s will *not* signal the start of the long-awaited economic collapse. They will instead be short and shallow, more like potholes on a path of steady economic progress.

The Argument

The forces that are converging to create the momentum behind a long-run global boom are multiple. There are developments in business and industry involving new forms of organization and new applications of technology. There are dramatic changes under way in the demographic profile of the working-age population, particularly, but not solely, in the United States. We are experiencing the beginnings of a major shift in the pattern of household spending that will make far more capital available for business investment and research and development. There are substantial positive changes taking place in government finance in almost all the industrial countries, including the United States. And, finally, developments in world politics offer the promise of a long-term, albeit slow, decline in both defense spending and the drain of talent into defense research. The net effect of all these factors will be a continued sharp rise in global output and productivity, a steady reduction of interest rates, high levels of capital investment in plants and new technology, low inflation, and steady economic progress for almost all sectors of society.

We will look more closely at each of these developments in this summary chapter and then explore them in depth in the chapters to come.

Any one of the factors and trends I listed would be a positive sign. What is remarkable, however, is that for the first time in a long time, *all* of the basic trends are pulling in the same direction. These are the kinds of dramatic convergences that Schumpeter wrote about. No one could have planned it or managed events to ensure such an outcome. The convergence of so many positive factors means that they will reinforce each other—in economic jargon, that they will create a "positive feedback effect." Developments in industry that are driving down costs and prices will help inflation to drop. Lower inflation will mean lower interest rates, because lenders will need less of an "inflation premium" to compensate for the loss of their loans' purchasing power. Lower interest rates will mean higher levels of business investment, which will reinforce the drive toward lower costs and higher quality, and so on.

In addition, the convergence of so many positive forces means that no *one* of them is crucial. We could have a setback on one or the other front without endangering the overall positive momentum. The margin for error, as it were, will be much greater in the 1990s than it was, say, in the 1970s.

Let's take a brief look at the converging positive forces. In the book, I group them in three sections—"Companies," "People," and "Governments."

Companies

The integration of the global goods markets is an entirely new force in the world economy. Everyone knows about global financial markets. Stocks, bonds, and bank deposits surge around the world in nanoseconds, riding the twinkling green blips on trading-room computer screens. Integration of the manufacturing economy is an even newer development. Trade and communications have progressed to the point where consumers in the industrial countries buy everyday goods from an essentially global marketplace. The steady reduction in the weight of most industrial products is reinforcing the trend—a piece of silicon carries as much value today as a ton or more of metal did fifty years ago. The result is unprecedented economies of scale in research and development, materials sourcing, and global production balancing. When a company runs out of capacity in Europe, or anywhere else, it can quickly move in product from other factories around the world to cover the shortfall. Ten years ago, the company would just have raised prices.

The globalization of almost every major industry has also meant a rapid diffusion of high-productivity manufacturing technology, much of it pioneered in Japan. Paradoxically, it is the local nature of global competition that is speeding the technology diffusion. Almost all executives of global companies I have talked to stress that the main competition in every market is still *local*. They must beat the local competitors at their own game—make products that meet local standards of design and function but do it at world-beating cost and quality. To do so, they are moving their marketing and manufacturing into their major local markets around the world. American and European companies have been doing this for years, and now Japanese companies are doing it. The global drive into local markets is squeezing out inefficient management or labor practices everywhere. Local companies must meet the global standard or die. The result is relentless global competition on price and quality, a steady, even startling, worldwide increase in manufacturing productivity, and sharp increases in real world output.

‖ People

The population profile of the United States has been wildly misshapen over the past twenty years. Tens of millions of young adults born during the "baby boom" years of 1946–1964, unskilled, semi-schooled, and very unsettled, streamed into the job lines. These were the same young people who generated a burst of elementary-school building in the 1950s and crowded the college campuses in the 1960s. In the 1970s and early 1980s, they left school, formed households of their own, and flooded the job market. Not surprisingly, they played havoc with the unemployment rate. But they also lowered the quality of American work output: New young workers are by definition inexperienced. And they lowered the American savings rate: Young adults tend to spend *more* than they earn, not less. The populations of Japan and Germany, by contrast, have been much more heavily weighted toward mature adults in their forties and early fifties—in their prime working years with high savings rates.

Starting just about now, the center of gravity of the American population is shifting radically once again; for most of the next two decades, the age mix in America will be very much like that in present-day Japan and Germany. About two-thirds of the baby boomers are already over thirty-five. For quite a while, forty- and fifty-year-olds will be the fastest-growing segment of the American population. The impact of the baby boomers on the American psyche in the 1990s will be every bit as powerful as it was in the 1960s and 1970s, but in the opposite direction. Where their influence was once disruptive and unsettling, it will now be a stabilizing force. The working population will grow very slowly, if at all. As workers become scarcer, companies will increase investment in labor-saving equipment. (For most purposes, workers were cheaper than machines in the 1970s.) Unemployment will decline. Output, income, and savings per worker will all go up steadily.

The aging of the baby boomers is not good news for the real estate industry. In fact, one of the most important positive developments in the 1990s will be a shift of household savings away from real estate into more traditional investments— bank deposits and CDs, stocks and bonds. As unattached young adults left home and formed their own households, they helped create a boom in housing that has lasted for almost twenty years. The boomers weren't the only contributors. The second fastest-growing population group was people over sixty-five. And, for the first time ever, *they* decided to keep their homes instead of moving in with their children, creating that much more pressure on the housing market. Housing prices tripled between 1970 and 1985, and housing costs absorbed about a third more of the average family's income than in the previous decade. Virtually *all* of the much-lamented decline in the American savings rate can be accounted for by the shift away from traditional savings instruments to real estate assets.

All of the demographic factors that caused the real estate boom, of course, will be running in reverse in the 1990s. The numbers of new young adults forming households will drop rapidly. The number of over-sixty-fives will stay roughly flat. Marriage rates are already rising and divorce rates are dropping—both signs of a more settled population and both bearish for real estate. Some analysts estimate that most of the baby boomers already have settled in their permanent homes, paying off their mortgages. Home prices should be flat through much of the 1990s and will drop in some parts of the country. That's bad news for people who were hoping to making a killing on their houses, but good news for everybody else. A declining real estate market will free up savings and income, drive down interest rates and inflation, and create a capital pool for higher business investment, increasing productivity and output and helping to keep the United States competitive.

Governments

The American federal budget deficit is one of the great bugbears of the gloom-and-doom school of analysis. The other is America's "international debt." I will show in detail later why the federal budget deficit has never had the ill effects mainstream analysts have been predicting for so long. And I will show why America's "international debt" is not the problem it has been trumped up to be. In fact, far from being the world's "largest net debtor," as the gloomsters insist, it is not even clear that America was a net debtor *at all* in the 1980s! A great deal of the apparent problem, as we will see, stems from governmental measuring conventions and loose interpretations of technical accounting terminology.

But whatever the effects of budget deficits, they are dropping fast throughout the industrial world. As a percentage of national income—the only sensible measure—the American budget deficit has been cut in half over the past few years. The same is true of all other industrialized countries except Italy. England is already in surplus, and Germany and Japan are almost there. Instead of worrying about budget deficits, forward-thinking investment managers are worrying about a coming *shortage* of government bonds! As government debt issuance continues to drop, government bonds could become scarcer than hen's teeth. That will raise the price investors are willing to pay for them. A higher price for a bond is the same as saying a lower interest rate for the investor—just one more force driving down interest rates and improving the investment environment. By 1995 or so, the long-term interest rate may be as low as 5 percent.

Finally, there is the possibility of a "peace dividend." If the United States spent the same percentage of national income on defense as its NATO allies, there would be no American budget deficit. If the Soviet Union and Eastern European countries continue to focus on repairing their battered economies instead of preparing for aggressive war, our own defense spending will gradually drop. Defense spending is not all bad, in economic terms. The Pentagon virtually created the microchip industry, for example, and is keeping America in the forefront of laser research. But about a third of America's best scientists and engineers are engaged in weapons and defense research and development. That's too much, and is a major reason why America has slipped in the *mid-technology* applications, like machine tools, that are the cutting edge of industrial competitiveness.

That, in a few pages, is an overview of the argument we will be pursuing in the chapters to come. As I said, the positive forces are building on all points of the compass, and their combined power will be overwhelming. This is not to say that there will never be problems. As I have already said, there will probably be occasional short recessions in the 1990s to work off one excess or the other. And the United States still has considerable work to do to restore fully its global competitiveness, although, as I will show, it has been closing the gap very fast and still enjoys an almost unassailable position in many key industries and technologies. And there is good reason to worry about ensuring that all Americans, including the "underclass"—the less privileged and the less educated—participate in the boom. No era is without its difficulties, but during the era of the coming global boom, there should be wealth, resources, and energy enough to deal with them.

Finally, in Chapter 11, I will offer some thoughts on how you, as a businessperson or as an investor, can organize your personal and business financial strategies to take advantage of the emerging global boom. I'd like to emphasize that this is *not* a "get rich quick" book. The simple fact is that over the short and medium term, financial markets do not always behave rationally. The wild market gyrations from August to October 1987, at a time when the basic economy was ticking along quite nicely, are final proof of the irrelevance of short-term market swings. But over longer periods of time, markets *must* fall into line with the underlying global trends. The powerful new currents that are operating in the world economy point to some obvious strategies for personal and business investing to insure the maximum personal benefit from the coming global boom.

I

COMPANIES

1

BIG BUSINESS GOES GLOBAL

One of the safest rules of thumb in political economics is that the conventional wisdom is almost always wrong. For example, if you believe the daily headlines, the world trade wars pose one of the most pressing economic problems facing the United States. The president; his trade representative, Carla A. Hills; and the secretary of commerce, Robert Mosbacher, have expressed their grave concerns. Congress has passed a welter of trade legislation to lay the lash on "unfair" foreign competitors and to protect home-grown companies.

But today's real industrial battles have almost nothing to do with trade. Look at the automobile industry. Lee Iacocca's recent television ads for Chrysler blared "Here's to you, America" as jet planes streaked red, white, and blue exhausts across the sky. It was a clever exploitation of the conventional wisdom: Buying from Chrysler is your patriotic duty. But in the real world, Chrysler and all the rest of the world's automotive majors are frantically forming alliances—in engineering, in manufacturing, and in marketing. They are literally carving up the world, forming what in another era we would have called "global cartels" to buttress their positions in a tooth-and-claw struggle for global car sales supremacy.

3

The emerging "Car Wars" are not between national car companies trying to ship cars into each other's markets, but between a relatively small, and rapidly shrinking, number of global companies who manufacture and market their cars all around the world. None of the national companies that dominated their home markets just a few years ago has proved big and powerful enough to win the global battle by itself. And it is still far from certain who the eventual winners will be. But what *is* clear is that only a relative handful of global companies will survive, and it is increasingly meaningless to speak of them as American or Japanese or European companies.

A relationship map of the global automobile companies is looking more and more like a family tree of the royals in nineteenth-century Europe, when so many of the crowned heads on the continent were Queen Victoria's cousins or uncles or nieces or nephews. Chrysler, to begin with, has long owned a major stake in Mitsubishi Motors, one of the Japanese majors, and Mitsubishi, in turn, owns 15 percent of the South Korean upstart Hyundai. Some of Chrysler's best-selling models—such as the Dodge Colt—come from Mitsubishi, and the two companies have teamed up as equal partners in the Diamond Star joint manufacturing venture in Normal, Illinois, which will be producing 240,000 vehicles under both Chrysler and Mitsubishi labels by the end of 1990. Of the Big Three, Chrysler has long had the highest percentage of foreign-sourced parts in its vehicles. Ironically enough, even the planes with the streaking red, white, and blue exhausts in Iacocca's ads were made in France.

Ford has always been the most global of the American companies, with about a third of its sales overseas. Ford recently made headlines by not-so-gently taking over the British luxury car manufacturer, Jaguar, which tried to fend off the Ford bid by rushing into the arms of General Motors. Ford also owns 25 percent of Mazda, one of the Japanese majors. Mazda makes the Ford Probe in the United States, and Ford will soon be making subcompact Bronco trucks for sale under the Mazda label. Over time, all the engines for the cars in Mazda's Flat Rock, Michigan, plant will be made by Ford, and the companies are planning joint production in Australia. Both Ford and Mazda own a piece of Korea's Kia Motors, which produces the Ford Festiva for export to the United

States. Ford also has extensive partnership arrangements with Japan's number-two car maker, Nissan. The two companies swap vehicles in Australia and are planning a joint mini-van program in North America. Nissan's Australian operation also makes cars for General Motors.

Nissan owns part of Subaru, and Subaru and Isuzu, both Japanese companies, are planning a joint car and truck plant in the United States. The biggest shareholder of Isuzu, however, with a 41.6 percent stake, is none other than General Motors. GM also owns 50 percent of Daewoo Motors, Hyundai's major competitor in Korea. Daewoo is a little global company all its own: It exports the Nissan Vannette to Japan, it is making a GM Europe-designed car for Isuzu to sell in Japan, and it makes the Pontiac LeMans for export to America. GM has also teamed with Japan's biggest car maker, Toyota, to make Toyota Corollas and the GM Geo Prizm in North America and Corollas and Camrys in Australia. The GM-Toyota American joint venture has been expanded to truck production and will be turning out a total of 100,000 mid-size vehicles by 1991.

Honda has avoided ties with the American Big Three but is expanding its American production so rapidly that it is on a course to replace Chrysler in the American number-three spot. Its Accord model was the seventh best-selling *American*-made car in 1988, and Honda hopes to be exporting 70,000 cars from the United States by 1991, although that's probably an excessively optimistic goal. Honda's American operations speak of themselves as an American company. In fact, I've spoken to some analysts who see the power balance within Honda shifting to the American subsidiary. The company sells more cars in America than it does in Japan, and there have been persistent rumors that the company may one day move its headquarters to the United States. About two-thirds of the components for Honda's North American factories are sourced locally, although a high percentage of them are made by Japanese component manufacturers who are frantically setting up shop in the United States.

One of the fascinating public relations battles of the past year or so is the spat between Honda and Chrysler about which is the more American company. Chrysler has claimed that Honda's export program is lagging and that 92 percent of its own parts come from North America, a much higher number than Honda's. Both companies, it seems, are cooking the books a little. Chrysler's sourcing numbers appear to exclude cars that are *completely* made abroad, while Honda's export claims, as I've mentioned, appear improbably high. The important point, of course, is that lines of national origin are becoming so confused that it is even possible for two companies like Honda and Chrysler to argue about which is the more patriotically American.

The European connections are no less entwining. Some of the British Rover's best cars are actually Hondas under the skin. Nissan and Germany's Volkswagen share production in Japan and Mexico. Subaru and Isuzu both have production and import agreements with the Swedish Volvo, which has a truck joint venture with GM in America. Isuzu also imports the GM Opel from Germany. Chrysler and the French Renault have extensive joint working arrangements throughout the world and are starting a fifty-fifty joint venture to manufacture mini-Jeeps under each other's label in North America and Europe.

Ford and Italy's Fiat have a joint venture truck operation in Great Britain, while GM owns a major stake in Fiat's component subsidiary and is 50 percent owner of Sweden's Saab. Ford and Volkswagen have merged their Latin American manufacturing operations and dealer networks and are also manufacturing trucks in Latin America for export to the United States. Germany's Daimler-Benz sells the Mercedes in Japan through a partnership with Mitsubishi and manufactures cars under Honda's label in South Africa.

Most of the press attention in Europe lately has focused on the aggressive entry of the Japanese companies in anticipation of 1992, when Europe, by plan at least, will become a single, unified economy. In one of the more comical recent trade disputes, France tried to bar Nissan Bluebirds, made in Birmingham with mostly European parts, on the grounds that they were Japanese cars. The British indignantly insisted that they were good English cars and eventually carried the day. But, ironically enough, the only truly European car companies, with manufacturing, marketing, and service facilities in place throughout the continent, are Ford and GM.

America's Industrial Humiliation

The picture of the world automobile industry is certainly one of industrial warfare, but it has little to do with the trade furor in Congress. It's an interesting question why the conventional wisdom still sees the problem in terms of a trade war. I think the reason is simply that it takes so long for a new idea to become the conventional wisdom. By the time a new awareness filters through working journalists, their editors, Congressional staffers, Washington opinion-makers, and the business and industrial elite and becomes a generally accepted "fact," the march of events has almost always passed it by.

The current conventional wisdom—the prevailing gloom among economists, the focus on trade wars—is still a reaction to the stunning series of industrial reversals we suffered in the decade that began with the OPEC oil price debacle in 1973 and that ended with the painful crash of 1982. And, indeed, it took almost the entire decade of the 1970s for America to wake up to what was going on. By that time, whole sectors of the manufacturing economy had been either totally wiped out or brought to the brink of destruction. All of our basic industries—the automobile industry, the machine tool industry, the steel industry, the textile machinery industry—sustained gaping wounds. Slothful management, careless workers, outdated plants, years of low investment, and declining productivity left them naked and vulnerable before a flood of low-priced, high-quality products pouring out of West Germany, Japan, and the "little dragons" of East Asia—Hong Kong, South Korea, Taiwan, and Singapore.

Just a few statistics convey the speed and extent of the humiliation. In 1975, America's machine tool manufacturers were among the world's leaders; by 1985, machine tool exports were virtually nonexistent, and German and Japanese machine tools were standard throughout American industry. In just a few years the American share of world semiconductor fabrication dropped from 60 percent to 35 percent. America's share of memory chips plunged even more—from 85 percent to about 15 percent. For all practical purposes, America simply exited the consumer electronics industry. *No* home radios, black-and-white television sets, phonographs, or cassette players are made in the United States any longer. American companies' share of the color television market is miniscule. No American company makes VCRs or CD players. Industry after industry told the same story. "We were oxyacetylened," said one Rust Bowl executive—it was like being taken out with a blowtorch.

In retrospect, the storm warnings had been flying for years. American companies had simply grown complacent and lazy, fat and sleepy in their big home market, running big-union, big-management cartels that turned out shoddy products that cost too much.

It was precisely the kind of situation that Schumpeter's analysis focused on. Whereas most economists endlessly tweak their models searching for the micro-impact of this change in the tax rate or that shift in government spending, Schumpeter looked for the sweeping forces—what he called "capitalism's perennial gale of creative destruction." Schumpeter's gale hit America with hurricane force in the 1970s, coming mostly from East Asia, but also from European countries like West Germany and Switzerland.

American companies are still adjusting to the onslaught. But they *are* adjusting to it. The point of this chapter, and much of the book, is not that the battle is over—far from it—but that, as economic citizens, as investors, or as businesspeople, we have to understand the adjustments that are going on. If we remain imprisoned in an outdated conventional wisdom, we risk making mistakes of the same magnitude as those we made a decade or so ago, when business and political leaders couldn't believe that "cheap" Japanese cars could ever be a success in America.

The most immediate and visible reaction to the foreign onslaught was a flurry of antitrade activity in the United States. The economist David Hale quite correctly points out that Ronald Reagan, despite all of his free trade rhetoric, was "the most protectionist president in history." Tariffs, quotas, and "voluntary restraint" agreements were quickly put in place covering automobiles, textiles, semiconductors, steel, and a host of other products. The total value of American trade covered by protectionist arrangements roughly doubled in the first half of the 1980s. If anything, George Bush will probably be even more protectionist than Reagan. Reagan's protectionist policies always were grudging, because he really seemed to believe in free trade. Bush's protectionism seems more enthusiastic. I will have more to say about trade in Chapter 7.

But much more important was the response by American industry, which greeted the onslaught from overseas with a burst of restructuring and capital spending, union-management productivity agreements and "givebacks," and reformed manufacturing practices that have generated a sustained surge of productivity improvement, one of the strongest on record, in almost every basic industry. I'll have more to say about that in the next chapter.

Most important of all was the profound reshaping of American business leaders' view of their businesses, their markets, and the new global nature of industrial competition. The broadening of business's world view has been all the more radical because American companies, at least since World War II, had always *thought* of themselves as world players. Coca-Cola and Hershey bars were everywhere. But American companies had always attacked *someone else's* market. The nasty shock of the last decade was that there were global competitors, led by the Japanese, who could win the war for consumer loyalty anywhere, including the American home market. At first, businessmen made excuses, blaming things like low foreign wages. But Japanese wages reached American levels a decade ago. The painful realization of the 1980s was that American companies were getting beaten, badly and on a global scale, and that "low foreign wages" or "unfair trade practices," while they were important from time to time in one industry or the other, were not at the heart of the problem.

There's no way, of course, to date shifts in world view precisely. But my own guess is that business leaders—and not just in America, but in Europe and Japan as well—had pretty well shifted their line of vision to a global perspective by about 1985. (The Japanese, in fact, have been rather late to make the shift. Competing globally is much different from merely exporting.)

I believe that the nearly universal shift to thinking of business competition in global-strategic terms is having profound implications for the world economy, for government policy, for financial investors, for unions and workers, and for businesses, both large and small, of almost every description. I will attempt to explore what those implications are in the first part of this book. The most important prerequisite for that exploration, however, is to shake off the old conventional wisdom. American—and European and Japanese companies—are engaged in titanic competitive battles, to be sure. But they are not battles between national companies for home markets, and they are, most emphatically, not battles to see who can ship the most goods into one another's markets. They are global battles for global markets between global companies. Companies or countries that are still fighting the battles of the 1970s are not going to be the successful competitors of the 1990s.

The Rise of a Global Marketplace

Kenichi Ohmae is the head of the Tokyo office of the international consulting firm McKinsey and Company. For more than a decade now he has been preaching to his clients and, in an enormous stream of books and articles, to anyone who will listen that the most important economic fact in the world today is the rapid convergence of consumer tastes and quality standards throughout all the industrialized countries.

Japanese consumers have the reputation of being the most insular in the world and the most resistant to foreign brands of any kind. But as Ohmae never tires of pointing out, Japanese buy their fast food from McDonald's: Nihon-McDonald's, or *Macdonarudo* to a generation of Japanese children, is Japan's biggest restaurant chain. They buy their soft drinks from Coca-Cola, their instant coffee from Nestlé, their luggage from Louis Vuitton, their shoes from Gucci, their disposable diapers from Procter & Gamble, their razor blades from Schick, and their Oreo cookies, Japan's newest food sensation, from Yamazaki-Nabisco.

You will have guessed already that none of these products is exported from America or from Europe. Even McDonald's couldn't keep its french fries crisp if it had to put them on a ship to Japan. But global businesses and converging consumer tastes have little to do with trade. The point is simply that, whether it's the elegance of a Gucci shoe, the consistency and cleanliness of a McDonald's, or the quality and compactness of a Sony Walkman, the similarity of consumer preferences in the rich countries has created global markets and global business opportunities on an unprecedented scale.

Take the world hypodermic syringe market. This homely little product, a far cry from the high-visibility battles between the likes of Chrysler and Honda, offers a nice example of how converging standards have created a global industry and how a middling-size New Jersey company, Becton-Dickinson, took advantage of it.

Not surprisingly, the people who set the standards for medical instruments are doctors, and particularly senior doctors in hospitals, since hospitals are usually the place where general practitioners look for continued professional training and consultation. For a long time, promising young doctors from around the world have gravitated to the United States for their education, since America is acknowledged to have the leading medical training centers in the world. As doctors trained in America rose to senior positions in their home countries, they created a demand for medical implements of a uniform quality standard all around the world—the first condition for a global industry.

But it was a technological development in syringe manufacture that created the possibility of taking advantage of the global opportunity. In the 1960s, reusable glass syringes slowly gave way to disposable plastic ones. Plastic syringes are much lighter than glass syringes and, since they are less breakable, are much easier to transport. At the same time, plastic syringes can be manufactured much more cheaply than glass syringes *if* they are made in very large volumes. By one calculation, the production costs of a syringe drops 20 percent every time volume doubles, and the research and development cost per syringe drops 50 percent. All the conditions were there. There was an emerging global quality standard and new technology made it possible to gain very large cost advantages by world-scale production.

Becton-Dickinson was the first to see the opportunity in the 1970s and to go after it. They put marketing teams in all

the major countries to promote a uniform, high-quality syringe. To a large extent, it was "missionary" marketing, because the teams were actually helping to create a demand for
a global product. Becton-Dickinson created manufacturing
and shipping and distribution centers all around the world.
With higher volumes and better access to raw materials, the
company was able always to undersell the local competition
profitably. Finally, Becton-Dickinson mounted a major market
push in East Asia to cut off an expansion route for a potentially
formidable Japanese competitor. In an era of high-volatility
currency swings, the company was able to shift production
from one country to another to take advantage of the most
favorable export position. Today, Becton-Dickinson has the
leading share of a new global market, with a long lead over
the second-place competitor, Japan's Terumo. Most of the
competitors that were in the industry a decade ago have
already dropped out of the market.

The Dynamic of Global Competition

Syringes illustrate the fundamental difference between global
markets and traditional theories of international trade. Tradi-
tionally, economists thought of international competition in
terms of "comparative advantage," an ancient economic doctrine that dates from David Ricardo, one of the early followers
of Adam Smith.

The doctrine of comparative advantage is straightforward
enough. If Honduras, say, is good at producing bananas,
because of weather and soil conditions, and Michigan is good
at producing refrigerators, because of steel and energy resources, then *both* Honduras and Michigan will be better off
doing what they do best. Since companies in Michigan will be
very bad at producing bananas—at the very least they would
have to build expensive greenhouses—they should concentrate on making refrigerators and export them to Honduras
in exchange for bananas, and vice-versa. The whole modern
theory of free trade rests, one way or another, on the doctrine
of comparative advantage.

But the traditional theory doesn't fit very well in a world of global competition. For one thing, it tends to concentrate too much on resources such as labor supply or energy and raw materials. In the modern world, these are only sometime things. Just look at the worldwide flight of the hand-sewing industry to see how evanescent a low-cost labor advantage is. In the last few decades, sewing has moved from Japan to Hong Kong and Taiwan, then to Thailand, then to places like Sri Lanka and Haiti, on its way to the People's Republic of China, whose billion blue ants may take in the industrialized world's sewing till the end of the century. Low-cost labor was a useful entering wedge into world industrial markets for countries like Japan, Korea, and Singapore, but galloping wage inflation quickly wiped it out.

Surpluses of resources may even be a *dis*advantage. Part of the reason for Japan's early focus on energy-efficient solid-state consumer items was its pressing lack of local energy supplies. In a similar vein, spacious American houses allowed the early American television industry to concentrate on making expensive furniture-quality television sets. Cramped living conditions at home, by contrast, forced the Japanese industry to concentrate on compact low-cost designs, leaving them ideally positioned to take advantage of the swing in American preferences to small portable sets once the living-room market was saturated. Michael Porter of Harvard notes that Holland has long dominated the world flower markets. Holland has extremely inhospitable growing weather, but has the world's most extensive and advanced greenhouses. To overcome a natural disadvantage, the Dutch created a technology that put them at the top of the flower industry.

Comparative advantage in the new world of global industries is likely to belong to *companies* rather than to countries. Comparative advantage may consist of being located in a home country with a huge market. Boeing's base in the world's biggest airline market, together with America's enormous military aerospace research and development spending, has helped it dominate the world civil aviation industry. Or advantage may stem from a knack for high-productivity manufacturing and a nose for market trends, the winning characteristics of the Japanese consumer electronics companies. And sometimes it may be a subtle and mysterious skill, like

Nestlé's, in managing brands. Nestlé is based in Switzerland, a small country that accounts for only 2 percent of its sales, but it has become the largest food company in the world by astutely developing brand-name foods throughout all the world's markets.

But more often than not, comparative advantage is a simple matter of scale. Becton-Dickinson recognized that if it could achieve worldwide operating scale, it could drive down the cost of manufacturing an individual syringe to the point where it could undercut any local competitor. IBM can afford a bigger research and development apparatus than most countries because the worldwide scale of its operations allows it to spread research and development costs over a huge sales base. The cost of a modern semiconductor plant has risen from $50 million just a few years ago to more than $350 million today. No company without a global sales base can afford that kind of investment. The cost of developing a new drug has risen to as much as $250 million and can take up to twelve years. Only companies that operate on a global scale can afford that kind of investment. The world civilian jetliner industry is evolving toward a pattern of shifting alliances between a small number of airframe manufacturers, engine manufacturers, suppliers, and governments. In an industry in which every new development comes with nine zeros on the price tag, global alliances are inescapable.

It's the rush to gain a competitive edge by moving operations to a global scale that is forging the intricate network of alliances between the automotive majors. That's why only five or six companies will survive the global restructuring of the industry. The ones who can't achieve sufficient operating scale will inevitably be at a disadvantage in research and development spending or raw material sourcing. Or they will find themselves shipping cars to a major market because their sales don't justify opening factories nearer to their customers. Ford is investing mightily in a computerized design and development system for a true world car, hoping to push the scale game to a new level. Its new line of smaller cars due in the 1990s is scheduled to have the same basic design and parts beneath the hood, invisible to the consumer, everywhere in the world.

The frantic pace of alliances among the automobile companies is merely the vanguard of a trend that is sweeping throughout large-scale industry. Texas Instruments and the Japanese computer maker Hitachi are partners in designing the next generation computer memory chip, the 16-megabit DRAM. Each company has a unique but risky approach to cramming millions of tiny components onto a tiny chip of silicon without burning up the delicate circuits. Bringing a chip to scale production takes years of effort and hundreds of millions of dollars. A wrong guess could literally sink a company. The argument for joining forces and sharing the risk was too compelling to resist. The same logic is behind the joint venture between IBM and Texas Instruments to tackle the industrial automation market.

The list goes on and on. The Japanese earthmoving equipment maker Komatsu is a partner with Dresser Industries in manufacturing and marketing throughout North and South America. The American equipment manufacturer J. I. Case has exited the diesel engine market and joined with Cummins Engine for production and/or licensing of the Cummins diesels throughout the world. Whirlpool has joined with the Dutch electronics giant N. V. Philips to operate six major appliance factories in the Common Market, making it the largest appliance maker in the world. Philips has also joined with a group of American executives and the Taiwanese government to create an advanced semiconductor-fabrication plant in Taiwan, where Texas Instruments is also building an advanced chip plant with a Taiwanese partner. Ball, of Muncie, Indiana, has entered into a series of joint ventures around the world to market and manufacture its light weight containers for the global soft-drink market. And so on: USX and Kobe Steel, Armco and Kawasaki Steel. The misnamed National Steel Company is a fifty-fifty joint venture between an American and a Japanese company.

Almost all of the European, American, and Japanese pharmaceutical majors have entered into extensive cross-licensing agreements for one another's products. None of them can afford the research base or the marketing structure to take on the world alone. The need to spread drug development costs over a bigger sales base is driving the recent wave of drug industry consolidations, such as the merger between Bristol-Meyer and Squibb, and Merck's joint ventures with du Pont to develop heart drugs and with Johnson & Johnson to develop over-the-counter drugs. Even in financial services, the big Japanese securities houses, Nikko Securities and Nomura Securities, have made major investments in the hottest American investment banking "boutiques," the Blackstone Group and Wasserstein, Perella and Company.

GE has made industrial alliances an express feature of its business strategy and has created a division explicitly charged with seeking out partnerships to advance its core global businesses. A GE/Bosch joint venture in Germany produces motors for Ford and a GE/Bosch factory is scheduled to open in Tennessee. Two Korean joint ventures produce appliances and air conditioners. GE has alliances in Canada, Australia, and Japan to produce its best-selling locomotive engines. Sales and marketing of electrical products in the Far East is through a partnership with Fuji Electric. The alliance between GE and the French government, SNECMA, is the world's leading producer of jet aircraft engines, and the company has recently entered into a broad-scale set of alliances with GEC (no relation) in the United Kingdom.

The Local Imperative

Paradoxically, the toughest hurdle to achieving global scale is learning how to compete *locally*. Michael P. Schulhof, Sony America's vice-chairman, points out, "The stiffest competition in each market is *local*. It would be much easier if we could face off against one or two global competitors. But we have to win competitively in each market. That's why it's so important to have your manufacturing and product development in the local market. Once you're in the market, your global position gives you an edge, because you can outspend local competitors on research and product development and source components worldwide."

The imperative of marrying local presence and market sensitivities to global scale is one that the best American companies, like IBM and Ford, learned years ago. It's one the Japanese are just learning. Sony, the world's premier consumer electronics company, was one of the first Japanese companies to move production into its targeted markets as an avowed strategy. Akio Morita, Sony's chairman, is probably the only Japanese executive well enough known to Americans that his face could appear in an American Express ad, and in Japan he became famous in the 1970s for making more than 300 trips to the United States.

Sony opened its first American television plant in San Diego in 1972, when American television companies, still playing the cheap-labor game, were moving their production *off*shore. Sony's consumer hardware sales were almost evenly divided between North America, Europe, and Asia, even before the acquisitions of CBS Records and Columbia Pictures. Sony's American operations are now its biggest overall revenue generator by far.

IBM is probably the outstanding example of a true global company. IBM opened operations in Japan in 1937, and IBM Japan, with about $8 billion in sales, is the number-two Japanese computer company, slugging it out daily with the local giants, Fujitsu, Hitachi, and NEC. (IBM recently regained the number-two spot from NEC. The company was number one until 1981, when Fujitsu took over the top spot. Fujitsu now has about a 15 to 20 percent lead.) IBM Japan is also one of Japan's top computer *exporters* with $2 billion in overseas sales, almost all of them to other Asia-Pacific countries.

In Europe, IBM has no peer; its sales are higher than the top three European computer companies combined, and its Zurich Research Center, with two Nobel Prize winners on its staff, is one of the leading basic research centers in the world. The chief executive of IBM Japan is, significantly, a Japanese; virtually all of the company's top staff and all but two of its board members are Japanese. (Sony's American chief executive is still a Japanese, Chairman Morita's brother.) Homare Takenaka, an IBM Japan managing director, says proudly, "Of course, we're a Japanese company. Not only that, the business press consistently ranks us as one of the best Japanese companies. We always are able to recruit the best university graduates."

Philips is an outstanding example of a company that has

converted from a loosely coordinated "multinational" company in the 1970s—essentially a polyglot grab bag of subsidiaries—to a true "transnational" company in the 1980s. After a painful fifteen-year restructuring, Philips has reached what appears to be a successful blend of truly decentralized local operations with scale opportunities in research and development, procurement, and global manufacturing. The company has been able to maintain remarkable diversity of development efforts. Its most advanced color television sets, for example, draw on a nearly "endless" set of product innovations from Holland, Canada, France, Australia, and the United States.

Only a few Japanese companies have achieved true global operations the way IBM, Ford, or Nestlé has. Significantly, the ones that have, like Sony and Honda, were considered mavericks in Japan. (MITI, the powerful Japanese economic planning agency, was strongly opposed to Honda's entering the automobile industry at all, since it thought there were already too many Japanese automobile companies.) In fact, it is probably the *lack* of market power in their home markets that have made Sony and Honda such effective global competitors. Like Philips, Nestlé, and Sweden's telecommunications giant, Ericsson, they have been forced to develop their global business skills to escape the shadows of more powerful competitors at home or constricting local markets.

There is, in fact, a striking inverse correlation between success in Japan and success abroad. Matsushita, for instance, is by far the most powerful consumer electronics company in Japan but has never been able to translate its highly centralized management style into a true global success. In the same way, Toyota, the leading Japanese automobile company, is still relying, rather timidly, on an exporting strategy—in effect giving hostages to the vagaries of currency fluctuations and national trade barriers. The Japanese consumer products giant, Kao, found itself scrambling in the early 1980s to fend off Procter & Gamble in its home market and has never, despite repeated attempts, managed to mount a credible threat to P&G's powerful position elsewhere in the world. The rise of the yen against the dollar after 1985, however, and the threat of comprehensive European trade barriers in 1992, however, is spurring the Japanese, pell-mell, to set up truly global operations on the IBM and Sony model.

The far-flung operating diaspora of true global companies puts some perspective on the political furor over trade wars. Japan is still primarily an exporting country. American companies have long since ceased to view exports as the primary way to sell in foreign markets. Alarmists who go on about our "trade deficit" fail to point out that the overseas branches of American companies sell more than three times as much as America exports, and about seven times as much as the trade deficit. About a third of the exports from aggressive trading countries like Taiwan, for instance, come from American overseas firms. In fact, about half the American trade deficit represents imports from *American* firms. Putting a car on a boat to cross the ocean is much less efficient than making it close to where it will be sold. As major industrial companies—GE, Fujitsu, or European giants such as Bayer or Imperial Chemical—globalize their operations, the obsessive charting of exports and imports will become increasingly meaningless.

Indeed, McKinsey's Ohmae suggests that in the next stage of globalization, companies will gradually lose their national identities altogether. McKinsey's board of directors, he points out, is already as international as its business. Investment banker Roger C. Altman, vice-chairman of the Blackstone Group, agrees: "A company like [computer manufacturer] Unisys has a much stronger position in Europe than in the United States. It would be perfectly sensible for it to be headquartered in Europe someday." Curtis Tarr, the dean of the Cornell School of Business, semi-whimsically expects global companies to begin incorporating in legal havens, much as tankers fly the Liberian flag: "A country with good beaches and golf courses for the annual meetings and the right set of corporate statutes could have a bonanza."

Sony's Schulhof says he would be hard-pressed to point to any peculiarly Japanese character of Sony. The company's stock is traded on eighteen exchanges outside Japan and has been sold in America for twenty-five years. Partly in response to protectionist pressures, it is accelerating its program to establish fully integrated American and European operations, from research and product development right through manufacturing and distribution. The board, he says, even once discussed moving its world headquarters to New York. A major recent step was the appointment of Schulhof and Jakob Schmukli, the head of Sony's European operations, to the Sony board, the first non-Japanese ever appointed to the board of a major Japanese company.

The New Battleground

The political and journalistic penchant for thinking about modern industrial competition in primarily nationalistic terms misses the most important new reality in the economic world. This is not just an American error. Japanese and European politicians think the same way. But the global companies are leaving them behind. The reordering of business enterprise is one of those fundamental forces Schumpeter always stressed. The implications for the United States, or for American businesspeople or citizens, is profound. Some are good and some are bad. But if we don't understand the phenomenon, we'll take the wrong actions and make the wrong decisions.

To understand the new phenomenon of global businesses, we need to look more closely at the technological changes that are making globalization possible. The management challenge for any global business has always been the exquisitely difficult one of achieving truly global scale while at the same time precisely adapting to the tastes and dynamics of each local market. The old style of trying to sell left-hand–drive cars in Japan (Japanese steering wheels are on the right, as in England) just won't wash, although some American companies still have not learned that lesson.

Until quite recently, very few companies—IBM is a notable exception—have managed to meet that challenge successfully. But a revolution in manufacturing technology during the 1980s is making it possible for a very large number of companies to balance local focus with global scale. The upheaval in manufacturing technology is spurring what one analyst has called the "Third Industrial Revolution." That will be the subject of my next chapter.

GE-FANUC

If Normal, Illinois, the home of the Chrysler-Mitsubishi manufacturing joint venture, is the heartland of America, Charlottesville, Virginia, must be part of its soul. Its rolling hills are home to Jefferson's beloved Monticello and the University of Virginia. Madison and Monroe were born nearby, and the portraits of all three hang in the local hotels. It is also the home of GE-FANUC, a fifty-fifty partnership between General Electric and Japan's FANUC, the world's leading robotics maker, to make control devices for automated machine tools.

Why the partnership? GE-FANUC's American CEO, Bob Collins, a youthful-looking fifty-year-old who wears sport jackets and casual shoes to the office, says, "We were faced with a fundamental decision. Either scrap our machine-tool business completely or do something drastic. We woke up one morning to find out that our machine-tool business just wasn't competitive. We just hadn't paid attention to what was going on overseas."

GE's controllers are devices, really miniature computers, that carry detailed instructions for a machine tool's operations. GE's inability to make competitive controllers was intimately tied up with the uncompetitive character of the American machine-tool industry as a whole. The rapid decline of the American machine-tool industry from a world leader to a tattered also-ran is a parable of the decline in all aspects of American manufacturing prowess in the 1970s.

Machine tools are machines that cut and form metal. They are the basic equipment of almost all manufacturing industries. Cutting tools drill holes and cut threads or gear teeth, grind and polish surfaces, or otherwise shape or taper metal into its final manufactured form. Forming tools use pressure to bend, stamp, or press metal into a final shape.

A complex manufacturing process may involve hundreds of different machining steps to turn out a finished part. The range of sophistication of machine tools is quite wide, from a simple machine that cuts and stamps steel wire into screwdriver blades to the complex array of tools needed to finish a jet-engine turbine blade. The delicate curvature of a high-precision blade may have a thousand distinct measuring points with tolerances specified to millionths of an inch.

21

The decline of the American machine-tool industry was so stark and so precipitate that it has become a major exhibit of American "industrial policy" advocates, who have been demanding concerted governmental action to recharge American industry. As I will suggest in Chapter 9, I believe the calls for an "industrial policy" are misplaced, but there can be no question about the near-total collapse of the American machine-tool industry. The 1970s were a period of rapid change in the industry, driven in large part by technological advances that were pioneered in America. The American industry simply did not keep pace, conceding much of the world market, and their home markets as well, to competitors from Japan and Europe—primarily Germany.

Machinists have always been among the most skilled and highest paid of industrial craftsmen. Setup of a conventional machining operation—involving precise measurement, task sequencing, and tool setting—can take from several hours to a full day or more. Machine-tool manufacturers in the United States reflect this craft tradition; they are typically small family-owned firms founded by a gifted inventor or tinkerer, often a machinist himself. Although the industry is now changing rapidly, it is still composed primarily of small firms—more than one-third of the manufacturers have fewer than twenty employees.

The technological change that revolutionized the industry was the introduction of "numerically controlled" or "NC" machine tools. As early as the late 1940s, American researchers working under U.S. Air Force contracts developed methods for automatic machine setup by feeding instructions to the machine on punched-paper tape. For certain highly complex operations, like maintaining a smoothly continuous curve on airplane wing parts, NC machines were not only much faster, but turned out much more consistent work.

Punched-paper tape controls gave way to solid state devices and finally to computerized, or microprocessor-controlled, "CNC" tools. More recently, the emphasis has been on developing flexible manufacturing stations, or "FMS" equipment. FMS centers combine a number of CNC tools linked together to perform complex machining sequences. As each part comes down the machining line, a computer relays the appropriate machining instructions to each tool, selects the required tooling (different sets of tools are waiting on arrays of tool palletes), sets the tooling in the machines, and monitors and controls the operation. Advanced machines use laser gauges to monitor tolerances and to achieve levels of consistent precision that were never before possible.

Although most advanced machining technology was developed in America, much of it under military contracts, the Japanese moved fastest to exploit it. Japanese machine-tool manufacturers were organized much like the American industry in the 1960s, but MITI, the powerful Japanese Ministry of International Trade and Industry, pushed the firms into a consolidation and restructuring in the 1970s. The number of firms was reduced from several hundred to just seventy, with about a dozen large firms controlling most of the market. In conjunction with the consolidation, MITI pressed the firms to concentrate on specific subspecialties. Okuma, Yamazaki, and several other firms have focused on lathes and machining centers, while Okamoto makes grinders, and so on. FANUC ended up with almost the entire Japanese market for controllers.

Most important of all, the Japanese manufacturers concentrated on making large volumes of off-the-shelf machines—figuring out how to employ the advanced American technology to make easy-to-use midtechnology machine tools. Through most of the 1970s, the home market absorbed most of the Japanese production. Indeed, advances in machine tools played a significant role in achieving the high quality and low costs that powered Japanese export successes in automobiles and other manufactured products in the latter part of the 1970s.

As their domestic machine-tool demand was satisfied, the Japanese used their high-volume production base to enter world markets, offering very high-quality equipment at very attractive prices. Between 1972 and 1986, the value of Japanese machine-tool manufacturing increased tenfold and Japan's share of world production roughly tripled, from 7.5 percent to 24.2 percent. The share of Japanese production that was exported rose from 13.4 percent to 41.3 percent, and the Japanese share of world exports increased about sixfold.

The other major world competitor, the Germans, roughly maintained their market share over the same span of years. German machine-tool manufacturers had always exported most of their production and have a long reputation for making very high-quality, very precise tools. While the German firms tend to be small, they are closely linked through trade associations and technical institutes. They were, in the main, slow to adopt NC and CNC technology, but by spreading the costs among loose associations of firms, they were able to move quickly once the imperative was clear.

The American industry, by contrast, simply stagnated. It was never export-driven, so its decline in world competitiveness tracked that of its most important customers, the big American manufacturers, who were still basking contentedly in their successes of the 1950s and 1960s. Since GE sold their controllers almost solely to American manufacturers, their products dozed along with the general decline.

"We'd always considered ourselves as having a big export business," says Bob Collins, "and strictly speaking, we did. But our exports were servicing American machine tools in overseas American factories. Our industry never really penetrated the world market the way the Germans did or the Japanese did later. Our clients, even our export clients, were Americans, and as it became clear that the American industry hadn't kept pace, we slowly realized that our own products had become uncompetitive."

Under its hard-driving chairman and CEO, Jack Welch, GE had adopted a policy of exiting any business in which it could not achieve a number-one or -two global position. GE's controller business was clearly unsustainable on its own, but before making the decision to shut it down, Welch sought out FANUC's legendary chairman, Dr. Seiuemon Inaba. After more than a year's negotiation, GE–FANUC Automation was created as a fifty-fifty joint venture, with three subsidiaries, in North America, Asia, and Europe. Dr. Inaba and a GE executive, E. E. Hood, Jr., are co-chairmen of GE–FANUC North America, with Bob Collins as president and CEO. Collins and Inaba are co-chairmen of both the Asia and European subsidiaries, with a Japanese and a West German as the respective CEOs.

FANUC, GE's new partner, is a most unusual company. The personal creation of Dr. Inaba, it reflects, among other things, his love of bright chrome yellow. All the FANUC buildings around the world are the same shade of yellow, FANUC workers wear bright yellow uniforms, all FANUC products are yellow, and FANUC executives all wear identical yellow ties with their dark suits. "We actually spent a lot of time on that," says Collins. "No way were we going to wear yellow ties or build a yellow factory in Charlottesville."

More important, FANUC may be the most profitable manufacturing company in the world, with over $1 million in sales per employee, manufacturing margins in excess of 45 percent, and pretax income margins of more than 30 percent. It is the world's leading manufacturer of industrial robots, and its hands-off factories at its headquarters near Mt. Fuji are the epitome of advanced Japanese manufacturing. FANUC's robot factories make robots with robots: There are typically *no* workers on the factory floor. All operations, from materials handling, line loading, machine operation, and so on, are carried out entirely by robotized tools.

FANUC is also something of a maverick among Japanese companies. In the first place, it is a spinoff from a larger company, Fujitsu (FANUC stands for "Fujitsu Automated Numerical Controllers")—a true rarity in Japanese business. Thirty years ago, Inaba was having problems selling his ideas about factory automation to his superiors, but finally talked his bosses into putting up the venture capital to create his own company.

That maverick streak in Inaba has also made FANUC one of the most successful Japanese companies pursuing a genuinely global, as opposed to a purely export-oriented, strategy. With his company's sales concentrated in Japan, and of only middling size, Inaba decided that FANUC needed partners if it was to grow to truly global stature. He has sought them out with single-minded dedication. Currently, besides the partnership with GE, FANUC has partnerships with General Motors in robotics manufacture, with the German giant, Siemens, in electronics, and FANUC has licensed a line of its plastic injection-molding machines to Cincinnati Milacron, one of the largest American machine-tool makers.

The entrance to the Charlottesville headquarters has a glass case containing a replica of two small statues that represent the guardian gods of Japanese Buddhism. The statues are facing each other and represent "Ah-Oon, or the state in which two people understand each other so well that they can read each other's thoughts."

"Inaba came and presented us with the statue," says Collins. "There had been a lot of questions inside GE about how a fifty-fifty partnership could work. The American assumption is that one party or the other must be in control. But Inaba was serious about that motto on the statue. If you sit down and are genuinely committed to reaching an agreement, you can work out almost anything. It's something of a different mindset for an American company, but I've found it a terrific experience.

"There had also been a lot of criticism inside GE that we were 'hollowing out the corporation,' in effect, giving away our technology to FANUC, because we couldn't be competitive on our own. But that's really not what happened at all. I think we've both benefitted a great deal and pretty much in equal measure."

FANUC, in fact, had much to gain from partnering with GE. GE's strong European distribution system gave FANUC immediate presence in what was, for them, almost a virgin market. GE also brought long experience in computer-assisted design, or "CAD," systems. "The Japanese are well behind us in software," says Collins, "so they are not nearly so advanced as we are in CAD. Now the entire GE-FANUC partnership has standardized on the GE CAD system."

Most important, GE brought a solid lead in the next generation of controllers, highly intelligent "programmable logic control" devices, developed while working for the U.S. Air Force. PLCs vastly simplify factory automation by distributing the control intelligence throughout the factory floor, instead of relying on a central computer. Collins's own GE career includes extensive experience in military program management.

"The heavy involvement in military programs is one of the strengths and weaknesses of American industry," says Collins. "We lagged FANUC in mid-technology applications, but we are really very advanced in the high technology areas, for instance, in computerized cell controllers [controllers that can manage entire banks of sophisticated machines through a whole series of precision operations]. The Japanese are masters at linking up individual work stations, but we have the more advanced technology for controlling whole groups of machines at the same time."

But FANUC brought a lot to the table. "Their factory controllers are the best in the world," says Collins, "and they've held nothing back. We make all their major products right here in Charlottesville. And, of course, they gave us access to the Asian markets."

Even more important, in Collins's eyes, were the Japanese lessons in manufacturing and design. "They were much quicker to market than we were. Their manufacturing, marketing, and product-design people worked as a cohesive team, and their designers are much more cost-conscious. They design against a hard 'cost-wall,' and a tight schedule. Americans tend to add features regardless of cost. Partly, that's because we're used to such a strong division between engineering design and manufacturing and marketing. If engineering has come up with a really great feature, it will usually end up in the product, even though it increases the cost, or throws off our marketing schedule, or makes the part hard to manufacture—or whether or not the customer really needs the feature.''

GE-FANUC designs the FANUC way. New product teams include engineering, manufacturing, and marketing members. The cost and marketing requirements are spelled out well in advance and rigidly adhered to. Manufacturing design is built right into the process. When the design is finished, the team knows exactly what the product will cost and how it will be manufactured. "We spend more time than we're used to getting the specs right up front," says Collins, "but then the rest of the process moves so much faster."

The combination of Japanese-style pre-design planning and GE's CAD techology has made it possible for joint design teams to work around the clock—each night, the Charlottesville designers download their day's work to a satellite link to Japan and carry on the next morning from where the Japanese left off.

The centerpiece of the Charlottesville controller factory is a maze of shiny tracks with parts palletes (stainless steel parts holders about the size and shape of the little *Star Wars* robot, R2D2) trundling along on stainless steel rollers. Each day's manufacturing schedule is entered into a small computer at the start of the line. The computer automatically retrieves the parts requirements and assembly sequence from its memory and downloads the required instructions to the remote controllers distributed throughout the assembly line. As the parts palletes move from station to station, the automated equipment retrieves the required parts, performs its operation, and returns the material to the pallete to proceed to its next station.

Custom-designed printed circuit boards are assembled by a bright yellow FANUC robot, which looks like a one-armed spider with a staring photoelectric eye. There is theoretically no limit to the number of different board sequences that can be stored in the robot's memory. Its whirring arm plucks tiny parts from component trays and inserts them into circuit boards precisely as programmed, all in a blur of jerky insectlike motions. "The factory is designed to get high productivity out of a custom business," says Collins. "Most of the controllers we sell are customized in some feature or the other, so we need to be able to produce in small lots. Now we can produce any part in any size batch without a cost penalty. Most orders come in with a lead time of a few weeks, but we can actually get any order out the door within four days of receiving it.''

Labor costs at the factory run about 5 percent of sales. "We're not trying to achieve hands-off manufacturing," says the plant manager Dick Spinazzolla. "Frankly, I like having people on the floor to oversee the machines. For instance, we could download a day's work schedules direct from our order department, but I like to have a supervisor enter them. That way she's more in touch with what's supposed to happen on the floor and is in a better position to trouble-shoot. We're taking people out of tasks that machines can do better, but we're making them supervisors of the machines.

"In some operations—in a very demanding clean-room environment, for instance—it's better to get people completely out of the process. But most of the time, there's some mix of people and machines that's ideal, and that's what we're looking for here. Our workers need to be smart, but they don't need special technical degrees. We can train them, and I think they find the work interesting and challenging. It's certainly a lot more fun than just stuffing pieces into circuit boards."

Although the GE-FANUC partnership is still young, based on its early results, it looks like a clear success. Global sales are still well behind Allen-Bradley's, the world leader, but they are growing at a roughly 25 percent annual rate. The sales growth is spread fairly evenly throughout the world, with a slight edge in the Asian markets.

"Partnerships and strategic alliances are not a zero-sum game," says Collins. "More and more American companies are learning that. Both GE and FANUC are much further ahead in controllers than either of us could have been on our own. Learning to work in partnership with foreign companies in global markets is one of the real challenges for American managers in the 1990s."

2

THE THIRD INDUSTRIAL
REVOLUTION

The Drive for Productivity

I recently visited an industrial equipment factory in Europe. As I walked through it—I spent about a half day examining the production system in some detail—it occurred to me that the factory was a living illustration of the changes that have swept through traditional manufacturing businesses over the past decade. For reasons that will become obvious, I won't identify the company by name.

The factory, along with a marketing and distribution network, made up a subsidiary of a much larger company. The parent manufactured a wide range of heavy equipment, all of it more or less related but sold into a variety of different markets. The factory's management were intelligent, enthusiastic, and aggressive, but the factory was not an impressive operation. It was organized like a typical middle-size American or European factory of a decade ago. The production line was awkwardly laid out. Materials handling—transporting heavy parts from one station to another—was fairly primitive, with most parts moving by rail on handcars. Most routine operations such as welding were done by hand. Indeed, many of them could *only* be done by hand, because basic parts had been modified and rejiggered over the years. As a result, the pattern of the welds had become very complicated, too much so to be easily adapted to robotic welding.

The plant managers were aware of all these problems and had developed ambitious plans for gradually reorganizing the production process into a more modern pattern. But the reason they were still proud and enthusiastic amid all of their problems was that, over the previous few years, they had roughly doubled their productivity and sharply improved their quality. And therein lies a tale.

Just a few years before, the manufacturing operation at the factory had not been organized as a subsidiary business. Regardless of all the different kinds of equipment made by the parent company, everything was managed as though it was just one big business. The factory I was visiting, along with many others, made parts for the parent company's products—"just bits and pieces," as the subsidiary manager put it. The workers didn't particularly know what the parts were for or where they would go upon leaving the factory. They rarely knew whether the parts they were making were in short supply or whether they were making too many of them. Above all, it was very hard to tell whether they were doing a good job. If a part met a specification, it was probably okay, but the workers—or the plant management, for that matter—had no way of judging whether that specification made any sense.

A breakthrough came when the parent company reorganized its various product lines as separate businesses, each with its own manufacturing and marketing arm. The factory I was visiting was designated as one of the subsidiary businesses and assigned to make the *entire* product. It was a sea change. The actual factory operations hadn't altered much. They still basically involved the forming and welding of metal parts, then assembling the metal frames and purchased subcomponents into a finished product. But for the first time, the workers could see the results of their work—could see, in fact, how poor it was.

That was the source of the big jump in productivity and quality. All the finished products were assembled in a "hospital" at the end of the assembly line and rigorously inspected. Problems with the welds showed up very quickly. The workers, chagrined, agreed to stamp their initials on the welds, and the quality approved remarkably. There were still problem welds, but it became obvious that they were in parts that had been designed so that the welds were very awkward to reach; it was almost impossible to do them right consistently. One by one, those parts were redesigned, again speeding production and improving quality.

A happy ending? No. The real moral of the story is that the factory was still a failure. The workers were working harder and better than ever, but the awkward layout and the lack of sophisticated manufacturing equipment meant that the factory was still much too slow and labor-intensive. Their main competitor was operating out of a brand-new factory and running at almost twice the volume. All handling of materials in the competitor's plant was by overhead, power-driven conveyors. All the welding was robotic. Parts were made right the first time, not patched up in a "hospital." The competitor's margins were probably three or four times higher. Ominously, market demand was heading into a cyclical trough. The competitor was already cutting prices to gain market share and keep his factory running at top volume.

There was no way the company could afford the investment to keep pace. The management and the workers had been making laudable, almost heroic efforts to improve their output and their quality. Ten years before, the results would have been outstanding. But in the new competitive world of the 1980s and 1990s, they were doomed to fall short. Without a first or second, or at least third, position globally, the sales volume couldn't support the heavy capital investment required to build a world-class factory. Shortly thereafter, in fact, the parent decided to put the business up for sale, while its good brand name and distribution system still had value to a larger competitor fighting for top-tier market share.

The Revolution in Manufacturing

The industrial equipment factory offers a parable for our times. All the stages of the manufacturing revolution are there. The first step, of course, was to realize that there was a problem at all. Until the late 1970s, when they were blindsided from East Asia, American and European companies didn't even know they had a manufacturing problem.

Manufacturing was the boring part of a business. As John Kenneth Galbraith put it in the late 1950s, business had "solved the problem of production." Advances in industrial unionism basically removed manufacturing as a source of competitive advantage—most companies in an industry had standard wage packages, shop floor job categories, and often standard manning profiles. Top company executives tended to come from marketing or accounting backgrounds, with little experience in, or even apparent interest in, getting product out the door. Instead of worrying about quality, "planned obsolescence" was the order of the day. The marketing and financial geniuses discovered that the faster their widgets broke down the more they could sell! The really surprising part about the Japanese onslaught is that it took so long to happen.

After the searing humiliations of the late 1970s and the 1981–82 recession, however, companies began to take manufacturing seriously. Honest executives couldn't avoid the fact that the Japanese were making basic products better than Americans did—making them faster, making them better, making them so they worked the first time and lasted longer. (Almost all Japanese quality practices, ironically enough, were taught by the American quality-control pioneers like Edward Deming, Joseph Juran, and Armand Feigenbaum, as part of the American effort to revitalize Japanese industry after the war. The Japanese, of course, have enormously extended the original processes, although the annual "Deming Award" is still the highest mark of Japanese industrial excellence.)

After the recognition of a problem, the next step in a manufacturing recovery is focus. Old-fashioned industrial-engineering lore tended to organize all factories as if they were huge process flows. Each worker did his tiny assigned task, following rules laid down from on high. Nobody seemed to realize that quality manufacturing is very difficult if workers don't understand what they're making and why. The Japanese taught Western manufacturers that workers are partners in the production process. If they understand what they are doing, they can help figure out how to do it better. This is a simple and powerful lesson that transcends most of the how-to recipe writing on "quality circles" and the like.

The *method* isn't what's important. If tasks are organized as whole units and management is genuinely interested in what workers think, the shop floor will invariably contribute a steady stream of small improvements to the production process. Most newer factories are being built around worker cells. In the joint venture diesel-engine plant run by Cummins and Case, for instance, most assembly tasks are organized to fit teams of about five workers. There are rigid specifications controlling team output, but within broad limits, the team can organize the work within the cell to suit itself.

But focus also means simplifying what a factory does. Most factories around the world are becoming much more specialized, making particular subunits and getting very good at making them. This is not the same as making "bits and pieces," because the subunits are usually completely functional parts. (The increased specialization of global companies is such an important force in the world that I will devote the whole of the next chapter to it.)

The next, and blindingly obvious, revelation was that some products are easier to make than others. Western companies have always had a rigid separation between engineering design and manufacturing. The walls have been battered down to a great degree over the past decade, but there is still too much separation in most companies. As GE learned from FANUC, designing for *manufacturability* was half the battle. When the California computer supplier Plus, Inc., contracted its "Hardcard" memory system to a Japanese manufacturer, JEMCO, its engineers were amazed how long the product design took. The Japanese manufacturing engineers participated in every stage of the design process, insisting on myriad minor changes, and finally developed special tools for each stage of the production. But when production started, the line could run full bore from the very first day, with high quality and reliability. When IBM decided to regain market share for its low-end printers, it designed a printer for automated manufacture and discovered that it could reduce the number of parts from 160 to just 63. Manufacturing quality immediately improved fourfold.

The next lesson is, in almost every instance, the overwhelming necessity to automate. American and European executives, for at least a decade, persisted in misunderstanding the source of the Japanese manufacturing advantage. It was *not* low-wage labor. Indeed, following the realignment of exchange rates after 1985, Japanese labor costs have become considerably higher than in the United States or in Western Europe. The advantage was capital-intensive automated manufacturing.

And many Western executives, it seems, still misunderstand the *reason* for automation. It is not to save labor costs. In many industries, labor costs have already fallen to only about 10 percent of sales costs anyway; in high technology industries, direct labor costs are often 5 percent of sales or less. Cutting out a few more workers here or there isn't going to make much difference. The reason to automate is *quality*. Few workers, one factory manager told me, can resist "filing and fitting" when a part comes down the line that doesn't exactly fit. An automated line will simply stop until you find out what is wrong and insure that every part fits exactly right the first time.

But effective automation requires obsessive attention to work flow and material flow. Japanese attention to work flow is the key to their famous "Just-In-Time" inventory practices. Ideally, a purchased part is supposed to arrive at a factory precisely when it is needed, no sooner and no later. Western executives, so many of whom come from finance backgrounds, usually assume that the point of "Just-In-Time" is to reduce working capital needs. ("Working capital" is the cash a business needs to finance its operations while waiting for sales revenues. Since a company has to pay for the parts and raw materials it buys, the longer they lie around the factory before being turned into something that can be sold, the more "working capital" the company will need. The interest cost of working capital is an important business expense item.)

Taiichi Ohno's production manual for Toyota, one of Japanese industry's management bibles, stresses that the main purpose of Toyota's "Just-In-Time" system is *not* to save working capital, although that is a clearly beneficial by-product. Inventory, Ohno says, is a "problem sink." Zero inventory can be achieved only if the production system is running perfectly. The reason for pushing toward zero inventory is that it forces you to squeeze out production-line inefficiencies relentlessly.

Thirty years ago, a British motorcycle company executive, Edward Turner, visited Japan to find out why Honda and other Japanese companies could sell motorcycles so cheaply in Europe and the United States. The answers he found were both startling and obvious. The Japanese were investing heavily in fully automated factories. They were taking a long-run view of their industry and pricing their products to increase their global market share to the point where it was cost-effective to buy specially made single-purpose production machinery. The bigger their share, the more they could automate; the more they automated, the better their cost advantage and the bigger their share.

Turner wrote in his report to his company, "Having familiarized myself with the situation as it exists, I have been giving considerable thought to what we might do, and a course to pursue to combat this situation, and I must confess that these answers are going to be hard to find . . . although nothing I saw was beyond our conception or ability to bring about in our own factories." The problem, Turner saw, was the scale on which the Japanese companies were determined to operate. "[Our industry's] safety has to some extent been that it has never attracted big capital and big enterprise. We have never made to date, even in these relatively boom times, 1,000 units of any one product in a week consistently, whereas many factories in Japan are currently doing this in a day."

Turner, it should be pointed out, was primarily worried about the Japanese threat to British *export* markets. Although he predicted that the Japanese were "bound to make some impact on our home market by virtue of the high quality of their product and low prices," he was not the first Western executive to conclude hopefully: "Personally I do not think the Japanese motorcycle industry will eclipse the traditional type of machine that the British motorcyclist wants and buys . . ."

It took almost another twenty years for American and European companies to wake up to the threat of high-productivity Japanese manufacturing. And, while the record is spotty in many industries, I believe there can be little doubt that the awakening has been real.

Caterpillar, the Peoria, Illinois, industrial equipment giant, for example, is reestablishing its global dominance after enduring a rough and almost wholly unexpected slugfest with Komatsu in the first half of the 1980s. The company is in the middle of a massive $2 billion capital-investment program—new automated production equipment, completely redesigned shop floors, computerized design centers, and an entirely new research-and-development center. Production lead times and inventories have been cut in half, factory floor space is down 21 percent (shorter flows are faster), and work flows have been totally re-configured in almost every major plant throughout the world. Costs are down, profits are up, and the company is robustly attacking a whole series of new global markets in medium-size construction equipment and diesel engines.

Xerox was getting badly beaten by Japanese manufacturers like Canon in the early 1980s before it embarked on a total quality improvement program—simpler, more robust product design, heavy investment in automated facilities, "empowered" workers who are part of a problem-solving team, a much-streamlined management structure. Over the past five years, the company has regained almost all of its lost market share, and consumers, of course, have a wider choice of much cheaper, better quality copiers than ever before.

One of Xerox's productivity tricks that is spreading rapidly throughout industry is the practice of "benchmarking." Productivity teams study the best in the world at a particular function and adopt that as their standard. Xerox's shipping department, for instance, benchmarks against L. L. Bean; its billing department benchmarks against American Express. Chaparall Steel, possibly the most productive steel mill in the world, benchmarks against the shipping costs of Korean steel. "If we can produce for less than their shipping costs," says one executive, "they can get their production costs down to zero and we'll still beat them."

There have been failures, of course. GM's early attempt at regaining market position by factory automation in the first half of the 1980s was an expensive fiasco. By some counts, the company spent almost *$45 billion* in plant investment— "enough to buy Toyota and Nissan," said one wag—but succeeded only in *raising* the costs of its cars by $1500 a unit. One former plant manager told me that he was given a quota for robot installation from the top of the company, with little thought for the effectiveness of the robots. "Most of the time we had to have so many people to watch the robots and keep them repaired that we ended up increasing the number of workers on the line."

To be fair, for all the show-boating hoopla that surrounded the early GM automation adventure, it helped call attention to the need for a manufacturing renaissance and has served as a kind of negative textbook example for other companies. Caterpillar, for instance, has been quite explicit about learning from GM's mistakes.

All mistakes aside, the rise in manufacturing productivity throughout the industrialized countries during the 1980s has been nothing short of startling. Manufacturing productivity in the United States has grown at an annual rate of 4.3 percent, one of the fastest sustained run-ups on record. (American steel is now actually cheaper than Japanese steel.) After slipping badly three years ago, Japan has surged back to the head of the productivity league tables, with a 5.9-percent growth rate over the same period. And right behind Japan is Great Britain, for twenty years the living symbol of "Eurosclerosis." Europe's second fastest rate of output growth was in Italy— that's right, *Italy*—just a hair faster than the United States. France, Germany, and Sweden are clustered behind the United States, but with quite respectable rates of improvement.

There is no mystery about the source of the productivity boom. All of the industrialized countries have sharply increased their factory investment since the 1982 recession. As a group, the industrialized countries have increased spending for plant and machinery twice as fast as GNP growth over the past seven years. In 1988, total plant and machinery investment grew by 11 percent, after taking account for inflation.

Gross plant and machinery spending in the United States since 1982, as a percentage of GNP, is the highest it's ever been in any comparable period since World War II.

Flexible Productivity

Remember Edward Turner's wistful confidence that British motorcyclists would never accept Japanese cycles. He was wrong, of course, but his hopes were not merely foolish. In 1960, highly automated, capital-intensive production—the source of Japan's emerging competitive advantage—was suitable only for long, high-volume production runs. Turner felt sure that the upscale segment of the British market would never be large enough to attract capital-intensive competitors. The "safety" of his industry, he said, was based on its small scale.

Until very recently, the basic problem in achieving global scale in manufacturing was that each market made slightly different product demands. From country to country, basic products have a different look or "feel." A global operating scale, it was thought, could actually be a disadvantage in a world of many small-scale niche markets. So long as a company's competitive edge depended on huge production runs of identical products, it usually ended up competing only in the low-end, price-conscious segment of a market, selling to consumers who repressed their taste in the interest of cost savings. The success of the original Volkswagen "bug" in the United States is a good example. It was not really a car to American tastes, but it was so economical to buy and operate that it was a signal success. The early Japanese entries into motorcycles and cars followed a similar strategy—low-priced, good value, mass-produced commodities for wallet-watchers.

But the manufacturing revolution of the 1980s—one that will not reach full fruition until the 1990s—is "flexible manufacturing." The advent of flexible manufacturing is what Stan Feldman, of Data Resources, Inc., has dubbed the "Third Industrial Revolution"—a fundamental shift in the production environment. Feldman argues that flexible manufacturing is another Schumpeterian phase change. It represents a revolution in production technology on a par with the original organization of the factory system (the first Industrial Revolution) and the later electrification of the factory floor in the United States, which made possible long assembly-line manufacture with a large number of free-standing power-driven machines.

Full-blown flexible manufacturing is the ability to produce a wide range of products in any quantity on the same assembly line with no loss of efficiency. The combination of flexible manufacturing with powerful global companies means that no local market is too small or too specialized to be beyond a global competitor's reach. It is a much easier matter to "tune" a production system to adapt precisely some specific percentage of output to a small niche market. The editor of the *Harvard Business Review,* Ted Levitt, waxes almost lyrical about the "possibilities of people having exactly what they wish as they wish things, and at mass-produced prices—prices that are low . . . because of global scale economies. The kinds of small market segments common in Switzerland now also appear in Sri Lanka and Swaziland. . . . Small preferences in many places cumulate into global bigness in all places. No product category—consumer or industrial, tangible or intangible, consumable or durable—is exempt."

Flexible manufacturing is still in its relative infancy. Allen-Bradley's new contact and relay factory in Milwaukee, Wisconsin, is a highly automated, very capital-intensive, large-volume operation. But it can produce any one of more than 1,000 products in any quantity, for all practical purposes, with no advance notice, "with zero defects and zero direct labor." Bob Collins, at GE-FANUC, says that his factory can ship any one of its multiple products within four days of receiving an order. More typically, the highly automated looms in Dan River's textile factories now routinely make profitable production runs only a fourth or a fifth as large as the standard runs of just a few years ago. Not quite a revolution yet, but substantial progress.

Flexible manufacturing is a *collection* of technologies rather than a single technology. Henry Ford's manufacturing breakthrough in the 1920s was to create a line of workers who each performed a small number of precisely routinized tasks in order to turn out identical parts in a highly efficient manner. The workers needed machines for many of the tasks, of course, such as pressing or forming heavy metals, but each machine needed a worker to operate it. The "automation" revolution in the 1960s did not tamper with that basic concept; it merely extended the range of tasks that machines could perform, allowing each worker to oversee more machines. In the pre-automation days, a worker would move a piece of steel into a heavy press, check the gauges, then push a button to activate the press. Post-automation, the part comes down an automated conveyor belt into the press station, and the press is activated when automatic sensors confirm that the part is in the right position. The worker merely has to stand by in case something goes wrong.

The factory-floor breakthrough in the 1970s was to add computer capabilities to the automation process. A semi-automated machine tool that performed five or six different operations, automatically moving a part from one cutting edge to the other, might take a skilled machinist several hours to set up. Computerized machine tools allow the operator to punch in the sequence of operations on a keyboard, vastly speeding up the setup time and ensuring a much greater degree of consistency and quality from one operation to the next. At the same time, microelectronics has made possible much greater measurement precision. I recently visited a factory that makes measuring devices that take up to 10,000 readings on a single silicon wafer only a few inches in diameter. Coupled with programmable tools, micro-measuring gauges ensure much greater manufacturing accuracy on every part.

The next step was robotics. Robots are automated tools capable of highly complicated interactions with the parts they are making. A traditional automated tool could react to one or two measurements. An automated press wouldn't activate until a part was in the right position; an automated machine tool wouldn't start another operation until a part had been ground to the right dimension. A robot is much more sophisticated. A robot that inserts tiny components such as transistors and diodes into a printed circuit board, for instance, will optically measure the next hole on a board, select the proper part from a tray (by "feeling" with its hand), and insert the part with absolute precision—all at blinding speed. The difference between the robot and a conventional computerized tool is that the robot is not performing a programmed sequence of tasks. It can stuff any combination of boards with any combination of parts in any order.

The 1970s also saw a parallel revolution in engineering. Computer-assisted design, or CAD, systems are now replacing the traditional engineering drafting board and blueprints with a computer screen. Designing on a computer screen is not only much faster than drawing by hand but, more important, is much more accurate. If a single bolt hole needs to go through three separate parts, for instance, the designer can "look through" the three part designs on the screen to insure that the holes are all aligned precisely. A hand draftsman will often have the holes slightly misaligned from drawing to drawing. And accuracy doesn't depend on the draftsman's skill with a ruler. If you specify a part dimension of .15 millimeters, for example, the computer will draw a part with exactly that dimension.

The real power of CAD, however, lies in the potential for linking up to the factory floor. Parts designed on CAD are already in computer-specified, digitized format. Instead of using an operator to translate a part specification into a set of instructions for a computerized tool or to set the initial tolerances and operating conditions for a robot, a computer can simply derive the detailed instructions from its library of CAD drawings—and do it instantaneously and do it consistently right. (I stress that this is the *potential* of CAD systems. Not many CAD systems are actually used this way yet; most of the CAD installations I've seen are used as just an efficient design tool, although more sophisticated applications of CAD are growing rapidly, particularly at bigger companies.)

It is the *combination* of robots and programmable tools, CAD, and electronic communications networks on the factory floor that make possible flexible manufacturing systems. I've already described the system at GE–FANUC, which is *almost* there. Once an operator enters in the day's parts schedule, the machines take over from there. The production line doesn't care what parts it needs to make, it just follows the instructions from the computer. FANUC claims that its model plant near Mt. Fuji has totally "hands-off" manufacturing. The machines take over as soon as the sales department punches in its final orders.

A Revolution in the Wings

Flexible manufacturing is a revolution that has clearly *not* yet happened. Most commentators seem to agree that the Japanese are ahead of the United States in the *application* of flexible manufacturing systems, while the Americans are ahead in *technology*. Japanese companies, for example, are typically much less advanced in the use of CAD systems than the United States and will tend not to have the sophisticated factory-floor electronic linkages that are becoming commonplace in American companies. To a large extent, both deficiencies probably reflect the continuing Japanese weakness in computer software, an area in which they are years behind the United States.

At the same time, a number of studies seem to confirm that the Japanese are much more creative in the use of existing flexible manufacturing technology than American companies are. One detailed survey by the Harvard Business School in the mid-1980s found that, with roughly comparable technology, Japanese companies were making ten times as many different parts with their flexible systems as American companies were.

An MIT survey found the same thing. American managers were charging ahead with the installation of flexible manufacturing systems, but they tended to use them the same old way. GM, for example, has made enormous investments in computerized manufacturing technology but tends to use it to re-route standardized production lines when stations go down. In other words, instead of ushering in better methods of manufacturing, GM is using the new technology simply to make an old-fashioned production line more efficient. This represents an improvement, to be sure, but it is still only a small part of the technology's potential.

One source of the Japanese advantage in applying new

manufacturing technology is simply the higher quality and discipline of Japanese factory workers. The American approach to manufacturing reform is instructive. In order to install "Just-In-Time" inventory systems, American companies usually begin by creating computerized data bases containing all their parts specifications. The computer becomes the essential tool for matching production schedules to parts and raw material needs and tracking the inflows and outflows to keep inventories as lean as possible. Detailed inventory tracking in a big factory is extraordinarily complicated, and it is inconceivable to an American manager that it could be accomplished without a mainframe computer. But the Japanese automobile companies began "Just-In-Time" inventory practices long before computers came to the factory floor. They just *did* it.

Japanese factories tend to have a much higher percentage of college-trained workers or advanced technical-school graduates on the factory floor, and their easy familiarity with high-technology machinery helps keep Japanese productivity so high. Robert Abbe is the president of ADE, Inc., the company that makes the sophisticated measuring devices I mentioned earlier. His company has a dominant world-market share in his small and specialized niche, including in Japan. But the measuring robots he makes for American companies, he says, "have to be foolproof—flexible, sophisticated, and highly intelligent." His competitors in Japan sell much less advanced equipment, "because they can count on having a worker sitting in front of the machine who is as flexible, sophisticated, and highly intelligent as any machine I can make."

Still, the key problem, most observers agree, is not American workers, but American managers. For all the progress of the recent past, American executives are still prisoners of the old categories of thinking. I've already mentioned the tendency at GM to use their sophisticated machinery to run old-fashioned production lines more efficiently. But the problems show up in many less obvious ways. American purchasing managers still buy primarily on the basis of competitive bids, playing one supplier off against the other to get the lowest price. But a "Just-In-Time" inventory system will work only if a supplier is precisely attuned to a factory's daily production schedule—if, in effect, it becomes a partner in the production process. High-quality supplier *service,* that is, may be much more important to high-value high-productivity manufacturing than the lowest supplier price.

Most American companies still maintain a rigid separation between design engineers and the factory floor. American designs tend to be too elaborate, contain too many advanced technologies at the same time, are too hard to manufacture, and overrun their cost objectives. Japanese product designers work in a team with manufacturing engineers, and are much more conservative in the application of new technology, preferring small incremental steps to home-run swings. It is a pattern that is particularly striking in the global semiconductor competition. Japanese companies' designers focus on making better and cheaper chips for standard applications. American designers are always pushing the edge of chip capabilities. Interestingly enough, IBM, probably the premier chip manufacturer in the world, follows a pattern much more like that of the Japanese.

But I also believe that much of the academic and other criticisms of American managers is too harsh. Some context is essential. The competitive weakness of American companies stems, to a large extent, from their world-spanning success of the 1950s and 1960s. American industrial success had been built on supplying standard products for a huge, homogeneous market. This was ideally suited to so-called hard automation systems—very efficient for standard applications—but very hard to retool in changing times. The Japanese actually tried to ape American factories in the 1950s and 1960s but found that their smaller market demanded much smaller numbers of a more diverse range of car and truck models, just the right learning laboratory for flexible manufacturing systems.

It is an old story. Runaway success conditions most people, and most companies, to believe they have the final answer, to rest on their oars. The drive to industrial recovery in Japan raised the stakes in global manufacturing competition in a single huge jump. American companies didn't realize what was happening until the Japanese suddenly came storming over the ramparts everywhere in the world. Bemused by the triumphs of previous decades, American companies missed out on an entire cycle of productivity technology until they woke up to how dangerously uncompetitive they were becoming.

But I believe the awakening is for real. I talk to many business executives; high-productivity manufacturing is almost always the first topic that comes up. American companies have been building a whole new cadre of manufacturing managers conversant with the new methods and the new technologies. They have been laying down a critical mass of factory-floor technology that holds the promise of massive productivity improvements in the years ahead. The effort is not the work of a single year or of a single decade, and it began for real, in my judgment, only after the shocks of the 1981–82 recession.

But some results are already apparent. For all the continued deficiencies in American automobile company management, the best American-managed factories are now neck-and-neck, in productivity terms, with the best Japanese-managed American factories, and just a hair behind the Japanese companies' performance in Japan. The *average* performance of American-managed factories still lags well behind Japanese factories, but that is largely because American factories are still so much older. At the same time, with the heavy recent pace of capital investment, the quality of the average factory is improving sharply. A detailed MIT survey, after taking a generally gloomy view of American competitiveness, concludes that the American automotive industry "is improving its international competitive position very rapidly. . . . In the early 1990s . . . it is likely that the U.S. trade balance will begin to improve substantially and that 'Made in America' will again be a respected phrase in motor-vehicle export markets." That may sound overly hopeful, for the Japanese haven't slackened their own investment pace. But it is a measure of the progress that has been made.

A Global Productivity Bonanza

I've been focusing in the last few pages on the productivity sweepstakes between American and Japanese companies. I believe American companies have been narrowing the productivity gap very rapidly. But the Japanese companies have not been standing still. With very large profits from their runaway exporting successes of the past ten years, very low interest costs, and very passive shareholders (Japanese companies rarely pay dividends), they have been making enormous capital investments. American steel companies have almost completely rebuilt their major plants and redirected their whole approach to steelmaking over the past decade. With the help of a falling dollar, they can now undersell the Japanese in the world steel markets. But they are spending much less than the Japanese on research and development spending and may find themselves far behind in the *next* generation of continuous-casting production technology.

The record varies from industry to industry. Automobile companies are much improved, although they face fierce global struggles. American computer companies are still the world leaders, and semiconductor companies seem to be recovering after the horrific battering of the past few years, although that is a complex story that I will tell in more detail in Chapter 9. *Process* industries, such as American chemical and food companies, have never been threatened and are strengthening a powerful global position against formidable European competitors. As one chemical-company director told me, "The Japanese are just not a factor in our industry." (Process manufacturing, such as chemicals or food, of course, is not well suited to the detailed, shop-floor focused Japanese production management style, but it does fit the more top-down traditional American approach quite well. It is a subtlety that is usually ignored in all the lamentations about the loss of leadership in cars and consumer electronics.)

But the relative performance of American against Japanese or, for that matter, European companies, is almost beside the point. What is important is that the struggle for global market share will be won or lost by the most productive companies. That tooth-and-claw struggle is driving truly spectacular productivity gains, with massive new gains from flexible computerized manufacturing systems still to come. I mentioned in the previous chapter that American companies' share of the American color-television market was miniscule. And so it is. But some 60 percent of color televisions sold in America are made in America. The workers at the American plants of Sony,

Panasonic, Philips, or Thomson probably don't much care that most of their company's stockholders aren't Americans.

There is almost no doubt that America is becoming a haven for high-productivity manufacturing, regardless of where the ultimate owners of a business live. American companies are rising to the challenge, and American companies will be the clear winners in some global industries. Some American companies that have taken the lessons of the last ten years to heart will be winners in every industry. And a large number of American companies won't make the grade and will be swallowed up by stronger Asian or European competitors, although it will be increasingly difficult for consumers or workers to tell the difference. The point is that no matter which companies come out ahead, consumers and workers all around the world, including in the United States, will be the winners.

Cummins Engine

Columbus, Indiana, the home of Cummins Engine, located in the rustiest center of the American Rust Belt in south central Indiana, proudly styles itself the "Athens of the Prairie," and, surprisingly enough to a jaded visitor from the East, it deserves the title.

Columbus, a town of only 32,000 people, is a veritable museum of modern American architecture. The quiet, leafy, streets are home to more than fifty architectural masterpieces by Eero and Eliel Saarinen, I. M. Pei, Kevin Roche, Skidmore, Owings, Merrill, and many others. The astonishing flowering of public art in Columbus attests to the longtime close relationship between the town and Cummins Engine, its chief corporate citizen.

Cummins was founded in 1919 by Columbus's leading banker, W. G. Irwin, and his family chauffeur, Clessie Cummins, a garage tinkerer who was convinced that diesel engines could be adapted for over-the-road transport. One of the conditions of the company's initial financing was that a portion of future profits be plowed back into the betterment of the town.

J. Irwin Miller, an Irwin greatnephew who took over the management of the company in 1934 and ran it for more than forty years, was responsible for the architectural boom. Miller personified the Platonic ideal of the corporate leader. A graduate of Yale and Oxford, he reads his Bible in Greek, plays Bach on his Stradivarius, was the first layman to be president of the National Council of Churches, and was a force in mobilizing the business community to support the civil rights movement in the 1960s. He is also an architectural buff—he owns two Eero Saarinen houses—and he picked up the fees for the town's design boom.

There is a park in the center of Columbus that could stand as a metaphor for big business in America at the beginning of the 1970s. The park is a serene little jewel; its design, of course, was financed by Cummins. Old men and young boys fish in a well-stocked pond, and gray-haired couples stroll hand-in-hand in the flowered walkways. To a visitor, the park seems an anachronism, almost a denial of the harsh social turmoil in the world outside. And as the 1960s drew to a close, Cummins, with growing markets and booming profits,

47

with a philosopher-statesman at its head, had—like most of American basic industry—no inkling of the decade of rude shocks that lay ahead.

From the late 1950s through the 1960s, Cummins' sales grew fourfold. As the interstate highway system was completed, truck transport gradually supplanted rail freight for all but the largest, longest loads. Long heavy hauls put a premium on engine durability and reliability, areas in which diesel engines had an unbeatable advantage. Truck manufacturers had grown up on gasoline engine technology, so when the industry shifted to diesel, the engines were typically outsourced, with the leading share going to Cummins.

Jim Henderson, at the age of fifty-five, the president of Cummins for a dozen years—in looks, speech, and mannerisms almost a Jimmy Stewart clone—was one of a small group of talented Harvard MBAs, including the present chairman, Henry Schacht, that Miller recruited in the mid-1960s to help him see the company through its rapid growth phase.

"The name of the game in the 1970s was *capacity,*" says Henderson. "We couldn't build plants fast enough to keep up with demand, so we went on a plant-buying spree. We bought millions of square feet of plant in those years. Of course, we tried to reduce costs, but still basically thought of them as a pass-through. We figured out our costs, added a profit margin, and that was our price, and the customer was only too glad to pay. Our problem was adding the capacity to keep up with demand."

The first rude shock was a bitter fifty-nine-day strike in 1972. "It was a warning that we were losing touch," recalls Henderson. "We'd always thought of ourselves and the workers as a family, and we were shocked at the animosities that had been building up. While we were concentrating on growth, we'd lost contact with the workers, even here in Columbus. In a way, we were fortunate the warning came when it did, because we resolved to become a much more people-centered organization. I think we have, and that stood us in good stead in the 1980s."

The next sobering realization, in the mid-1970s, was that the heavy truck engine market was flattening out. The conversion of the North American fleet to diesel was practically completed, and except for a few markets, such as Australia and the United Kingdom, the pattern of haulage and the highway systems in most other countries did not suit the big tractor-trailers that Cummins had built its business around.

"We discovered in fact," says Henderson, "that heavy trucks were only about 10 percent of the diesel market, and there were lots of other applications, from buses and smaller trucks to marine applications that we had barely touched." Faced with a choice between stagnating or plunging into new markets, the company resolved to embark on a billion-dollar expansion program, an audacious move for a company with barely that much in annual sales.

A lighter and more fuel-efficient engine for heavy trucks, the L10, already represented a major capital commitment. But now, Cummins began work on two brand-new engine lines, the "B" and the "C," covering a range of power configurations that would reach down to the pickup-truck level. The B and C developments followed another design effort at the top of the engine line—a massive diesel for high-speed double-trailered loads—one that was eventually squelched by the ongoing energy crisis.

Miller had retired from active management by the mid-1970s, but one of his legacies to the company was a modern technical center (designed by Harry Weese) and a strong research and development staff, so Cummins was able to pursue its ambitious development program. As the 1970s drew to a close, the future seemed bright. The new L10 engine looked to be a sure winner and the company's expectations for the B and C line were high.

Then came the rudest jolts of all, although it took a while before Cummins realized it was faced with a mortal threat. Cummins had long licensed its heavier engines to Komatsu for manufacture in Japan. The first mini-shock was the realization that Komatsu was selling a Cummins knockoff, admittedly with some different features that made it more suitable for the construction market. Clearly, Komatsu, and as it turned out, other Japanese companies, such as Hino, Nissan, Toyota, and Isuzu, could make world-class diesel engines. Cummins marketing people began to report to headquarters that some of their key customers were experimenting with Japanese engines.

Henderson visited Komatsu in the early 1980s and toured their diesel plant. "I was really impressed," he said. "They were clearly turning out engines more efficiently than we were." Henderson extended his trip in Japan and visited other diesel plants. "The more I saw, the more I came to this terrible realization that we were getting beaten. The way their plants were laid out, the way they used their labor, the attention to detail. Some of it was simply astounding. There was a truck assembly line at Hino where almost every truck was different. And they had an engine line running in parallel, so each engine was ready for each separate truck at almost the same moment the truck was ready. They were doing this without a lot of fancy automation, but with phenomenally good management, almost a fanatical attention to every detail of the operational flow. "Just sticking my finger into the wind as I went through the Japanese factories, I figured they had a 30-percent cost advantage, easily. It had nothing to do with wages. Their wage package seemed lower, but when you added housing benefits and a whole host of other subsidies, our wage costs were really about the same."

Henderson started preaching the Japanese threat inside Cummins with such fervor that employees dubbed him "Hender-san." He sent a series of management teams to Japan, who all came back with the same conclusions. The Japanese had a substantial cost advantage, and there was no mystery how they had achieved it. They had invested heavily, both in money and time, in plant layout and design, and their operational flow was immaculate. They displayed great respect for their employees; the work force was of very high quality and was deeply involved in improving every aspect of the daily operation.

"And," says Henderson, "they had a wonderfully simplifying approach to complexity. An American manager looks at a complex operation and sees complexity. A Japanese manager sees aggregations of simplicities. That attention to detail allows them to look through surface complexity and see just a series of very simple, and very simply interconnected, operations."

The question at Cummins was how to respond. The management teams that returned from Japan, impressed as they were, typically wrote reports, then went about their jobs in the same old way. But the situation called for radical reform.

It was not until 1984, Henderson recalls, that Cummins really bit the bullet. There was now no question that Japanese diesels were a major threat. In particular, since the Japanese had more experience with smaller engines, the threat to the new B and C engines was potentially lethal. Cummins' new downsized engines were just beginning to come off the production lines. If they were priced out of the market before they had even a chance to build customer loyalty, much of the massive investment over the previous decade would be wasted.

Cummins also had the sobering benefit of having been a close-range observer of the Japanese assault on the American automobile industry, where the pattern was chillingly familiar. The Japanese would target certain major manufacturers, sell hard, win market share, and gradually build distribution capability. Then they would move their plants directly into the market and, with a choice of siting, locate close to strategic American customers—often enjoying state and local tax incentives at the same time—Cummins' major customers were sympathetic, but they were all under severe financial pressure themselves. They professed loyalty to Cummins, but only up to a point—there was no way they could overlook the real cost opportunities the Japanese were offering. Without dramatic action, the future looked bleak.

At this point, most American companies ran to their congressmen. "We can't compete against the Japanese cost advantage," they would say, "so impose quotas, impose tariffs, do something so we can keep our customers, and your constituents can keep their jobs." Cummins seems not even to have considered a political approach. "When a country imposes protectionist legislation," Henderson says flatly, "its industry loses its global competitiveness."

The crucial decision, Henderson recalls, was not made all at once in a single flash of insight. "We inched up on it over the space of a couple of years." At first, Cummins merely lowered its price expectations for the B and C engines. The company's long-run budget assumed a series of price increases for the B and C, so Cummins decided to increase prices at only half that pace. Then they decided to hold the price flat. "But it was obvious it wasn't enough," Henderson says. "If we were going to protect our markets, we had to be able to meet, or beat, the Japanese on price. No one questioned the quality of a

Cummins engine. But the hard reality was still that 30-percent price advantage.''

The final—and extraordinary—decision was simply to cut engine prices, on all engines, to whatever level was necessary to maintain market share. It was a decision that guaranteed years of losses. The gamble was that the company could survive the losses and learn how to produce engines profitably at whatever price the market demanded. To make matters worse, the economy boomed. Since Cummins lost money on every new engine it produced, it was counting on a recession and low demand to see it through the transition period. As demand for its new engines soared, the losses just piled up faster and faster.

"It was a total shift in psychology," says Mark Chesnut, the vice-president of human resources and a key manager in implementing the new strategy. "For the first time in our history, we didn't have control over pricing, just passing through our costs. The price was a given, it was set by the market, and we had to find out how to manufacture profitably at that price, or get out of the business."

In the early 1980s, when American industry was clamoring for protection, the Cummins decision was virtually unique. The course of the automobile industry stands in stark contrast. The automobile companies, besieged by Japanese imports, won a "voluntary" restraint agreement—by dint of threats of much more heavy-handed protective actions—that limited Japanese imports to 20 percent of the market. Since the quota effectively ended price competition, Japanese profits boomed and were reinvested in American plants—the 20-percent limit applied only to imports. Within a year or two, the Japanese "transplant" factories in America will have captured roughly 20 percent of the market as well, giving Japanese companies a total market share close to 40 percent. For the sake of a few years' price relief, that is, the American companies gave away the heart of their markets. The whole sorry sequence of events is an outstanding example of the executive shortsightedness and outright cowardice that marked so much of American business's initial reaction to the competitive onslaught from East Asia.

Of course, it is easy to understand why so many American companies took the easy way out, for the road Cummins took was a rocky one. After big losses in 1986 and 1988 (and a narrow profit in 1987), the company achieved a healthy rate of profitability in the first half of 1989. But a sharp downturn in heavy truck orders in the third quarter of 1989 meant more losses. Some analysts have voiced sharp criticisms of Cummins' strategy: "The company to date hasn't exhibited extraordinary interest in helping its shareholders," said one.

In fact, Cummins has achieved most of what it set out to do. After seven years of inflation, the company is still selling at 1987 price levels. That is, a comparable engine that sold for $100 in 1982 dollars would sell for $78 in

1989 dollars. In real terms, that is, correcting for inflation, the price cuts are on the order of 45 percent. "Jim's guess that there was a 30-percent Japanese cost advantage was about right," says Chesnut. "We ended up taking out 22 percent of our costs—and we're not finished—but the flip in the yen-dollar exchange rate after 1986 took us the rest of the way."

The more important victory is that the Japanese have, for all practical purposes, no presence in the American diesel engine industry. Komatsu has exited the "loose engine" business—that is, it has virtually stopped trying to compete as an engine seller to Cummins' traditional customers. Although Komatsu still makes engines for much of its own equipment, outside of Japan, it is increasingly buying engines from Cummins.

In addition to its Komatsu business, Cummins has recently begun to win major export orders from other Japanese majors, like Kawasaki and Hitachi. There are few comparable examples where a basic American industry met the Japanese on their own terms—and effectively on their own turf, which is cost-effective manufacturing of basic products—and came away with such a clear-cut win.

Meeting the cost-reduction goals meant rethinking almost everything the company did. Like most American companies, Cummins always had a sharp separation between its design departments and the factory floor. Now a significant portion of the engineering staff has been decentralized to factory-based units. Manufacturing designs have improved markedly: A typical Cummins engine now has only about 60 percent as many parts as its leading competitors. Fewer parts means easier manufacture, lower costs, and fewer failure points.

All of the company's people-management programs had to be revamped. Cummins had made a major effort to improve worker involvement in the 1970s, but taking a cue from the Japanese, Cummins had to carry the process much further. In the newest plants, all Cummins workers are salaried and there are no time clocks. There are few work rules or rigid job assignments. Each production unit is manned by a worker team with considerable flexibility for organizing its work and allocating assignments among the team members. On the other hand, workers are expected to work hard, and they do; there is much less standing around than at traditional plants. And while there is no piece work, bonus payments are tied to productivity and profits.

The company has had to match its high expectations for the work force with much greater investment in screening and training. One manufacturing executive, Dave Hoyte, a GM veteran, says, "In the auto industry, we'd take them as they came—the only requirement was passing a physical. Then we'd give them about an hour's training—you screw in these three bolts this way, that type of thing—and that's all." The training period at Cummins' plant in Rocky Mount, North Carolina, extends for sixteen weeks (shortened from seven months, which the company finally decided was unnecessarily long).

The Rocky Mount plant, a joint venture with the tractor giant, J. I. Case, to produce the B and C engines, is a sparkling model of automated efficiency. But Cummins could not afford to rebuild all of its plants. In many ways the company's most impressive achievement has been to get world-class cost and efficiency out of its older installations.

"One of the legacies of our rapid-growth period," says Chesnut, "is that we had too many plants. So a lot of people and a lot of time was spent shipping inventory back and forth, coordinating schedules, and tracking materials." A typical older plant now looks cramped. "That's a Japanese trick," explains Mike Cantrell, manager of the main engine plant in Columbus, Indiana. "You don't leave any space for parts and inventory to pile up. Everyone is forced to work more efficiently. Japanese think our plants still have too much space."

Every production line was re-configured. The re-configuration involved moving every one of the one-hundred-odd machining lines. Machining is a major manufacturing process at Cummins. Cast-iron engine blocks need hundreds of machining operations—grinding, polishing, drilling, tapping, etc.—before they can be assembled into a finished engine. Machining lines can be up to a half a block long, giant conveyors that move the raw blocks from one work station to the next. The cost of the re-configuration ran into hundreds of millions of dollars.

The new layouts are an ingenious mixture of old and new technology with Japanese concepts of plant management. Much of the machining operations, for example, have been reorganized as work cells—four or five different machines run by a single worker, who is responsible for turning out a finished piece of work. The machines in the cells are for the most part older machines, but since the worker must see an operation through from start to finish, productivity and quality have risen sharply.

The most modern, computerized, flexible machining stations have been intermingled with the old-fashioned, rigid, "hard automation" machining lines. Customers require a wide variety of different mountings and attachments on their engines, but old-fashioned machining lines must perform exactly the same operations on every block. Cummins could neither afford the labor for the customized operations nor the cost of rebuilding all the old lines, so its engineers separated out the standard and customized operations. Automated conveyors pull engine blocks off the old-fashioned line in a computer-controlled sequence. Flexible machine tools then perform whatever series of customized operations a particular engine block may require, before returning it to the standard line.

Space and work flows are kept to a minimum. "We really try to measure the distance a part has to travel," says Cantrell, "and we keep it as short as possible. That often costs money—extra loading bays, decentralized quality control stations, and so forth. It flies in the face of everything I was taught in school. Looked at from a strict cost-accounting standpoint, it doesn't seem to make sense, but in the long run, it takes costs out and moves quality up."

"When we first started the process," Henderson recalls, "I was really stressing quality. We always had good quality, but we wanted to move it up to a whole new level. The typical response was that we couldn't afford it. But the Japanese lesson, which we're still learning, is that you can't afford *not* to have the highest quality. Higher quality means lower warranty repairs, less rework, smoother production lines, less down-time. It means doing it right the first time. Quality *saves* money."

Cummins executives freely admit that they made a multiplicity of mistakes along the way. The transition took much longer than they originally hoped and cost more money. Some of the redesigns were rushed into service and cost hard-won quality gains. Some of the initial attempts to foster worker autonomy were naive. The manufacturing managers are still groping for the right mix of flexible and hard-wired automation.

But the results are impressive. Plant space has been reduced 25 percent, and the engine work force is down a third, while unit volume and sales have roughly doubled. Overall productivity is up by about 50 percent. The Japanese have been beaten off; Cummins has kept its dominant share in the North American market and is now expanding aggressively overseas.

But there is no sense of complacency in Columbus. Indeed, as this is written, the company is still not out of the woods. The announcement that the 1989 third quarter would show another loss prompted an outcry from stock analysts. Hostile raiders, sensing vulnerability, are circling in the woods. Caterpillar, its profits recovering rapidly after surviving a Komatsu onslaught into the construction-equipment market, has targeted the mid-range diesel as an area of rapid growth, and is moving aggressively into Cummins' markets. The 1991 and 1994 fuel emission standards pose daunting technical problems.

"But the challenge is still the Japanese," says Henderson. "I'm sure they'll be back. They're just very good. We're so much better than we used to be, but we're not there yet. Some of their best factories look like they've been choreographed, everything goes so smoothly. We're good, but we're still not that good."

Chesnut recalls that Cummins recently took delivery of sample pistons from a Japanese supplier. "A piston is actually a complex product with a large number of measuring points. When we checked their samples, we thought our gauges were broken. Every measure was right in the dead center of the tolerance range. It was eerie. They'll be back."

GLOBAL "DIS-INTEGRATION"

The Heroic Model

Most of us, when we think of a global company, envision a huge industrial monolith—a giant, vertically integrated, self-contained business empire. Until relatively recently, that was an accurate picture. For a century or more, the organization of giant companies tended to imitate the models laid down by J. Pierpont Morgan and John D. Rockefeller during the heroic age of American enterprise.

Few people realize that Morgan's creation of U.S. Steel, measured in the purchasing power of today's dollars, was the biggest leveraged buyout in history until it was nosed out of first place by the $25-billion RJR Nabisco deal in 1988. After a decade of titanic industrial wars, Morgan succeeded in welding together the world's largest industrial enterprise, the first billion-dollar company. The weapon he used, in the disapproving jargon of the day, was "watered securities," essentially the same as today's junk bonds.

Morgan's new company included a whole range of previously independent baronies—the Nail Trust, the Tin-plate

Trust, the Barrel-hoop Trust, the Bridge Trust; Andrew Carnegie's giant ingot mills; Rockefeller's Lake Superior ore deposits and mining companies; a whole network of barges, steamships, and railroads. Morgan's steel empire was entirely self-sufficient. From mining the ore to distributing the nails, the wires, and the tin cans sold in rural general stores, all was carried out within the corporate labyrinth of the new United States Steel Corporation.

Rockefeller's methods were different—he was the consummate manager, not primarily a financier like Morgan. But with a lethally accurate sense of market trends and opportunities, he built Standard Oil into probably the first truly global company in the modern sense, an empire that eventually exceeded even Morgan's in size and power.

Like Morgan, Rockefeller built his empire by consolidating thousands of different enterprises—pipelines, oil refineries, railroad lines, tank farms, local cartage companies, and wholesale and retail distributors. Each time he entered a new market, he used his growing financial strength and incomparable operating efficiency to squeeze prices until the competition either succumbed or agreed to march under the Standard Oil banner.

Rockefeller took the *Standard* in his company's name seriously. He was fanatically concerned that his products be of absolutely uniform and reliable quality, and his drive for consolidation was motivated as much by his search for the perfectly efficient production and distribution system as by a raw urge to power. At one point, he even bought huge tracts of Canadian pine forests and immersed himself in the details of the barrel-stave craft to insure that every Standard Oil barrel stave was made precisely to the highest specifications.

Rockefeller's and Morgan's organizational model was standard for virtually all great American companies, from GM and Ford to IBM and AT&T, with its famous Western Electric manufacturing arm and the Bell Laboratories research centers. General Motors long took pride in manufacturing virtually all the components in its cars; Ford still operates its own steel plant. No company, of course, could make everything in-house, but the American industrial empires often came close to it. IBM long had a policy of keeping *some* in-house manufacturing capability even for its outsourced parts. That way, it always had first-hand experience for evaluating its suppliers' costs and could plausibly threaten to bring the component's manufacture back in-house if suppliers showed signs of getting out of line.

In most big integrated companies, supplier relations were always semi-hostile. The goal of the purchasing department was to maximize the company's market power. Purchasing policies at the American automotive majors illustrate the pattern. The Big Three consciously tried to keep their suppliers small and fragmented—by some counts, GM, Ford, and Chrysler buy from more than 50,000 suppliers. The companies have different degrees of integration. Even today, after a substantial period of increased "outsourcing" GM still makes 70 percent of all the parts in its cars, and Ford makes about half its own parts, while Chrysler, partly under the duress of its period of insolvency, now buys about 70 percent of its parts externally.

The fundamental principle of automotive outsourcing was always price. The in-house design bureaus produced rigidly detailed specifications and put them out to competitive bid, often encouraging new companies to enter into the bidding process to keep the pressure on established suppliers. The whole system was designed to produce maximum economic leverage for the Big Three purchasing departments. And it succeeded, but at a heavy cost.

The Big Three purchasing systems are a classic example of carrying a laudable objective—securing the best possible price for outsourced parts—to such an extreme that it becomes self-defeating. The point is that price is only *one* of the objectives of a purchasing system. The semi-hostile buyer-supplier relationship meant that the supplier typically took no responsibility for improving quality. So long as the supplier arguably met the purchasing department's standard, he was entitled to his price, so corner-cutting became the order of the day and shoddy parts become standard in the industry.

The supply system also caused high inventories. A weak supplier would deliver ahead of schedule to improve cash flow and certainly had no interest or ability to participate in "Just-In-Time" inventory controls. And since the purchasing relation was semi-hostile, the purchasing department quite legitimately needed substantial resources and time to inspect incoming deliveries, causing inventories to accumulate even more. Finally, the supply system tended to freeze designs. A major priority of the design bureaus was to enforce design compliance. If a supplier changed a design, the assumption was that he was trying to cheat the company. Clearly, suppliers had no incentive to improve designs.

The problems of the automotive supply system illustrate the shortcomings of the traditional, quasi-military American style of business organization and the dominance of financial over manufacturing managers. The dominant intellectual error in the United States in the 1960s and 1970s, I believe, was a faith in our ability to rationalize and measure everything. If you couldn't measure it, it wasn't worth talking about. The insistence on measurement often meant overlooking everything that was important. Remember the "body counts" in Vietnam? The Pentagon counted dead guerrillas and strategic hamlets while utterly missing what was really going on.

Businesses made the same error. Extraordinarily detailed performance-measuring systems were the order of the day, and inevitably they focused on the one or two most easily measured items. For purchasing departments, it was price. Manufacturing departments were measured on downtime— the imperative was to keep the line running at all costs. Design departments were supposed to turn out a specified number of designs. It never seemed to occur to anyone that a good price could be a poor bargain if it meant higher inventories. Or that "filing and fitting" to keep the assembly line running meant poor production rates and quality over the longer term. Or that designs that were hard to manufacture were worse than worthless.

For many years, American business has been dogged by the problem of "spurious specificity," or "misplaced concreteness." Almost all businesses have elaborate capital-budgeting processes to justify new investments. Managers must carefully spell out all future costs and revenues associated with a new idea to prove that it will earn an adequate rate of return.

A recent study, *Dynamic Manufacturing*, by three Harvard professors, demonstrates how misleading such exercises are. It's almost impossible to be sure that all relevant cash flows are properly accounted for. There is always an enormous amount of guesswork underlying all the future assumptions.

The intangibles, such as the positive message that a new investment program gives to market and employees, are never included. The same applies to cost accounting—the surface precision can be wildly misleading. The bald fact is that businesses that invest tend to be market leaders. All of the much-touted financial modeling emanating from the business schools tends merely to deter investment.

The Triumph of the Intangibles

Leading Japanese companies, and particularly the big automotive companies, took a radically different approach. Partly because Japanese industry was capital-starved after the war, the big car makers chose a strategy of assembling parts provided by other companies. Because they were so dependent on their suppliers, but also because of the Japanese style of problem-solving, the new automotive companies concentrated on building long-term relations with a relatively small number of suppliers, in sharp contrast to the American preference for keeping the supplier community small and fragmented. Although the Japanese companies outsource a much higher percentage of their parts than the American companies, they use only about a tenth as many suppliers. GM needs 6,000 buyers to deal with its suppliers; Toyota, which produces about the same number of vehicles, has fewer than 350. The average GM plant deals with 1,500 vendors; the average Toyota plant deals with about 175. The sharp recent improvements in Xerox's market share and product quality were accomplished in part by reducing the number of suppliers from about 5,000 to about 400.

In the Japanese automotive industry, relations with key suppliers are reinforced with cross-ownership and other arrangements that weld the disparate companies into a semblance of a unified team. About 40 percent of Nissan's parts come from some 110 companies, the *Takawakai,* that supply only Nissan. Almost all of Toyota's outside sourcing comes from three Toyota "families," each with a different specialty, involving fewer than 300 companies.

It is the long-standing and stable working relationships between the Japanese automotive companies and their suppliers that make possible such striking innovations as the fabled "Just-In-Time" inventory system, where suppliers deliver parts to the assembly line precisely as they're needed. It is also the source of much of the Japanese advantage in rapid design change. In contrast to the American companies, the major or "first-tier" Japanese suppliers usually carry primary responsibility for design and research and development for their specialties. When it's time for a new model design, the whole first-tier supply family is brought into the process, and the major components of the design proceed in parallel.

The typical American design process, again in sharp contrast, was shrouded in secrecy—partly because the adversarial relation with suppliers created a high probability that new designs released prematurely would be leaked to competitors. The automotive company design bureaus would typically refuse to release designs until they were completely finished, even to supply divisions within their own companies. That kind of design process obviously takes much longer than the Japanese process. Even worse, it virtually insures that some specifications will have to be redrawn because they were developed without the input of key suppliers.

Not surprisingly, Japanese model development cycles are much faster than those in America or Europe, about 50 percent faster through much of the 1980s, according to one study. The Japanese companies developed twice as many new designs as the Americans and Europeans, with two-thirds the design manpower. The net result is a design cycle that is about a year and a half shorter, meaning that new Japanese product ideas will hit the market that much sooner than new American or European products. The same speed to market, for much the same reasons, was also a major source of competitive advantage when the Japanese consumer electronic companies were decimating their American and European competition a decade ago.

All of the American automobile companies, at least rhetorically, are beginning to adopt Japanese-style supplier relations, although, partly because of union objections to outsourcing, the pace of change is slow. Ford has begun to enter into five-year contracts with major suppliers, and the newly anointed

American first-tier parts suppliers are assuming responsibility for research and development of entire subsystems. Rockwell and Mitsubishi have a joint venture to supply complete suspension systems. The Budd Company (hardware) and ITT (electronics) are working together to build complete door systems. GE Plastics and Sheller-Globe (a major interior parts supplier) have teamed up to supply plastic molded components. Key suppliers are also expected to be able to meet sourcing needs throughout the world.

My own impression from working with a number of automotive suppliers is that the transition still has a long way to go. In some instances, the automotive majors may be creating the worst of all possible worlds for their suppliers. They are using long-term contracts to require year-over-year price reductions, but at the same time the design bureaus are still keeping rigid control over designs and specifications. In other words, suppliers are being tasked to reduce costs and improve efficiency, which is fair enough, but aren't being given the flexibility to redesign a part to reduce its cost or to improve its manufacturability.

But it should be no surprise that there are transition problems. The American mode of manufacturing organization was brought to its highest point of development by the automotive companies and dominated the industrial world for almost half a century. Success breeds deeply furrowed habits. But at the same time, as Samuel Johnson said, "The imminence of execution concentrates the mind wonderfully." The productivity data I cited in the previous chapter demonstrate that the American companies are changing both their methods and their outlooks, and they are changing them rapidly.

One of the most significant events speeding the transition process may well have been the recent rejection of the United Automobile Workers Union in the election held at the Nissan plant in Smyrna, Tennessee. Paradoxically perhaps, I believe that rejection will prompt a reduction in union objections to sourcing more production from outside suppliers, at least over the medium term. The Nissan election dashed any union hopes of organizing a significant fraction of Japanese-owned American factories for the foreseeable future. The unions, therefore, will not be in a position to enforce homogeneous manufacturing practices on the American industry, as they succeeded in doing before the advent of the Japanese "transplant" factories. Manufacturing practice will continue to be a major source of competitive advantage in the 1990s, as it most emphatically was not in previous decades. To preserve their own unionized companies, the unions will have to become partners, to an even greater extent than they are already, in implementing the best manufacturing practices, even when that means cooperating in the outsourcing of work to companies beyond their control.

The move toward increased outsourcing at the automotive majors is just an example of a trend sweeping through large-scale industry. IBM, long one of the most self-contained companies in the world, made a radical break with past practices when it entered the personal computer market in 1981. The original IBM PC depended on more than a thousand suppliers—Microsoft supplied the software for the operating system, Intel supplied the key microprocessor, controllers came from Chips and Technologies. And the PC would never have been a success at all if it were not for the vast libraries of software supplied by hundreds of unrelated vendors such as Lotus and WordPerfect.

After the initial PC breakthrough, IBM has been pursuing the new strategy across a wide range of products and technologies; it has just joined with Toshiba, for instance, to develop a new generation of high-resolution display screens. As George Feiger, a partner in McKinsey's London office, who makes a specialty of following global industrial developments, says, "No company can go it alone anymore. Market developments are just too fast."

The new trend toward "horizontal globalism" is behind many of the global alliances I mentioned in Chapter 2. Instead of large, integrated companies on the Morgan-Rockefeller model dominating a global industry, the trend is toward global specialists supplying their specialties to end-product manufacturers in all the industrialized countries. Along with global scale and the advent of high-productivity flexible manufacturing systems, the disintegration of the old industrial monolithic structures into sharply focused worldwide specialty producers is a powerful force driving a radical reordering of world manufacturing. It is one more compelling piece of evidence that the industrial world is moving through a Schumpeterian phase change, a series of fundamental re-structurings that will underpin sustained gains in productivity and output for many years to come.

Horizontal Globalism

The frantic wave of corporate acquisitions, divestitures, and re-structurings that has swept through American and European industry over the past few years sometimes seems like mindless financial churning. And, of course, sometimes it *is*, as investment banks dream up improbable deals for the sake of generating high fees. But much of the re-structuring process, disorderly as it sometimes seems, is actually following a rigorous industrial logic. Companies are stripping away non-essential businesses and focusing on one or a few specialties, where they have a chance of winning a dominant market share. Even a conglomerate like GE, for all the wide range of its businesses, has been steadily increasing focus through a decade of rapid-fire divestitures and acquisitions under its chairman Jack Welch. It now has sixteen businesses in which it can legitimately claim a number-one or number-two global market position.

The textile industry—contrary to the conventional wisdom, one of the most profitable, productive, and highly automated of American manufacturing industries—has undergone a sweeping re-structuring. Freddie Wood, a partner in Kurt Salmon Associates, the world's leading textile consulting firm, says, "You can go through every industry segment—corduroys, denims, sheets and towels, auto-body cloth—where there used to be ten or fifteen players, now there are four or five at the most. Every major company used to think they had to be all things to all men—home furnishings, yarn-dyed, knitting, weaving, carpets, whatever. Now West Point Pepperell and Fieldcrest Cannon do towels and sheets, J. P. Stevens and Collins and Aikman do auto-body cloth. It's the same pattern throughout the whole industry. And most of the specialization has come from buyouts and spinoffs. Companies are focusing on just a few items and getting very good at them."

It was the threat of hostile raiders that forced Goodyear to re-focus on its core tire business, selling off a confusing collection of oil and gas holdings, a resort hotel, an aerospace company, and a pipeline operation. Similarly, Union Carbide exited from a wide range of consumer-oriented businesses to return to ethylene-based and specialty chemicals—its traditional strength. It was the discipline of an LBO that pushed Revlon to leave the health-care business and to concentrate on beauty products. Beatrice sold off a host of unrelated companies to focus on a handful of food companies.

Anyone can find examples, of course, that don't fit this general pattern—RJR Nabisco, the biggiest of them all, is one. But I think few people will disagree that, in the main, the cycle of 1980s re-structurings has greatly increased companies' focus. For the most part, the old-line, 1960s-style conglomerate has become a thing of the past. The fashionable academic theory of business organization in the 1960s was the notion of a "portfolio of businesses." The basic idea was that some businesses, such as big-ticket manufacturing or businesses tied to residential construction, were inherently cyclical. A wise company chairman would balance off a cyclical business like industrial equipment manufacturing with a business such as food retailing, which tends to have fairly steady sales through the economic ups-and-downs.

The "portfolio theory" wave of mergers in the late 1960s is a good example of the eclipse of basic business common sense by academic financial theory. The academics didn't realize that heavy manufacturing companies might not be very good at running stores. Exxon predictably botched its attempt to make a line of typewriters and other office equipment, while Mobil wasted its shareholder's money on circuses (Ringling Bros.) and deparment stores (Montgomery Ward). If investors want to diversify their portfolios, they can do it themselves much more efficiently on the stock market. The theme of the 1980s re-structurings has been a total reversal of the "portfolio balancing" logic: The rallying cry is "Stick to your knitting." Build your business by doing a relatively small number of things better than anyone else in the world.

The manufacture of major civilian aviation aircraft demonstrates the process of global specialization in its most advanced stages. There are only three airframe manufacturers in the world able to produce jet transports with more than seventy-seat capacities—Boeing, with about 60 percent of the market, McDonnell Douglas, at about 10 to 12 percent, and Europe's Airbus Industrie, with the rest. But, as McKinsey's Feiger points out, "Boeing is a wing specialist and systems integrator. Its engines come from Pratt-Whitney or another engine supplier. The avionics come from Rockwell or someone else. Boeing manages the whole process and assembles the final product." Boeing's critical technology, according to an MIT study, is its program management, or its capacity for enforcing a high level of performance on thousands of subcontractors and bringing all the processes and all the components smoothly together at its airframe assembly plants. It is a model much more in the spirit of the Japanese approach to the automobile industry than to the traditional American one. (Boeing, of course, never had much choice in the matter. No single company could master the multifarious technologies that go into a modern jumbo jet.)

Beneath the level of the airframe manufacturers as well, there is both a high degree of global presence and a high degree of specialization. There are only three big-ticket civilian aviation engine manufacturers—GE–SNECMA, a French-American alliance and the current market leader; United Technology's Pratt-Whitney; and Great Britain's Rolls-Royce, only recently resurrected from bankruptcy. And there are only a handful of companies worldwide, such as Howmet and Precision Cast Parts, that can supply the precision turbine blade castings used by the engine manufacturers. The same applies to the avionics and other advanced systems used by modern aircraft.

The consequence, of course, is a fantastically convoluted set of supply relationships. All of the major subcontractors work with each other and the three airframe companies. The three airframe companies sometimes even subcontract back and forth to each other. Although Airbus Industrie was created to be Europe's answer to American dominance in civilian aircraft manufacture, about 30 percent of the average Airbus is still built in America. By the same token, Boeing, partly in order to maintain its exclusive lock on Japan's civilian aviation business, has been gradually taking in Japanese subcontractors for its newest planes. Feiger muses on the "complexity of the international relationships" that are developing: "The multinational links in the aerospace industry are quite extraordinary. It's probably no coincidence that the only countries that have wars these days are countries that don't have much in the way of modern economies."

Developments in the semiconductor industry may presage a similar trend toward specialization in that hotly contentious field. Japanese semiconductor companies, on the whole, have a lead in chip manufacturing over American companies—with the exception of IBM, which does not sell its chips. One reason is that the Japanese concentrated early on relatively standard lines of memory chips, particularly the so-called DRAMs (for "dynamic random access memory"). By concentrating on standard lines, they generated the production volumes required to justify high levels of investment in production technologies. As mentioned, the capital costs of a modern chip plant are enormous. Advocates of government assistance to the American industry usually point to the huge capital requirements of playing catch-up—most of the American companies are too small to manage that level of spending by themselves.

But the United States still enjoys a long lead over the Japanese in the most advanced chips, such as logic chips, including the Intel and Motorola microprocessors that are at the heart of the powerful new generations of personal computers. Analysts disagree over the sources of the American edge in chip design. The Japanese have mounted richly funded catch-up programs and are making headway in many areas, but the American design houses are continuing to innovate at an extraordinary pace and are building a strong competitive position in the newest chip concepts, such as RISC and ASIC chips—which I'll describe in more detail in Chapter 9.

One reason for the American lead in chip design is the huge American lead in software. Chip designers prefer to interact with software writers when they are working on a new application. Or it may simply be that the individualistic

American culture turns out more people with the artistic flair necessary to design new generations of chips. The consequence, however, is that while most American computer companies must buy a great part of their standard chip supplies from Japanese competitors, Japanese computer companies typically license their microprocessors and other advanced chips from American companies.

MIPS Computer Systems in Sunnyvale, California, is one of the hottest new chip companies in the industry. Founded only in 1984, its 1989 sales are estimated at $100 million. MIPS' RISC chips are powering DEC's newest high-speed computer work stations. Competition in the RISC marketplace is fierce, but there are still no Japanese contenders. IBM was the original developer of the RISC chip. Sun Microsystems, which has grown to $2 billion in sales in less than ten years, has licensed its own RISC chip to AT&T and Fujitsu. Hewlett Packard has a RISC chip it has licensed to Hitachi, among others, and Motorola and Intel have entered the market aggressively. Significantly enough, MIPS does not *manufacture* RISC chips; it only designs them. Manufacture is contracted to five "manufacturing partners" throughout the world—three in America, one in Europe, and one in Japan— that make the chips to MIPS designs.

There is, in addition, the first glimmer of a trend toward specialized chip-manufacturing companies that will concentrate purely on contract manufacturing—for example, as suppliers to the automotive industry do. James Dykes is the president of the Taiwan Semiconductor Manufacturing Company, a venture founded by Morris Chang, a Taiwanese who is a former CEO of General Instruments and a group vice-president at Texas Instruments. Dykes and most of his top management team come from GE. The financial backers are the Dutch firm Philips and the Taiwanese government. Dykes's goal is to create a "manufacturing partner" with the advanced chip houses: "The customer delivers a design, and the foundry delivers a finished part." Dykes expects that within a year his foundry will be operating at sub-micron tolerances—the most advanced current technology for high-volume production. Two American chip makers—National Semiconductor and Sierra—are engaged in a joint venture to develop a similar foundry with the Singapore government.

It would be feckless and dangerous for America not to have world-class chip manufacturing capabilities. But it will not be true that the only successful chip companies will be those with large-scale manufacturing plants. Some successful companies may be primarily designers and creators of chips, while others may be primarily manufacturers, specialists in production technology rather than in chip design. Or a pattern may emerge where a number of design-oriented companies manufacture through a special-purpose consortium, like the aborted U.S. Memories.

Factories as Design Boutiques

The revolutionary promise of high-productivity manufacturing is still some years away, but the pace of the revolution is accelerating. Consider the implications of the trends I have been discussing in this and the previous two chapters—competition on a global scale, flexible manufacturing systems, and the re-structuring of industry into "horizontal" global specialists.

The factory of the future will be radically different from the long assembly-line operations that dominated manufacturing twenty years ago. Instead it will be a high-speed, highly automated assembly shop bolting together a wide variety of parts from specialist manufacturers into many small lots of precisely targeted final products.

The world's largest manufacturing industry, the automotive industry, is leading the way. The process of global specialization is being carried forward so rapidly that the day is not far off when most cars will be assembled from virtually identical parts supplied by the same worldwide suppliers. A middling-size British firm, GKN, dominates the world market for the constant-velocity joints used in most four-wheel drive and front-wheel-drive vehicles. Intermet Inc., of Atlanta, Georgia, the world's largest independent iron foundry, sells a small range of parts to most of the major automobile manufacturers everywhere in the world. Germany's Robert Bosch and Alfred Teves, along with America's Allied-Signal's Bendix Division, dominate the world market for brake systems. Bosch is also the world's leader in fuel-injection systems. Rockwell's Automotive Body Systems Division is a worldwide supplier of complete "kits" and "cassettes," as it calls them. For example, it supplies door units—complete with windows, window winders, stereo speakers, and locks—for Italy's Fiat; for GM's British Vauxhalls, it supplies complete sunroofs, including glass and electric motors.

Virtually all the European and American subsystem specialists have entered into joint ventures with the Japanese majors to supply the new overseas Japanese factories and are beginning to compete for business in the Japanese homeland. At the same time, the semi-captive Japanese suppliers are slowly breaking away from their exclusive intra-"family" supply relationships to compete on a global scale. The far-reaching alliances between the major vehicle manufacturers mean that cars are getting increasingly similar under the hood.

One consequence is a rapid compression of the quality differences between cars. Lloyd Reuss, a senior GM executive, has said that such previously burning competitive issues as fuel economy, safety, reliability, and manufacturing quality are rapidly on their way to becoming "non-issues." "In the future," he adds, "it's personality and image, more than anything else, that will sell cars and trucks."

The best example of what Reuss is talking about comes, once again, from Japan. Mazda's sporty new convertible, the Miata, designed for the American market, has been such a success that by the end of 1989 car buyers were shelling out $3,000 to $4,000 premiums to go to the head of the delivery list. There was nothing fundamentally new about the Miata except the design; the parts were basically the same as in other Nissan cars or, for that matter, in the cars of many other manufacturers. Instructively, the home-run-hitting design came from a young Californian designer, Bob Hall, whose father is a senior designer at GM.

Some analysts are predicting the advent of design-it-yourself manufacturing. As final product manufacturers more and more become assemblers of mixed-and-matched subcomponent modules purchased from global specialist suppliers, the variety of potential final products will be nearly infinite. Stan

Feldman predicts that in the near future the turnaround time from ordering a car to producing the finished product in a factory will be just a few days. A customer will select a customized vehicle from a wide range of feature combinations for manufacture to order with no penalty in delivery time.

The gains in cost and efficiency will be enormous. Under the current system, the automobile companies must guess at each year's model demand and start turning out cars in the hope that their forecasts are right. On average, it takes several months for a finished car to work its way through the dealer chain to a final sale. The result is an enormous floating inventory of more than a million unsold cars. The quasi-permanent overhang of unsold vehicles is a major source of industrial volatility, a financing drag on all the automotive companies, and a huge, continuing economic risk.

The automobile companies are merely an outstanding example of the rapid progress of the new modes of manufacturing organization. The manufacture of most electronic products, from television sets to personal computers, is following the same trend, if anything even more rapidly. Flexible manufacturing from modular parts holds the promise of vastly reducing product inventories and financial risk, at the same time as it greatly increases consumer choice.

At some time in the future, we will have to worry that a small number of global specialist suppliers, no matter what the industry, may develop so secure a dominant position that they become an obstacle to innovation, protecting their markets by obstructing technological progress. But for the decade of the 1990s, the continuing reshaping of global manufacturing into a lean, high-productivity, highly flexible process of assembling modular subcomponents into final products of unprecedented variety will be a major force for rapid economic growth, low inflation, and a long, steady rise in real per capita output.

Intermet Foundries

Steering knuckles, the Intermet annual report brags, are "not pretty things." Indeed they are not. Awkwardly angled iron brackets, they are a vital stress-bearing part in a car's or a truck's steering linkage. Steering knuckles are the major product at Intermet's Archer Creek Foundry in Lynchburg, Virginia, the largest of thirteen Intermet foundries throughout the world and capable of turning out some 6,000 steering knuckles a day.

At Archer Creek, the newly cast knuckles emerge from their beds of oily black casting sand and, glowing dull red, cascade by the hundreds down giant slow-turning barrels that clatter away the clinging sand with blunt iron teeth. The din in a big iron foundry is fearful, the atmosphere Stygian. Even casual visitors walk away with grit in the crevices of their skin.

Metal casting is one of the world's oldest industries. Along with fixed-site agriculture, it is one of the key technologies that propelled primitive man into the modern era. At least seven thousand years ago, men learned to collect metal ores strewn over the earth's surface, melt them with forced-draught fires, pour the liquid ore into molds (casting), and beat it into final shape as it cooled (forging) to form metal objects of incomparable hardness and durability. It was the bronze weapons of the Indo-European chariot warriors that allowed them to sweep away the tribes of Europe and Central Asia and impose their language over one and a half continents. Thousands of years later, the descendants of those charioteers, still armed with bronze, fell before the much more formidable iron swords of the Romans.

Remnants of ancient foundries dot the world. There are even two-thousand-year-old iron foundries in Central Africa, with their furnaces ingeniously constructed of mud, giving a tantalizing glimpse of more advanced civilizations of centuries ago. Oddly, for all their megalithic engineering skills, the native civilizations of the Western hemisphere never discovered metal casting, which sharply limited the technological paths open to them.

Intermet is the world's largest independent iron foundry, although its $400 million in annual sales make it only about a fifth as big as the biggest of the "captive" foundries, the General Motors Central Foundry Division. Intermet

71

and the GM Foundry Division also differ in other, more critical, ways. GM's Central Foundry is one of the world's most unprofitable multibillion-dollar businesses. GM does not publish the divisional financial results, but trade sources estimated its 1988 losses in the $250 million to $500 million range. Intermet has always been a highly profitable company.

Intermet's founder, CEO, and major shareholder is George Mathews, a native Georgian who conceals a hard-driving business ambition beneath a relaxed "good ole boy" air. Mathews achieved local fame in 1946 when he and Georgia Tech teammate Frank Broyles scored touchdowns in the last two minutes of the game against Navy to pull out a victory. Mathew's score came on a ninety-six-yard return of a fumble recovery. Mathews went on to become a College All-Star and was drafted by the New York Giants, but he gave up football to go to the Harvard Business School. Broyles went on to become the head football coach at the University of Arkansas and is now a member of the Intermet board.

In the late 1960s, Mathews worked in marketing and sales for the Columbus Iron Works in Columbus, Georgia. While he was there, he convinced the owners to invest in a foundry. About a year after he left Columbus for a job in Atlanta, the Columbus owners contacted him to report that their foundry was losing money and to invite Mathews back to sell it for them. After some months of hesitation, "my gambling instincts won out," says Mathews, and with the help of a hefty loan from a local businessman, he bought Columbus Foundry himself in 1972 for $1 million. Its best-selling product was backyard barbecue grills.

Mathews is not a metallurgist—he studied engineering and business at Georgia Tech—but he had a clear idea of where he wanted Columbus Foundry to go. Before he had left Columbus, he had heard of a young metallurgist there, a University of Alabama graduate, preaching the virtues of ductile iron. Alabama's metallurgy department at Birmingham, working closely with the local iron-and-steel industry, had developed, over a number of years, a low-sulphur, high-nickel iron alloy—ductile—that could be cast as effectively as standard or "gray" iron, but was much lighter and stronger. Mathews shifted the focus at Columbus toward the automotive industry and toward ductile. As Columbus became profitable, Mathews added another foundry, then began to grow by acquisition. After buying a German foundry from Bendix in 1976 (the time of the name change to "Intermet"), he more than doubled the company's size by acquiring the Lynchburg foundries, including Archer Creek, from Mead Corp. in 1983.

Mathews has since opened another German foundry, bought Volvo's foundry in Sweden, and opened a joint venture in Korea with a local partner. Intermet is also operating two joint ventures in the United States, one with Ford and one with Aisin Takaoka, a member of the Toyota supplier "family" that is aimed at the Japanese transplant factories in the United States.

With a reputation as one of the few Western companies that can run a high-quality foundry profitably, Intermet receives inquiries almost weekly from manufacturing companies around the world, all of them with loss-making captive foundries, wondering if Mathews wouldn't like to take the foundries off their hands. Intermet already controls the majority of outsourced automotive ductile iron castings in North America and makes the brake calipers for almost all cars manufactured in Europe. Since most automotive companies in Europe and North America are shedding internal manufacturing operations in favor of outsourcing—on the Japanese model—the company expects continued strong global growth.

The history of the American foundry industry in the 1960s and 1970s is one more illustration of the rule that rapid growth and high profits will sooner or later attract aggressive competition. When the competition does emerge, the companies that have grown complacent will suddenly find themselves struggling to survive.

The 1960s and most of the 1970s saw strong growth in iron castings. The automotive, the household durable, and the farm-equipment markets were all booming, and foundries were hard-pressed to keep up with demand. Growth was particularly strong among the independents as the big integrated manufacturers began to outsource their overflow work when their captive foundries hit the capacity wall.

The Lynchburg foundries, before Intermet took them over, were one of the industry leaders among the independents. They were acquired by Mead Corp. in 1968, at the height of the late-1960s fad for industrial conglomeration. "We were the Cadillac of the industry," says Al Singleton, a forty-three-year Lynchburg veteran, who is now president of Intermet and who enjoys a reputation as one of the foremost foundrymen in the country. "Everyone knew we had the highest-quality product, and we didn't pay much attention to price. If someone complained about our prices, we would tell them to go find a lower-quality foundry."

"We began to hear about George Mathews and his Columbus foundries in the late 1970s," says Stan Atkins, the marketing vice-president at Intermet and another Lynchburg veteran. "There was even some talk at Lynchburg that we should buy him. George was preaching low price *and* high quality, and we knew about his success with ductile iron. But it was hardly a time to be worrying about prices. Capacity was so tight that even quality-conscious companies like Caterpillar and Chrysler were coming into our plants and mining our rejects—'we can use this one, and that one, don't throw those out'—that kind of thing."

But by the late 1970s, the straws were swirling in the wind. In the first place, foreign foundries had finally discovered the huge American market. "We'd never seen foreign castings in our market before," says Singleton. "And at first we assumed it was just cheap junk. But we gradually realized that a lot of the foreign castings were good quality and they were shipping them in at lower prices than we could make them for." By the end of the 1970s, foreigners had more than 20 percent of the American casting market, estimates Singleton, and their share was growing year by year.

Then came the 1979 energy crisis. The automobile companies had shrugged off the 1973 oil-price increases, but the threefold increases in 1979 wrought a fundamental change in transportation economics. Cars, engines, and all the castings that went into them had to be much smaller and much lighter. Foundries were used to marking up profits as a percentage of costs. But iron was their biggest cost item. Weight reductions meant less iron in each product, a lower cost base to mark up, and lower profits.

The 1981–82 recession was the *coup de grace* for much of the industry. Auto and consumer durable sales plunged. The farm-equipment market disappeared. Big American foundry customers like Caterpillar, Cummins, and the automotive majors began to lose market share to foreign competition. The foundry industry, beset on all sides, was gasping just to survive. About a third of all American foundries simply rolled over and died.

For Mathews and Intermet, it was a time of unparalleled opportunity. The weight reduction in cars served to highlight the advantages of ductile iron. There was also a substantial trend toward aluminum castings for pistons and other automotive components. But aluminum does not have the strength required for high-stress parts like steering knuckles, brake calipers, and crankshafts—all major products for Intermet.

At the same time, the generally poor performance of the big 1960s-style conglomerates had been thrown into sharp relief. A frantic re-structuring drive in most old-line industrial companies meant that a number of traditional gray-iron foundries were going on the auction block at fire-sale prices. Mead Corp., for one, was shedding companies left and right as it struggled to refocus on its traditional paper and forest products businesses. Mathews picked up the Lynchburg foundries, now the heart of the Intermet North American capacity, for about half the cost of building a new foundry.

"Mead was a wonderful company to work for," says Singleton, "and I still feel a great deal of loyalty to them. But it really made a difference to work for a company with a single focus. The week after the deal with Intermet closed, I prepared my capital budget. It had a number of major investment items. The normal capital budget cycle at Mead was four to six months or so, because approvals had to go through the various corporate offices. Instead, I flew to Atlanta and spent the morning with George going over my proposals. We worked out an agreement, he signed it, and I came back to Lynchburg the same day ready to go. It was almost hard to believe."

In the early 1980s, American foundries produced about $30,000 worth of product per employee, or about a third the level routinely achieved in Japan. Most of the foundries Mathews was acquiring were performing at about that level. By 1987, Intermet's foundries, on average, were neck-and-neck with the Japanese, turning out better than $100,000 of product per employee.

"There were no magic tricks," says Singleton, who now runs all the foundries. "It was simply a question of what you paid attention to." Singleton visited a number of Japanese foundries after the Intermet acquisition. "What impressed me was that they got eight hours' worth of work out of each employee each day, their planning was very thorough, and their customer follow-up was very good. Their level of automation was about the same as ours at Archer Creek, which at the time was our newest foundry. They weren't doing anything that we couldn't do."

Intermet is a perfect illustration of the dawning realization on American business that there was no conflict between low cost, high quality, and good customer service. Bill Hopkins, the general manager at Archer Creek, says, "In fact, low costs and high quality go hand in hand. High quality means doing it right, exactly the way the customer wants it, the first time. It means maintaining your equipment better, less down-time, lower scrap, fewer customer rejects. You get to the point where you can do all of that, your productivity soars, your customers are happy, and your costs go down. Your employees are working harder, but they're actually happier because they know they're doing a good job."

The drive for quality and productivity at Intermet was strongly supported by the automobile companies. "We were introducing much greater use of statistical process control," says Hopkins, "and the automobile companies sent teams into the foundries to review our procedures and help us upgrade them." Intermet has won all the top quality-supplier awards—the Chrysler "Pentastar," the Ford "Q-1," the General Motors "Spear," the Caterpillar "Certified Quality Supplier" award, and many others. "All these awards involved regular audits," says Hopkins, "and they really helped us sharpen up our internal controls."

Productivity improvement at Intermet is the net result of a host of individual small improvements. To begin with, the single-minded focus on ductile iron and the automotive industry has in itself been a major force for improved quality and productivity. With a big network of foundries, Mathews has focused each one on a family of products—Archer Creek on steering knuckles, the European foundries on brake calipers, and so forth. Whereas the bigger foundries were working from as many as 300 patterns a few years ago, each now typically makes only a couple of dozen. "You can get very good if you specialize," says Atkins. "Intermet has made more disc-brake calipers than anyone in the world. Nobody, no matter where they're from, is going to beat us on quality or price on disc-brake calipers."

The trend toward specialization at Intermet has been reinforced by standardization in the automotive industry. Chrysler has moved to two basic car platforms for all its models, using only two different kinds of brake calipers. Ford is moving rapidly to one or two standard sets of most parts for all its cars worldwide. Almost all European-made cars use Alfred Teves brakes (with

Intermet calipers). Japanese cars are standardizing on a small number of brake sets from Japanese brake specialists—with Intermet working hard to become the supplier of choice at least to their American plants.

Intermet has also invested extensively in automating its foundries. The new foundry built with Aisin Takaoka may be the most highly automated in the world. But the veterans insist that automation was only part of the reason for the productivity upsurge. Their proof lies in the fact that Archer Creek now probably one of the half dozen or so most productive foundries in the world, built only in 1973, was already highly automated when Mathews took it over. "For one thing, we began to pay attention to our own rules," says Hopkins. He gives three examples—"stickers," temperature control, and melt control.

In a sand casting operation, as at Archer Creek, customers supply precision-machined steel casting patterns that are mounted on stamping machines. Automated molding lines fill a long train of twin palletes with an oily sand mixture, and the palletes move under the stamping machines where a "negative" of the top and bottom casting shape is stamped into the sand. Workers insert "cores" into the hollowed-out sand moldings by hand, and check the alignment of the moldings. (The cores are a special sand and wax mixture in the shape of the hollow sections inside a casting. When the hot metal hits the core, the core will melt away but leave the hollow space in its wake.) After the cores are inserted, the top sand molding pallete is closed over the bottom half, leaving holes for pouring.

At the other end of the line, a giant magnetized crane is loading scrap iron into a huge electric-arc furnace, where it melts at a bright orange 2,800-degrees Fahrenheit. The melt is poured off into giant holding ladles, "slag" or other impurities like sulphur are scraped off from the top and siphoned out from the bottom, and copper, nickel, and other elements are measured in to adjust the metallurgical content. The molten iron is transferred to pouring ladles and poured into each pallete as it passes beneath on the transfer line. The filled palletes wind through a cooling room as the metal hardens, then dump their contents unceremoniously into the barrel shaker to knock off the sand. The castings are transferred from the barrel into an abrasive spray-cleaning chamber and finally to a machining line where a mixture of human workers and robots grind off the metal burrs remaining from the casting operation.

If a casting pattern begins to wear, explains Hopkins, it will leave a small blank space on the sand molding that will cause a "sticker" (a bump on the finished casting) that will have to be machined away either at the foundry or by the casting customer. "In the old days, we hated to stop a line," says Hopkins, "so we used to let stickers go through, and we'd end up with a lot of wasteful machining and extra rejects. Now we're constantly measuring the moldings, and we change the patterns at the slightest sign of an irregularity. In the end, we save time. We do a lot less machining, our scrap rate is well under 2 percent, down from 8 to 9 percent some years ago, and our customer reject rate is less than 0.1 percent."

The same applies to temperature control and melt control. "We're supposed to pour molds within a hundred-degree temperature range," says Hopkins, "usually between 2,500 and 2,600 degrees. But we used to pour 'a little hot' or 'a little cold.' Now that's unheard of. The same with melt control. We have rigid rules on alloy content, and we would never dream of bending them, although it used to be routine. When you tighten up like that, the whole process gets crisper, and the work force reacts to it. They know they're doing a precision job and they put in a much better day's work."

The new crispness is most evident in customer service. A foundry is at the bottom of the product chain. In the automotive industry, for example, the car companies more and more are becoming designers, marketers, and assemblers. Brakes come from specialty suppliers like Bendix or Teves. The brake manufacturers buy specialty parts, such as calipers, from Intermet or, as often as not, from specialty machine shops that do the final machining operations on Intermet's castings. The massive industry movement toward "Just-In-Time" production, which squeezes out inventories at every stage of the process, inevitably pushes inventory down to the very lowest level in the product chain—to companies like Intermet. Intermet's biggest customers will typically refuse to stock more than one or two days' supply of castings. "At the same time," says Hopkins, "they would go through the roof if they ever ran out, because it would mean shutting down all their machining lines. It's up to us to have one day's supply there every day."

A decade or so ago, average inventories at Intermet foundries would be in the sixty-to-ninety-day range. Now it's typically in the week-and-a-half range. Archer Creek normally has a week's supply of scrap iron on hand—scrap dealers are still not well-organized, so some safety stock is essential. And it has a total of about two days of work in process and finished goods *including* an average twenty-one-hour shipping time to major customers. Scrap iron going into the melting furnace on Monday morning is in finished-product form and on a truck by Monday night or Tuesday morning, in the customer's shop late Tuesday night, and on the customer's machining line sometime on Wednesday, or Thursday morning at the latest.

"Ten years or so ago, we shipped almost all of our product by rail," says Hopkins. "You never knew where anything was. Stuff could sit on a siding for weeks. Sometimes the railroads would actually lose it." The economical shipping loads by rail were also necessarily much larger. "When you're working on one- or two-month lead times, with a lot of slack built in at every step, everything just runs a little sloppier."

The changing technology of intermediate product distribution is nothing less than a quiet revolution, and it illustrates, as much as any other factor, the new tautness and rigor marking the response to the industrial challenge from

Asia. Intermet has a completely computerized inventory control system that links directly to the computers controlling inventory levels at its major customers facilities. At any moment, the Intermet production control staff know how many steering knuckles, say, Chrysler has in inventory and can plan their day's run accordingly. (Automated molding lines can change products on a dime—in the time it takes to switch the casting patterns.) The new quality-award system that most big companies have instituted usually eliminates incoming inspections at the customer's site. Once a supplier achieves top-quality status and maintains that rating through follow-up audits, its product goes right to the customer's production floor.

The transformation of the foundry industry from small, sole-proprietor-type shops into a modern global industry has taken place within Al Singleton's career span as a foundryman. "It's not that long ago that you didn't need much technology to run a foundry," Singleton recalls. "A furnace, a fifty-five-gallon drum of sand, and a rammer, and you could make castings." For many years the industry moved forward only slowly. The captive, dominant foundries fossilized under the weight of complacent management and rigid unions, snoozing away behind the barriers of supposedly impregnable markets.

The competitive challenges of the 1980s have been wrenching, but Intermet is a good measure of the progress that has been made. With a research and development foundry, a metallurgy lab, CAD systems, computerized links to customer inventory systems, and a host of advanced quality-control capabilities—from spectroscopic, magnetic particle, ultrasonic, and X-ray and gamma-ray technologies to sophisticated statistical-control methods—Intermet symbolizes the transformation of an old-line industry. Its world position in a small number of parts also illustrates one of the fundamental trends driving the recent worldwide manufacturing productivity increases—the disintegration and increased focus and specialization that have accompanied the reach for global scale in most basic manufacturing companies.

SUMMING UP

The 1980s have seen a fundamental re-structuring of large-scale business enterprise, a restructuring that will continue through the 1990s. The result is a transformation of the productive process on a grand scale, the kind of radical reordering of the economy that Schumpeter suggested presages a prolonged period of business expansion—an economic "golden age."

The transformation is multifaceted. The competitive arena for basic industries is shifting from a national or regional scale to a global one. The onrush of global competitors into all local markets of consequence is causing a rapid diffusion of the most advanced productive technology and steadily escalating standards of consumer demand. At the same time, the enormous capital requirements of modern large-scale manufacturing is spurring a spreading network of strategic alliances in pursuit of global competitive advantage. The result is intense competition at the local level between competitors who can draw on the financial, technological, marketing, and research and development resources of globally based enterprises.

From the standpoint of the factory floor, the method of industrial organization—the "hard-wired," standard-product assembly system—that was the basis of the American economic success in the 1950s and 1960s is giving way to new systems of "flexible manufacturing." The new manufacturing systems are designed to produce many small batches of diverse products without any loss of productive efficiency compared to the more traditional methods. Particularly in the

United States and Western Europe, the coming of flexible manufacturing has been hastened by the broad-scale application of computer technology to basic production problems, from design, through parts and inventory management, to the control of intelligent machines.

Flexible manufacturing technology combined with a global competitive arena, in turn, is forcing a "dis-integration" of traditional vertically organized industrial monoliths into a new pattern of "horizontal globalism." Most subcomponents of standard consumer products, from memory chips in video cassettes to anti-skid braking systems in new cars, are sourced from a small number of highly focused global specialist businesses that are driving the advances in production technology and product design more rapidly and aggressively than was possible in the typical vertically integrated firm.

The convergence of all these forces has sparked a decade-long run-up in manufacturing productivity in all the industrialized nations. Despite the widespread fears that the world has been teetering on the thin edge of economic catastrophe, intense global competition and rapid advances in production technology have generated a long run of strong economic growth with relatively low inflation.

The organizational and technological transformation of global industries is still in its earliest stages, and the process will continue at an accelerating pace for at least another decade, possibly considerably longer. If anything, the evolutionary process will be hastened as more and more countries, from emerging regional superpowers like Brazil to the centrally planned economies of Eastern Europe, and possibly even of the Soviet Union, opt to join the Western economic system.

II

PEOPLE

4

THE AGING "ARCHIPELAGO OF YOUTH"

The Boomers Take Over

The disappearance of men's ears, which happened about the middle of the 1960s, was, I've always thought, one of the significant social events of recent American history.

The Beatles came to America for the first time in 1964 and appeared on national television, on "The Ed Sullivan Show." One of the Beatles' gimmicks was their long hair—long hair on men was so unusual in 1964 that it worked as a theatrical trademark. At the high point of their songs, they would shake their hair and their audiences would shriek and squeal ecstatically.

Within just a couple of years, men all over the country, of all ages and in all walks of life, were wearing their hair like the Beatles. Sargent Shriver, President Kennedy's brother-in-law, set off for Paris as the American ambassador to France with a Beatles haircut. There was a string of baseball contract disputes as club owners tried to make the players keep their hair cut short. Even policemen and construction workers suddenly had hair bushing out awkwardly from beneath their caps and hard hats.

It was a signal example of the power of the 1960s "youth culture" to impose its own tastes on the rest of the country—whether in hair styles, rock music, garish colors in clothes, or—as the college campuses amply demonstrated—in social, philosophical, and educational ideas.

The influence of the youth subculture in the 1960s and 1970s is a fascinating example of how the *rate of change* in a population group has so much more impact than absolute numbers. At the peak of the "youth culture" in 1970, eighteen to twenty-four-year-olds made up only about 12 percent of the total population. But the rate of change in the number of eighteen to twenty-four-year-olds was very fast. There were 16 million eighteen to twenty-four-year-olds in 1960 and 24 million in 1970, and *that* was a 50-percent increase.

Why should *rates* of population changes in subgroups have such a disproportionate impact? My own guess is that so long as all age groups more or less maintain their share in the population, social and economic institutions are well adapted to deal with them: Change is perceived as gradual and evolutionary. But when one age cohort is changing faster than any of the others, the allocation of social resources is continually disrupted, and the pace of change suddenly feels revolutionary.

Certainly, the impact of the "baby boomers" has always felt revolutionary, ever since the huge wave of births in the aftermath of World War II began to wash over American institutions in the 1950s. Most demographers date the "baby boom" births between 1948, when births first began to pick up, and 1964, when the postboom "birth dearth" began. The peak birth year was 1958.

Why a baby boom? It seems that *three* distinct generations of women all had their children at the same time. The first group were older women who had postponed bearing children during the Depression years in the 1930s. (Birth rates were sharply down during the Depression, interestingly enough, well before the advent of modern birth-control methods.) The second group comprised the women who came of age in the 1940s and had to postpone families because of the war. The third group were the women who normally would have been starting families in the 1950s anyway. And *that* group was temporarily inflated because, in the euphoria after the war, women got married younger and had children sooner.

On top of the fact that so many women were having babies at the same time, the average *number* of children per family went up. Interview data show that the preferred family size actually didn't change. But in the generally balmy economic climate of the 1950s, women became more relaxed about limiting births, so there were more "accidental" third, fourth, or fifth children. And since the age at which a woman had her first child dropped sharply in the 1950s, the average woman's prime child-bearing years covered a longer span than normal.

The baby boomers' lives were governed by those rate-of-change data I mentioned above. In the ten years after the war, for instance, the number of babies jumped by 50 percent. There was a rush to build hospitals as obstetrics wards overflowed and women in labor lined up in hospital hallways. Then there was the rush to build schools and playgrounds and a rush to train teachers when schools were forced into double and triple sessions.

In the 1960s, the rush to build colleges and universities was even more frantic. Prior to the war, only a little more than a third of all young people actually were graduated from high school, and only about a third of them—or about 10 percent of the total—went on to college. In the 1960s, 75 percent of the baby boom generation was graduating from high school, and half of them, or more than a million a year, were entering college. During the decade, higher education enrollments doubled to almost 10 million. For the first time ever, the nation had more college students than farmers. And in the scramble for available places, students became as nerve-wracked and anxiety-ridden as the administrators who were scrambling to make places available for them.

No generation ever had more money or leisure than the young people who were coming of age in the 1960s. Their market power is attested to by the absolute conquest of rock music. With teenage spending behind it, rock music swept all other forms of popular music off the boards. The retail record industry took in a billion dollars for the first time in the early 1960s, virtually all of it from rock. Adults strained their sacroiliacs learning the Twist and the Mashed Potato.

The economist Richard Easterlin offers the provocative hypothesis that the relative size of a birth cohort compared to the one just preceding will have profound economic and social effects. His prime exhibits are the baby boomers and their immediate predecessors—the generation born during the low-birth years of the 1930s.

Men born during the 1930s, Easterlin argues, since they were born at a time when the birth rate was significantly depressed, were an economically favored generation. When they entered the job market in the 1950s, they were a relatively scarce commodity. And, in fact, the entry-level wages paid to young men in the 1950s were quite high compared to the wages paid to older men. Older men's wages were still higher, but the gap between older and younger men's wages was unusually small.

Easterlin suggests, in fact, that the relatively high wages for younger men had a lot to do with the "nesting" phenomenon of the 1950s. For the first time in decades, young husbands were earning enough by themselves to support a rising standard of living for themselves and their growing families, with all the trappings of lawns, suburban mortgages, backyard barbecues, and wives devoted full-time to home and children.

Most people regarded the "working wife" phenomenon of the 1960s and 1970s as some kind of aberration. And compared to the standard practice in the 1950s, it certainly was. But women's participation in the labor force had been growing rapidly and steadily through the entire twentieth century up *until* the 1950s, when it suddenly dropped sharply—presumably because men were making enough money to support their families by themselves. The aberration, that is, wasn't the growth in female labor force participation in the 1960s and 1970s, but the low participation rate in the 1950s.

Much the same can be said about most of the rising indicators of social dislocation of the 1960s and 1970s. They appeared all the more dramatic because the 1950s were so remarkably stable. The rise in crime, for example, had a devastating impact in the 1960s and 1970s. But it took until the mid-1970s for the crime rate to catch up to the high level of the 1930s. The burgeoning crime rate was so painful because of the contrast with the 1950s. Mid-1950s crime rates were the lowest since reliable records were kept and were probably as low as at any time in American history.

Divorce rates illustrate the same effect. The low divorce rate in the 1950s was actually an aberration. During the 1950s, divorce rates dropped for the first time in half a century, slipping far below the historical trend line. The soaring rates of divorce in the 1960s and 1970s almost exactly balanced out the drop in the 1950s, simply moving the overall rate back to the trend line.

The Baby Boomers Hit the Labor Market

Economists have debated the details of the "Easterlin hypothesis" for a decade, and there is a lot of disagreement over the actual impact of the baby boom generations on one social indicator or the other. But there is little question about the impact of the baby boom generation on the labor markets.

The picture of the American labor market during the 1970s and the 1980s is remarkably schizophrenic. On the one hand, the "Great American Job Machine" has been the envy of the world. The United States has created jobs for 38 million new workers since 1970, for 17 million in the last seven years alone. Employment in almost all the other industrialized countries has remained basically flat. Rates of unemployment in Germany and England hit previously inconceivable double-digit levels. But in the same breath, economists lament the slowdown in American productivity. With the recent exception of manufacturing, the output of American workers has been roughly stagnant since the early 1970s.

The strong performance in job creation and the weak performance in productivity are, of course, two sides of the same coin. The same 50-percent rate of change that dominated the lives of the baby boomers from their birth on had a powerful impact on their earnings power and severely restricted their job opportunities. When the baby boomers finished school and began looking for work in the 1970s and 1980s, they swelled the total work force enormously and caused a sharp downward shift in average age and experience. In 1960, the most experienced and productive workers, men aged thirty-five to fifty-four, made up about 30 percent of the work force; only a bit more than a third of all workers were under thirty-five. By 1985, half the work force was under thirty-five, and only 20 percent of workers were men aged thirty-five to fifty-four.

Not surprisingly, unemployment rose and real wages steadily declined, particularly for younger men. The gap between the wages of younger men and older men, which had narrowed dramatically during the 1950s, yawned wide once again. The psychological impact was severe. Easterlin points out that the relevant standard of economic success is not one's age group peers, but one's *father*. Men who entered the labor force in the 1950s did very well compared to their fathers; but *their* sons, who were starting careers in the 1970s and 1980s, did relatively poorly.

Economists tend much too often to overlook the kind of forces that Easterlin identified, the same kind of deeper trends that Schumpeter focused on. A good example of the tendency is the obsessive focus on marginal changes in tax rates. The business press has trumpeted for many years how cuts in the capital gains tax create new businesses by increasing incentive. The prime exhibit is the capital gains tax cuts in 1978, which were followed by a sudden burst of entrepreneurial activity. The rate of new business formation in the late 1970s, insofar as data are available, was quite spectacular—one of the highest in history.

But I suspect that the capital gains tax cut had very little to do with it. (When the capital gains tax rate was *raised* in 1986, the venture capital industry predicted doom, but the rate of business formation seems to have been unaffected.) A personal anecdote will help explain what I mean.

I had a relatively senior position at an international bank around 1980. I was forty years old; in fact, the average age of the people in comparable positions—about forty executives—was just about forty years old. We reported to nine executive vice-presidents, whose average age was about forty-five. The president of the bank was forty-two, and the chairman was fifty-three. Most of these executives had joined the bank after college, just before the baby boom generation began to enter the labor force. Their paths to senior positions were relatively unobstructed.

But the careers of younger executives were radically different. I took an informal survey of the hundred-odd professionals in the group I was responsible for. The average age was about thirty-two. Most of them came from professional or semi-professional families and were well educated. But they were earning only middling salaries, and their careers, for all practical purposes, were utterly blocked. Most of the executives on my level had twenty or more years to go before retirement. There was no possibility that more than a tiny fraction of the thirty-year-olds could advance higher up the corporate ladder for many years.

When I talked to the bank's customers—they were all executives of *Fortune 500* corporations—they said the situation was exactly the same in their own companies. The top slots were filled by executives in their early forties, and the competition in the next lower ranks, occupied by men and women in their thirties, was both fierce and desperate. Because big companies as a whole *reduced* their management ranks as part of the slimming-down process of the 1980s, the job competition among the younger executives seemed all the more hopeless.

And, of course, *that's* the reason for the burst of new entrepreneurial activity. If a young executive wanted to move up rapidly, there was almost no alternative but to start a new company. Consider how long it would have taken Steven Jobs (one of the founders of Apple Computer) to work his way to the top of IBM—I suspect he never would have made it. Violent demographic surges affect the total economy in ways that are not even suspected. But economists prefer to plug their economic models with more easily measurable variables—like changes in the tax rate—that are more likely than not simply swamped by tidal changes in the real world.

Whatever the effect on entrepreneurial activity, there can be no doubt that the shift in labor-force age structure accounted for much of the sharp increases in unemployment during the 1970s. Younger men and women have always had higher rates of unemployment than older people. In the early

1970s, the number of young men aged twenty to twenty-four entering the labor force went up by more than 8 percent per year. (Compounded, that's a very high rate of increase; carried on for ten years, it would double the number of young men in the labor force.) Total unemployment soared, from about 4 percent in the late 1960s to as much as 8 percent in the mid-1970s.

With the large increase in numbers, earnings dropped relative to older workers. For example, in the mid-1950s, men aged twenty to twenty-four made, on average, about 75 percent as much as men aged forty-five to fifty-four. By the mid-1970s, the ratio was down to only about 56 percent. Younger women's earnings in the mid-1950s were virtually identical with older women's. By the mid-1970s, they had slipped to 80 percent.

With the huge increase in college attendance, college graduates suffered the most relative disappointment. The rate of increase in college graduates was the fastest of any sub-group, running as high as 15 percent a year for men in the mid-1970s, and over 20 percent for women. The value of a degree slipped proportionately. Data are available only since 1967, but it appears that young male college graduates earned about 1.35 times more than same-age high-school graduates in 1969, but only about 1.2 times as much by 1975.

To make matters worse, as men's earnings went down, women entered the work force in greater numbers than ever before. Some of the increase in female workers reflected changing social attitudes toward women working. The change in labor force participation was the most dramatic for younger women. Only about a third of women aged twenty-five to thirty-four worked outside the home in 1948, but almost three-quarters of them did so in 1988. But much of the shift in working patterns, particularly in working-class families, had nothing to do with "liberation." It was driven by sheer economic necessity. Most important, the average new female entrant to the labor force, regardless of her age, had little previous work experience, so she helped skew the experience level of the work force even more sharply downward.

The overall slippage in national labor productivity should have come as no surprise. With lots of cheap new workers mobbing the doorway, companies quite naturally increased hiring instead of investing in labor-saving machinery. A fancy industrial robot can cost as much as a million dollars, or about as much as the yearly wage of a hundred entry-level workers. And, not surprisingly, the business success stories were companies like McDonald's that learned how to mine the gold in that low-wage pool. The productivity debacle of the 1970s had more to do with sheer numbers of inexperienced workers than with a sudden burst of incompetence on the part of American managers or malicious slothfulness on the part of workers.

The baby boomers are still moving through their generational life cycle, with the same profound influence at each stage—the proverbial "pig in a python." But for the first time, that influence will not be disruptive. The same babies that generated a 50-percent overcrowding in obstetric wards in the early 1950s, then created a 50-percent upsurge in primary-school students a few years later, then crowded the college campuses in the 1960s, and mobbed into the work force in the 1970s and early 1980s, are now getting older. And their influence, for the first time, will be almost entirely benign.

The Comforts of Demography

During the 1990s, the American population and the American work force will suddenly become middle-aged. The chart (page 92) tells the story dramatically. Young adults in the eighteen-to-thirty-four age group will drop by about 11 percent in absolute numbers, and their share in the population will fall from 28 percent to 23 percent—that's an 18-percent drop. Older adults aged thirty-five to fifty-four will increase by 28 percent. Put another way, in 1990, there are about ten adults aged eighteen to thirty-four for every nine aged thirty-five to fifty-four; ten years from now, there will be thirteen adults aged thirty-five to fifty-four for every ten persons aged eighteen to thirty-four. As the chart shows, the most dramatic change will be among the oldest and most productive sector of the adult population, those forty-five to fifty-four years old, whose numbers will increase by a full 46 percent—roughly the 50-percent change at the margin that has defined the impact of the baby boom generation upon society.

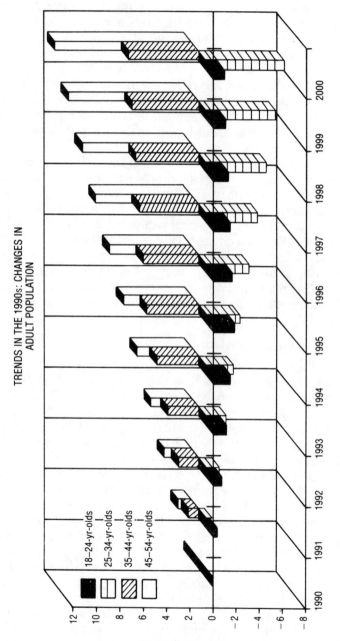

TRENDS IN THE 1990s: CHANGES IN
ADULT POPULATION

18–24-yr-olds
25–34-yr-olds
35–44-yr-olds
45–54-yr-olds

CHANGE IN MILLIONS

12 10 8 6 4 2 0 −2 −4 −6 −8

1990 1991 1992 1993 1994 1995 1996 1997 1998 1999 2000

Source: U.S. Dept. of Commerce, *Current Population Reports*

The baby boom generation has had a profound, sometimes violent impact on society as it has moved through each stage of its life cycle. There is no reason to assume that that impact will diminish as it moves into middle age. But it implies quite a different kind of America than the one we were forced to come to terms with in the 1960s and 1970s, and the impact on the economy should be dramatic.

In the first place, of course, the labor force will stop growing. The rate of natural increase will drop to less than 1 percent a year, and the age of the average worker will jump up by almost a full ten years. (The number of new young adults entering the labor force will drop but the number of retirements will slow by just a little more, so the total labor force will keep growing slowly.) The actual labor force may grow by slightly more or less than the rate of natural increase, depending on changes in labor force participation rates, particularly among women. But even assuming that female labor force participation continues to go up—it is already historically high—total annual labor force growth will still be a gentle 1.5 percent or so. The unemployment rate will continue to go down. Rates of unemployment in the 1990s should approximate those in the 1960s, before the youthful influx of workers hit the job lines. Prudential-Bache Securities projects an unemployment rate of about 4 percent by about 1993.

Some economists worry that, as labor force growth slows down, companies will become desperately short of workers and will touch off a fierce round of wage inflation as they bid for available workers. I think that is extremely unlikely. We have already seen how global competition is clamping a firm lid on price increases. A company that simply inflates its wage bill won't survive. Companies will have no choice but to increase capital spending and improve employee productivity. That has already been happening in the 1980s—despite the generally high prevailing interest rates—and will continue throughout the 1990s. (Gross capital spending, leaving out residential construction, has averaged between 11 and 12.5 percent of GNP in the 1980s, the highest levels since World War II, up from 9.5 to 11 percent in the 1960s and most of the 1970s.)

We have already seen how rapidly manufacturing productivity has been increasing in the 1980s—not only in the United

States but almost everywhere. The sharp productivity increase in the 1990s will come in services. Services accounted for all of the American productivity slowdown in the 1970s and early 1980s, because services absorbed essentially all the new young workers. As that supply of new workers dries up, services productivity—or output per worker—will go up.

A fashionable worry among connoisseurs of doom is that it is not possible to improve services productivity the way it is possible to improve manufacturing productivity. That is simply not true. Some of the most outstanding productivity increases in history have been made in services. The telephone company's replacement of telephone operators by dial phones in the 1950s is just one example. The highly automated dispatching and parcel handling system invented by Federal Express is another. Automated bank teller machines are a third. Home health care is another—in California, for example, it is now common for patients requiring intravenous feeding to receive it at home. The patient or his family is trained in monitoring techniques, and a traveling nurse checks in at programmed intervals. The productivity gain and the cost savings are enormous.

Next time you are in a modern supermarket, watch the checkout clerk run your purchase under a bar code reader. The bar code reader is registering the proper price for the day—no need for the clerk to look up the list of the day's specials. It also stores sales data that will be funneled into a central computer to measure the success of price reductions and advertising programs. It then updates the computer that keeps track of inventory and generates automated purchase orders when stocks fall below a programmed level. That's productivity. Not long ago, all those tasks took a small army of clerks and a mountain of paperwork—if they were done at all. The careful tracking of the impact of sales incentive programs, for example, just wasn't possible a decade ago.

The problem with productivity improvement in services is not that it is hard to achieve, but that it is hard to *measure*. One of the little secrets of the gloom-and-doom school of economic analysis is that the services productivity statistics, which have provoked so much lamentation over the past decade or so, are almost completely meaningless. It is comparatively easy to measure the output of new cars per manufacturing worker, for instance, or the quarts of strawberries produced by farm workers. But there is no easy way to measure most productivity gains in services like the computerized tracking of sales incentive programs in supermarkets.

Government statisticians, confronted with the necessity of producing productivity data in services, are forced to fall back on either price changes or labor input changes to construct indexes of improvement. In a service business, however, price movements often conceal major productivity changes. If a securities firm, for instance, switches from typed customer statements to much more useful computerized statements incorporating data from a number of different customer accounts and credit cards, there obviously has been a significant productivity advance. But if a firm doesn't *charge* extra for the service, it will be lost in the productivity data. Using labor force changes as a proxy for productivity improvement can be even more misleading. I don't doubt that service productivity really *did* go down during much of the 1970s, simply because of the influx of so many young workers. But there is good reason to believe that the lag has been substantially overstated, particularly over the past decade or so.

The financial services industry and the retail sales industry are two examples of industries that have made substantial capital investments and sharply increased the machinery and equipment backing up each worker. In particular, they have both made massive investments in computerization and telecommunications. The impact on the way they conduct their businesses has been revolutionary. A half trillion dollars is traded electronically every *day* on the world's foreign exchange markets, for instance, an inconceivable volume just a short while ago. If foreign exchange trades were measured like quarts of strawberries, the productivity improvement would be stupendous. But the statistics show that the productivity of financial services and retail sales has been lagging for a long time. Bad management? No, bad statistics.

A last crucial result of an older population should be a sharply higher savings rate. The American savings rate, in fact, has already been edging up again after hitting an all-time low in 1987. Personal savings, of course, is the ultimate source of all productive investment. It is the high Japanese savings rate—apparently as much as 18 percent of all personal income in recent years—that has financed Japan's global industrial conquest. It is the high savings in other countries as well that have allowed America to dance through the economic raindrops in recent years—foreign capital picks up the tab for the American budget and trade deficits.

Like productivity data, the personal savings rate is another of those much-quoted, anxiously watched, but in reality extremely imprecise and uncertain, statistics. "Personal savings" as defined by the U.S. Department of Commerce is merely the residual of two other huge data series. Each month the department calculates Americans' personal income—using thousands of data sources and making myriad estimates, interpolations, and seasonal adjustments in the process. Then it calculates personal spending, using thousands of *different* sources and making a different set of estimates, adjustments, and interpolations. Then it subtracts one from the other and the difference is called American "savings."

Obviously, tiny estimating errors or changes in method in the two big series will cause proportionately enormous swings in the residual. The savings numbers are subject to continual revision and reestimation long after they are produced and should be used with much greater caution than they usually are. *International* savings comparisons, as one might expect, are even more fraught with statistical perils, since different countries use different data series and data collection and estimation methodologies. Researchers at the University of Pennsylvania's Wharton School, for example, have estimated that if Japan calculated its savings rate the way that America does, it would be only about half as high as it currently appears. The Japanese savings advantage would still be strong, but at a level much more within Americans' reach in the 1990s.

Ed Yardeni, the chief economist at Prudential-Bache Securities, has estimated that the American personal savings rate should recover to about 10 percent in the mid-1990s, roughly double what it is now and a dramatic improvement over the all-time low of 3.2 percent in 1987. His reasoning is simple: People under thirty, particularly those with lower incomes, don't save. In fact, they "dis-save"—they spend more than they earn. It is people over forty, particularly those with higher incomes, who do most of the saving. And, of course, people over forty will dominate the economy in the 1990s.

It is fashionable to lament the poor American performance in productivity, in savings, and in investment per worker, particularly when compared to Japan and West Germany, the two economic stars of the 1980s. Americans, by comparison, appear feckless, coddled, unwilling to bend to the grindstone like Japanese and Germans, unable to put out the little extra that ensures success.

But, in fact, the three countries have had much different population profiles over the past few decades. On the whole, Americans have been much younger than Japanese and West Germans. Not surprisingly, Americans acted that way. The differences are clear in the following table—and in demographic terms, they are enormous. But strikingly, the age profile in America during the 1990s will be moving rapidly to approximate that in Japan and West Germany in the 1980s.

PROPORTION OF YOUNG AND MIDDLE-AGED
ADULTS IN POPULATIONS OF U.S., WEST GERMANY, JAPAN

	U.S.		Japan		W. Germany	
	% Aged 20–34	% Aged 35–54	% Aged 20–34	% Aged 35–54	% Aged 20–34	% Aged 35–54
1985	26%	23%	21%	30%	23%	28%
1990	25%	26%	20%	30%	24%	20%
2000	20%	31%	21%	27%	19%	30%

Source: World Bank Population Projections, 1987–88

Although it is not apparent from the table, the demographic tides in Japan will begin to put extreme pressure on its economy. The generation of Japanese workers currently in their fifties—the star worker bees that have contributed so mightily to Japan's success over the past twenty years—will retire in the 1990s. An IMF study says that the impact of demographic change in Japan will be "the most extreme" of any of the industrialized countries. The number of aged dependents will double starting about 1995, straining the most ungenerous pension system in the industrialized world. The very high Japanese savings rate will drop as retirees begin to draw down their savings—at about the same time as American savings begin a long rise. I will focus more on trends in Japan in Chapter 9.

In the case of America, it is hard to overestimate the impact of the demographic trends. Before the mid-1980s, the baby boom generation had always been a *dependent* population. They *consumed* wealth and services and produced very little. When they were babies and children, they consumed medical and educational services. When they became adolescents, the great American wealth accumulated by their nose-to-the-grindstone parents in the 1950s and 1960s allowed them to indulge their tastes for music and clothes and prolong their adolescence in college. College ended in the 1970s and they plunged into the cold water of a labor pool that was suddenly overwhelmed by their presence.

But the baby boomers' adolescence and their labor force apprenticeship is over. They are entering their middle years and, for the most part, acting the way adults in their middle years have always acted. They are acting, that is, the way American adults acted in the 1950s and the way German and Japanese adults acted in the 1970s. They are settling down in their jobs and getting better at them. They are making more money and will save more of it. They are getting and staying married, raising children, and beginning to pay off their mortgages. As Bill Cosby remarked in horror after going to a class reunion, "All my friends looked like *parents!*"

And, in their inimitable way, by sheer force of numbers, they will impose their values on the rest of the country, just as they always have. Unemployment rates will go down, savings and productivity will go up, and America will become a much more competitive country than it was a decade ago. There is already much evidence that all of these trends are taking hold. An older, more stable working population will make the industrial adjustments I described in Part I much easier for Americans to manage. Indeed, I believe it means that America will survive the global industrial battles in very good fettle indeed.

No adjustment comes without some pain. There will be some surprising, and temporarily painful, consequences of the shifts I've been describing here, benign as the overall trends may be. I'll describe one of the most important in the next chapter.

Club Med

In 1973, Ed and Linda Burke, recently married, recently out of graduate school, took a week's vacation at the new Club Med Caravelle located on a stunningly beautiful beach on the Caribbean island of Guadaloupe. (Guadaloupe, in fact, has a paucity of good beaches. By being one of the first large-scale developers on the island, Club Med, as it always tries to do, locked up one the very few picture-perfect beaches on the island.)

For a young couple in their twenties, without kids or a great deal of cash, Club Med was the obvious vacation choice. It advertised freedom, informality, sports, action—a week in the sun with other young people in bikinis—at a relatively low and relatively all-inclusive price. Even the extras, such as bar drinks, were paid from strings of currency beads worn around the neck, reinforcing the Club's image of primitive simplicity—the "antidote to civilization."

In 1989, in their early forties, with a co-op apartment in Manhattan, two children aged eleven and five, and demanding jobs—Ed is a financial executive, Linda is in real estate—the Burkes took a family skiing vacation in Switzerland. Their choice of ski resorts: the Club Med ski village at St. Moritz.

"Club Med was the obvious choice," says Ed. "We knew it would be clean and well-run. The price was reasonable and covers everything: instruction, guides for the glaciers, whatever. But most important is the way Club Med is set up for kids. There's a program for them all day, but it's totally flexible. If you want them with you one morning, that's fine, and if you want to ski by yourself the next morning, that's fine, too. But you're not dumping them. The activities for the kids are really well organized, and they just loved it."

Club Med, in the words of a Harvard Business School research report, is a "marketing classic." More than any other leisure services company, it has succeeded by inspiring intense loyalty among its customers—up to 75 percent of its guests, or *gentils membres* (gentle members) are repeats, an almost unheard-of level in the resort industry. Club Med has been able to retain such loyalty by consciously evolving along with its customer base, matching the lifestyles of couples like Ed and Linda Burke, as they mature and their needs and tastes evolve. It is one of very few companies that has successfully marketed to America's baby boom generation in both their 1970s and 1980s incarnations, and it plans to continue doing so in the 1990s.

Jean-Luc Oizan-Chapon, the ebullient chief operating officer of Club Med, Inc., the subsidiary that operates the resorts selling primarily to the North American market, insists there's no secret to the Club Med "magic:" "Club Med is a family, and families grow and change. It's nothing new for us."

Oizan-Chapon points out that the parent company, Club Méditerranée, had already managed a generational transition with its French customer base before tackling the North American market. (The Club Med subsidiary trades on the New York Stock Exchange. The parent is a French company. About 35 percent of total sales still originate in France compared to about 22 percent in North America.) "Last year in France," Oizan-Chapon says, "we had four generations from one family in the same village—starting with an eighty-two-year-old man who was one of our first members, down to his six-month-old great-grandson. It's our job to make them all feel happy, to feel part of the family."

Oizan-Chapon talks about the Club Med "family magic" with a zealot's fervor. In his mid-forties, he has been with Club Med for twenty-five years, starting as a volleyball instructor in the Mediterranean while he was still in college and working his way through various *chef du village* postings to chief financial officer of Club Med, Inc., before assuming his present responsibilities in 1989.

Club Med was not, as many Americans think, organized as a paean to the swinging-singles lifestyle of the late 1960s or 1970s. Its roots go back to postwar France, a time when "everybody was unhappy," says Oizan-Chapon. "They were difficult, sad times. We were still surrounded by the destruction of the war. People needed a chance to relax, to play sports, to renew themselves."

The actual beginning of the Club was a newspaper ad that Gerard Blitz, a Belgian-born diamond cutter and water polo champion, placed in the Paris *France-Soir* in the summer of 1950. Blitz and his friend, Gilbert Trigano, whose family was dealing in U.S. Army surplus tents, wanted to organize an informal club of sports-minded people for a tent vacation on the Mediterranean. Neither man planned to make a profit on the venture, and they hoped that forty or fifty people would respond. To their amazement, more than two thousand people signed up for the trip and sent in their money, plunging the two men into a frantic round of assembling tents, organizing food services and sanitary facilities, creating a sports program, and laying out the very first village of what eventually became Club Méditerranée.

Trigano converted the "Club" into a profit-making business in 1954 and opened the American subsidiary in 1972. By 1989, with Trigano's son Serge at the helm, the Club had grown to be the ninth-largest resort organization in the world, operating 243 separate villages, villas, spas, and ski resorts, spread throughout five continents, from Thailand to the Caribbean, from Switzerland to Saharo Mountain in Japan, drawing 1.1 million *gentils membres* worldwide, including a newly burgeoning East Asian market, with sales edging toward the $2 billion mark.

The success of the Club's laid-back vacation style is built on hard economics. First of all, by packaging every aspect of a vacation, from travel, hotel services, and food and drink to leisure activities and sports, the Club can exert its considerable buying power to deliver a total vacation for perhaps half the cost of an "unbundled" trip. Just as important, the trip is relatively risk-free: The adventures will be *on* the beach or the ski slopes, not in trying to *find* the beach or sign up for ski instruction. With its broad range of resort choices and strong brand identification, the Club is an attractive offering for most travel agencies, and it has focused on building a strong distribution network of "expert" travel agencies, reinforced with frequent agent-training programs.

The Club also keeps operating costs low. Its traditional villages are spartan, but clean. Accommodations are two to a room—singles are assigned same-sex roommates—and service costs are low. There are no radios, TVs, clocks, or telephones. True to its French heritage, the Club pays considerable attention to the quality of its food, but service is buffet-style in a common dining room, usually with eight to a table. And the Club has had enormous success attracting legions of enthusiastic young workers, the *gentils organisateurs,* such as Jean-Luc Oizan-Chapon himself twenty-five years ago; they sign on for average stints of two or three years of hard work and hard play at low pay in a series of exotic climes all around the world.

And, unlike most resorts, the Club manages to capture a very high percentage of its members' vacation spending power. The villages are laid out on generous spaces with landscaped walks, secluded settings, and a blur of activities to induce members to spend their entire vacation within the Club's special ambience, its *je ne sais quoi,* as the Club's advertising literature puts it.

But the most powerful feature of the Club's program, a device that both keeps the spending dollar within the Club's confines and builds the strong brand loyalty that keeps guests returning again and again, is the conscious fostering of a group atmosphere. It was the senior Trigano's insight that belonging to a "club" could be such a powerful marketing device. Building a sense of group cohesion pervades every aspect of the daily program. According to one study, the Club Med "magic" was managing to "transform a group of uptight urban professionals—who start out as total strangers—into a fun-loving, relaxed group of friends and acquaintances, 'converts' who assist the staff in welcoming the next group of uptight urban professionals into the village."

The young staff are the key element in building the group feeling. They function as friends and participants as well as instructors and servants. Seating at the dining room is a random mixture of staff and guests. Although the day's activities offer a wide range of sports or leisure options, the evenings are quite structured. Every night the staff puts on an impromptu stage show, with an emphasis on comedy, and then leads the group in a Club Med ritual, the "crazy signs dancing," a set of complicated hand motions performed to French songs. In the family villages, the evening programs will be seasoned with children's performances.

The point of the evening exercises is to break down social barriers and sweep the whole group into the feeling of infectious enthusiasm displayed by the staff. As one guest puts it, "To see those kids putting out that kind of energy and enthusiasm especially after doing a full day's work, makes *me* feel like a kid again."

The centrality of the young staff to the Club's success points up a central conundrum of modern service industries—how to bring production-line styles of efficiency, productivity, and standardization to a business that depends to a very large degree on the personal interaction between customers and the very lowest level staff. As employment continues its long-term shift toward services with the automation of factory production in all the industrialized countries, the effective management of service personnel will loom ever larger as a critical component of business success.

A brief digression is in order here: The shift toward services employment in the United States is commonly cited as evidence of America's "deindustrialization," or the "American disease." The deindustrialization hypothesis, as the first part of this book argues, is simply not true. Manufacturing accounts for almost the same share of GNP in 1989 as it did in 1948. But since manufacturing productivity has risen so rapidly, manufacturing accounts for less and less *employment*—which is not the same thing as "deindustrialization."

As William Baumol and others have recently pointed out, the shift of labor away from manufacturing toward services is the long-term trend in every industrialized country. The trend began in the United States somewhat earlier than elsewhere, and America has a slightly higher percentage of its work force in services than other countries (or did in 1980, the end point of Baumol's data series). But the shift toward services is actually proceeding much faster in almost all other countries than in the United States—at a 31-percent annual rate in Japan, for instance, and a 30-percent rate in France, compared to only 10 percent in the United States.

The causes of the shift toward services are straightforward and universal in their operation. In the first place, as manufacturing workers generate more and more wealth, they both produce the income to buy additional services and free up the workers to provide them. Secondly, as manufacturing productivity rises relative to services productivity, the cost of services necessarily rises relative to goods. Since GNP is measured by the cost of final sales, services will inevitably make up a greater and greater portion of apparent GNP. Measuring conventions help reinforce the trend. Since we tend to underestimate services productivity gains, we overstate the gap between services and manufacturing productivity and so overstate real services costs.

In addition, as companies strip down to the basics, they generate substantial employee reclassification, creating an illusion of greater services employment. To take an example, at GE the in-house public relations staff that served several of the company's units was recently "spun off": That is, the former staffers formed their own company and now provide services to GE in competition with other independent public relations firms. It is a small example of a trend toward "contracting out" that is sweeping through large-scale industry, covering everything from data processing to cafeteria services. ("Contracting out" is the services parallel to the "dis-integration" of manufacturing production we saw in Chapter 3. A specialized, competitive payroll service, the reasoning goes, will provide payroll services more cheaply and efficiently than an in house operation, in the same way that Intermet outperforms the Big Three captive foundries.) But each instance of contracting out generates a statistical increase in services employment. When the GE public relations staff received salaries from GE, they were classified as "manufacturing" employees; as soon as they formed their company, they automatically entered the "services" sector.

Improving the quality and productivity of services activities will continue to grow in importance as the industrialized economies mature. Companies like IBM have long since recognized that the responsiveness and follow-up of their services are at least as important as their hardware in maintaining their customer base. And it is their generally poor service performance that accounts for the failure of Japanese personal computer makers—who, as one would expect, turn out high-quality, economical machines—to gain a larger share of the American PC market.

Probably the outstanding services success story of the last twenty years is McDonald's—a true pioneer in pointing the way toward achieving production-line efficiencies in a service operation that depends on a far-flung network of entry-level workers. Every aspect of producing a standard serving of a McDonald's hamburger and order of french fries has been painstakingly engineered. The french fries scoop, the clips that position the french fries bags, the cash register keyboard are all cunningly designed to produce exactly the same product quality at every location in the world. Quality control is reinforced by detailed training for managers and franchisees at the famous "Hamburger University" at the company's headquarters in Oakbrook, Illinois. With food-handling simplified and standardized to the maximum degree, McDonald's managers can focus on maintaining the pleasant and friendly demeanor of their front-line staff, the critical variable in ensuring repeat customer visits. The McDonald's conception of a service product is being applied to a host of poorly organized service activities—beauty parlors, automobile oil and lube services and routine repairs, even funeral parlors.

Club Med approaches the service quality problem with extensive training at all staff levels, obsessive attention to detail, and standardization of most basic services. Each village features a set of locally derived menu choices, for example, but the basic dining choices will be standard throughout the world. Sports instruction, in particular, is rigorously standardized. Guests receiving ski instruction at one ski resort, for instance, should be able to pick up precisely where they left off at a different resort the following year.

Club Med reinforces its commitment to quality standardization by a rigidly enforced staff rotation policy. Each year is divided into two seasons, and *all* village staff change locations every season. The goal is to make every staffing unit interchangeable—no cliques, no local procedural variants, no village-specific lore or "solutions." The company freely admits that its rotation policy is a high-risk, high-cost strategy but argues that the impressive degree of standardization that has been achieved is evidence of its success.

The challenge for the next decade will be to maintain the Club's appeal to its loyal members as they continue to age and prosper. Club Med is working hard to maintain its gradual evolution along with its customer base. Just as the 1980s saw the evolution of "Mini-Clubs" and "Baby-Clubs" to take young children off Mom and Dad's hands, the 1990s will see a slow shift toward sports such as golf and horseback riding as alternatives to volleyball and tennis for aging baby boomers.

And the Club is consciously reworking its image to appeal to the more upscale clients to keep pace with its guests' move up the economic ladder. New or refurbished, more upscale villages will offer restaurant settings in addition to the traditional buffets, more elaborately appointed rooms, and extra touches of personal service. Even in the common dining rooms, seating will be four to a table, instead of eight, to permit greater privacy. One spectacular new venture, with a decidedly upscale appeal, is the *Club Med I*, the world's largest sailboat—virtually a sail-powered *Queen Elizabeth*, with a fully appointed onboard set of Club Med facilities. The boat will sail from port to port, traveling at night—"We sail at sunset, the most beautiful time," says Oizan-Chapon—leaving the day free for beach sports, shopping, or other excursions.

Another major innovation will be the introduction of "Flexi-stays." "Say you're a lawyer," says Oizan-Chapon, "you've got money and you've just won a big case three days earlier than you planned. It's Tuesday afternoon, and you're starting another big case on Monday. You should be able to call your wife or husband, make sure they can clear their schedules, too, and be on a Club Med plane the next morning. When you get to the village in the middle of the week, and you want to start scuba lessons or tennis, it's our job to tailor the lessons to start when you do—no rigid weekly schedules, everything totally customized. That's hard," he says, "and we can't do it yet, but that's what we're working on. That's where we want to be."

But the company still insists on its family image and does not want to get caught up in serving a single social stratum or age group. "In the 1980s, when you were ten years old, you went to a Club Med with Dad," says Oizan-Chapon. "In the 1990s, when you're eighteen, and Dad's heading for a Club Med golf vacation, you don't want to go with Dad. You want to go with your girlfriend. And we'll have the vacation for you. And we intend to keep on being the place of your choice. Because that's what belonging to a family is all about. We change right along with you."

5

THE COMING REAL ESTATE BUST AND WHY IT'S GOOD FOR AMERICA

The Great Housing LBO

For about ten years now the financial press has been marveling at the wizardry of the leveraged buyout buccaneers—Henry Kravis, Carl Icahn, T. Boone Pickens, and their like. The leveraged buyout, or LBO, game involves buying a business with borrowed money. The trick is to put up only a little of your own cash and float loans secured by the assets of the business you're going to buy.

Since the LBO entrepreneur puts up only a little cash, he doesn't lose much if the business goes bankrupt. The lenders will have to look to the assets of the business to get their loans repaid. But if the business is at all successful, the returns can be enormous. Here is a simple example: Assume Blackbeard the Raider buys a business for $100 million, putting up $10 million of his own cash and borrowing the rest. And assume the business is a mild success: Sales grow slowly, and there is a general inflationary rise in stock prices. Blackbeard therefore is able to sell out five years later for $150 million. He pays off the $100 million in debt and is left with $50 million.

The value of the company increased by only 50 percent—from $100 million to $150 million, or about 8.5 percent a year. Nothing spectacular there; it's about the same as the return on treasury bonds in the 1980s. But the $50 million that Blackbeard had left over after paying off the debt *quintupled* his original investment of $10 million. That's about a 40-percent annual rate of return, and that *is* spectacular. (The ratcheting up of returns that results from buying with debt is the source of the term "leverage.")

And that's the magic of the LBO. Since the required equity investment—the initial cash out of pocket—is so comparatively low, relatively modest rates of increase in a business's value will result in very large returns on the initial invested cash. And since the stock market rose so rapidly throughout the 1980s, almost all businesses experienced substantial growth in their stock market values, so almost all LBO buyers made very large amounts of money.

In effect, as Peter Peterson, the chairman of the LBO boutique, the Blackstone Group, has pointed out, the LBO game could be viewed as just an evasion of SEC margin rules. (The stock market rules laid down by the Securities and Exchange Commission say that a private investor may borrow no more than 50 percent of the price of a stock purchase. The borrowed money is the "margin.") From that perspective, the LBOs were a device for investors to buy into companies on 90-percent margins.

So long as the stock market continued to rise, it was very hard to lose money on LBOs. In fact, if an investor had LBO'ed any large random sample of the Standard and Poor's 500 companies in 1982, he would have made about a 70-percent annual return by 1988—rather a better rate of return than the LBO experts actually achieved.

But if stock market prices stop growing, so will the return opportunities. And as this is written in late 1989, there's a good argument that the stock market is relatively fully priced. Not surprisingly, a number of LBO venturers who were counting on continually rising stock prices—(for example the Canadian financier Robert Campeau who paid a very high price for Federated Department Stores (Bloomingdale's, A&S) in 1987)—are finding that they have overpaid for their businesses. To their shock, they may have trouble making any return at all on their investment, and some may lose all their equity investment.

But LBOs are not the private preserve of the world of high finance. The man in the street plunged into the LBO business with a vengeance twenty years ago. The only difference is that instead of using debt finance to buy stock market companies, he used debt finance to buy real estate. And the returns, like those on business LBOs, have been nothing short of spectacular.

Consider these numbers. From 1968 to 1988, the market value of residential real estate rose from about $600 billion to about $4 *trillion*. Over the entire period, home prices grew about 2 percent per year faster than the rate of inflation— almost 3 percent a year over the inflation rate during the 1970s and a little over 1 percent a year in the 1980s.

Any investment that so consistently beats the rate of inflation for such an extended period is obviously a good deal, but it's even better if it can be leveraged. The debt incurred to buy a house doesn't change with inflation, so from the buyer's point of view, inflation is a good thing—the debt just keeps getting smaller and smaller as a proportion of the expected resale price. Assuming normal leveraging, that is a cash down payment in the 10- to 20-percent range, the average return on cash invested in housing in the 1970s was well above 20 percent *per year*. Returns dropped in the 1980s but were still in the double-digit range. The average house purchased with a 10-percent down payment in 1969 would have produced a 14.5-percent *real* annual return, that is after stripping away the effects of inflation, when it was sold in 1989.

These returns, spectacular as they are, are probably understated. Until well into the 1970s, commercial and savings banks had very large pools of low-interest consumer deposits in checking and passbook savings accounts. Since consumers didn't demand market rates on their deposits, mortgage lenders competing for business charged lower than market rates for their mortgages. The real rate of interest on home mortgages was actually *negative* for much of the 1970s; that is, the interest rate on the mortgage was lower than the rate of inflation. (Strictly speaking, when real rates of interest are negative, mortgages could be considered *assets*.) If we factor the federal tax advantages for mortgage interest and the various favorable tax provisions to shelter housing capital gains, home ownership was, without question, the best possible investment for the average family.

The spectacular investment returns from housing lend some perspective to continuing laments over the high cost of housing for young people. The worry over how young couples can afford housing has been a staple item in the financial press for the last two decades. Although figures on housing costs are slippery, data compiled by Comstock Partners, an investment advisory firm, show that the hours a blue-collar worker needed to work to meet his monthly mortgage payment went up about two-and-a-half times from the early 1960s to the early 1980s. No wonder that women entered the labor force in such numbers.

But overlooked in the laments was that working to support a mortgage was an entrepreneurial undertaking in the 1970s. At a 20-percent return on investment, putting a spouse to work to help carry the mortgage payments was, in economic terms at least, the best possible use of time and money. That is the simple explanation of what the financial writer Adam Smith called the "absolute frenzy of house-buying and mortgaging, a thrashing shark pool."

Nor should there be any mystery about the drop in the personal savings rate in the 1970s and the 1980s. The share of personal income that went into savings accounts went down as the share of income that went into housing went up. That's not the whole story, of course. As we saw in the last chapter, the baby boomers' emergence into adulthood caused a sharp downward shift in the age of household heads. Young people consume more of their income and save less. The available data on savings and spending, as I've noted before, are quite shadowy, for all the decimal-place precision of their presentation. But data compiled by Comstock Partners, and other data series, like those compiled by Townsend-Greenspan Co. for the 1970s, show a clear shift of household assets toward real estate and away from financial instruments, like bank deposits, CDs, stocks, and bonds. That shift would show up in the U.S. Commerce Department's data series as a drop in the personal savings rate.

The Lumbering Herd

Markets, I've always been convinced, despite their reputation for efficiency, are dumb, slow-footed animals. It took five or six years for stock market prices to catch up to the values that LBO buyers were willing to pay. And, similarly, it took a long time before house prices began to reflect the extraordinary capital-gain opportunities that were available. But once slow-footed animals pick up speed, they usually have trouble stopping, and markets are no exception. The "Great Stock Market Crash" of 1987 was the consequence of a bad case of overenthusiasm driving prices to unsustainable levels.

The same overenthusiasm has also driven house prices far too high. A good indicator is the spreading gap between house and apartment rentals and house and apartment purchase prices. In economic terms, a purchase price is just the capitalized value of a stream of future rents, so in a normal market, rents and purchase prices should move more or less in lockstep. And in the computer industry or the airline industry, for instance, they do. Over the life of the equipment, it costs about the same to lease a commercial jet or a mainframe computer as it does to buy it, and companies decide whether to lease or buy based on purely internal financial management considerations. But over the past two decades, house prices have increased almost twice as fast as rents, and the divergence was still accelerating through 1988.

The disparity between the cost of buying or renting a home is clearly driven by buyers' anticipation of capital gains. Just as the prospect of ever-rising stock prices drove LBO spectulators into bidding ever higher prices for companies, the chance to make a killing in real estate has driven house prices through the clouds.

But if the capital gains don't make up for the cost of carrying the debt, home buyers will find themselves in the same uncomfortable position as Robert Campeau did when he discovered he had paid too much for his department store chains. Consider what happens if home prices just stop rising—not fall, just stop rising. In the Northeast, for example, a "starter" executive home—presumably three or four bedrooms, a family room, a couple of baths, a decent yard—costs easily $300,000. It's the kind of house a young professional couple with one or two children buy. Assume they put down $50,000 and take on a fixed-rate thirty-year 11-percent mortgage. Assume that the tax benefits of ownership cancel out the costs of maintenance.

If the couple has to move five years later and the house's value is still stuck at $300,000, they will take a bath. They would still owe $243,000 on the mortgage. After paying off their bank and covering normal transaction costs, they would end up with only about half their original down payment. (That's an annual 13-percent *loss.*) Their total shelter costs over the five years would have been in excess of $30,000 a year. With such heavy housing costs, they would have had little chance to add to their savings. They may decide to stay put after all.

Why the Boom in Housing?

The housing boom is usually attributed to a squeeze on living space caused by the baby boomers. But that's only half true.

In the first place, the baby boomers *do* account for much of the demand. A 50-percent increase in young adults in less than a decade was bound to put pressure on the housing stock.

But changes in behavior in all age groups were just as important. The baby boomers, perhaps, should take part of the blame for that as well, because the 1960s and 1970s ushered in the "Age of Aquarius," with freer, looser lifestyles that helped break up traditional nuclear-family living patterns.

The baby boomers themselves moved out of their parents' households sooner, and, just as important, they got married later and settled down later than previous generations had done. "Unattached individuals" was the fastest growing category of household during the 1970s. The pattern of delayed marriages, as we saw in the last chapter, was partly a matter of raw economics. In a crowded generation, it took longer to get settled into a decent job, so it made sense to delay forming a family. But in the meantime, there was a substantial increase in demand for separate housing.

But the second most important generator of housing demand was the over-sixty-fives—nothing to blame the baby boomers for there. Social security and corporate pension benefits were increased substantially during the 1970s. When Congress tied social security benefits to the rate of inflation in 1973, the formula they adopted, until it was changed recently, actually had the effect of increasing social security benefits faster than inflation. Medicare benefits provided much better support for older people's health care needs.

At about the same time, Congress passed the ERISA legislation that tightened standards for private-sector pensions and ensured that funds to pay pension benefits would actually be available. Pension benefits had been a major focus of union bargaining in the 1960s and early 1970s. The combination of improved private pensions, much better social security benefits, and government health insurance, taken together, meant that people retiring in the 1970s were much better off financially than previous generations had been.

One of the unexpected consequences was that a more affluent older generation hung on to their houses. In previous generations, owned houses were often passed down to family members. Or if Grandma was a renter she moved in with the kids when Grandpa died. (Previous generations of children thought that Grandma *wanted* to move in with them. But as soon as grandmas as a group became self-supporting, they showed that they much preferred independent living. Let the kids hire someone else to do their baby sitting.)

Over-sixty-fives grew from just under 20 million in 1970 to 28.5 million in 1985, a 46-percent increase, a rate almost as fast as the increase among the baby boomers. In the last chapter, I commented on the importance of changes in population groups *at the margin*. It wasn't the total size of the youth generation in the 1970s that made it so disruptive but how fast the numbers were changing.

Anyone who doubts that might reflect on the vast increase in political power exercised by oldsters as their numbers increased rapidly over the past two decades. The late Senator Claude Pepper's social security lobby and the "Gray Panthers" of the American Association of Retired People became a political instrument that struck fear into the hearts of vote-conscious legislators. Not surprisingly, now that population growth among the over-sixty-fives is leveling off—it will be fairly flat for the next twenty years—politicians are slowly becoming more willing to speak negatively of the high cost of federally supported retirement benefits. The fastest growing population group for the next two decades will be people in their prime tax-paying years.

Political consequences aside, the impact on the housing market was that a large number of homes were effectively taken out of inventory and kept by older couples or older people living alone. That increased the bottlenecks in the housing supply, particularly for family-size homes, and helped push up prices.

Even the adult cohorts whose numbers didn't change contributed to the housing crunch by changing their behavior. Divorce became much more acceptable in the 1970s; in some big cities, broken families were the norm. The consequence, again, was more demand for separate housing.

Finally, the 1970s were a period of extensive regional migration. When the oil boom in the Southwest coincided with the collapse of the Rust Bowl in the mid-1970s, hundreds of thousands, possibly millions, of families moved to sunnier climes. Many of them moved back again when the oil economy collapsed in the early 1980s. Housing in the wrong place is as good as no housing at all. There was a residential building boom all throughout the South and Southwest in the 1970s, driven primarily by population movement.

All told, sheer demographics caused about half the upsurge in housing demand in the 1970s, while behavioral changes of one kind or another accounted for the rest. The rate of new home building during the 1970s was 50 percent higher than during the 1960s. (From the 1950s to the 1960s the rate of home building was roughly constant.) New construction, of course, accounts for only a small part of the housing stock. The rapid run-up in the market value of existing homes was even faster than the increase in construction, which suggests that even the accelerated pace of building didn't manage to keep up with demand.

Poking a Hole in the Real Estate Bubble

Almost all of the demographic trends that drove the housing boom will run in reverse over the next decade or so. As we saw in the last chapter, the number of young adults will drop fairly sharply. In addition, the number of old people will be relatively stable for the next few decades, or so, before the older population starts growing very rapidly again about 2020. Taking the adult population as a whole, the demographically driven component of housing demand will *drop* by about 35 percent from 1985 to 1995.

Housing demand, as we saw in the last section, depends on more than sheer numbers. Behavioral changes accounted for about half the increased demand for housing in the 1970s and early 1980s. Obviously, it's very difficult to predict behavioral changes. But it's hard to conceive of behavioral changes that would lead to further family fission than there has already been—recognizing that the "hard to conceive" style of forecasting is fraught with pitfalls.

But there are straws in the wind suggesting a return to greater family stability—in other words, behavioral changes may actually reinforce the demographically driven decline in housing demand. The American divorce rate almost doubled from the mid-1960s to the mid-1970s. But it has stabilized since then and has actually dropped slightly during the 1980s. More stable family units mean less demand for separate housing.

As the baby boomers settle down into marriages and families, if quite belatedly by the standards of previous generations, their children are creating a small "echo boom." People in their thirties and forties, particularly people with children, move only about half as frequently as younger adults. There should be less of the frantic mobility of the past two decades and less "churning" in the housing market. In analytic terms, the number of people per house will go up, dampening overall housing demand.

Some analysts see hope in the steady aging of the baby boomers. People in their forties, as they reach their peak earning years, are likely to want to move up to bigger, more expensive homes, into the so-called luxury housing market. But they will have problems financing the move. In the 1970s and early 1980s, people "moved up" at absurdly high price levels by cashing in their equity gains in their current houses. Paying $300,000 for an ordinary four-bedroom home may seem ridiculous. But it's not so ridiculous if the price of your current three-bedroom has risen to $225,000 or so. In fact, after selling the three-bedroom and making a minimum down payment on the four-bedroom, you ended up with cash in the bank. The mortgage payments were heavy, but didn't look so bad as long as you expected the value of the new house to rise to $400,000.

The problem facing the luxury housing market in the 1990s will be that, with the falloff in younger adults, the prices of starter homes will stop growing. The capital gains that have been flowing into the luxury housing sector will dry up, and the price reverberations will be felt all up and down the market. When couples are faced with a loss of their equity investment by selling at depressed prices, they will be more likely simply to stay put, keep their heads down, and work at paying off their present mortgages.

Charles Clough, chief investment strategist at Merrill Lynch, thinks the housing deflation has already started. The inventory of unsold houses has been rising sharply over the past few years. "You don't see the falloff in home prices in the data yet," he said (speaking in October, 1989), "but that's because people are keeping their houses on the market longer. The data don't reflect the big build-up in inventory. If it takes longer to sell an asset, that's the same as a price cut as far as the owner is concerned. I don't think house prices will actually fall, but the days when real estate was an inflation hedge, let alone a source a capital gains, are gone."

Analysts who have looked closely at the real estate market disagree mainly about the speed and the violence of the coming transition. The investment advisors Comstock Partners take seriously the possibility of a true price collapse "as For Sale signs give way to surrender flags." But even the Comstock analysts concede that an actual drop in real estate prices would be "highly unusual." Ed Yardeni of Prudential-Bache Securities tends to agree with Clough that prices will not actually fall. He expects them to rise gently in the 2 to 4 percent annual range, barely keeping pace with inflation. (Between 1981 and 1984, it is worth noting, the rise in home resale prices failed to keep pace with inflation for four consecutive years, the first time that has happened in a long, long time.)

While developments in the residential real estate market are most directly relevant to the thesis of this book, similar trends are afoot in the commercial real estate sector. The volume of new construction rose mightily during the 1970s and 1980s—from about $100 billion a year in 1972 to more than $300 billion by 1986. Although the factors driving the commercial real estate market were different from those driving the residential real estate market, there are some broad similarities.

Negative real interest rates in the 1970s and highly favorable tax treatment spurred a sharp run-up in commercial real estate prices. The spectacular capital gains from highly leveraged real estate investments drew even more money into the market. The Tax Reform Act of 1986, which ended the most egregious tax preferences for real estate investment, paradoxically, added fuel to the investment boom as speculators rushed to close projects before the new rules took effect.

The boom in residential construction carried certain commercial sectors along with it. In particular, the steady growth of suburbs and apartment complexes created a demand for more urban and suburban shopping malls. The rapid growth in the financial services industry sparked steady price increases for office space and a boom in office construction. The decentralization of American business away from traditional business centers in the Northeast and Midwest greatly increased business travel and caused an upsurge in hotel construction.

Virtually all of these trends have run their course. Financial services industry employment is suddenly trending down. In addition, most of the big banks and brokerage firms still have relatively antiquated back offices and are much too labor-intensive. Pressures to cut overhead costs will be severe in the 1990s and should result in rapid computerization and reductions in clerical staffs. Office vacancy rates have already quadrupled, from about 5 percent in 1979 to just under 20 percent in 1988. And those are nationwide figures. The situation in hard-hit office markets like Denver, Houston, and Dallas is much worse. Even in relatively healthy economies, such as Atlanta's, there is roughly a ten-year space surplus. The hotel industry tells the same story. Nationwide occupancy rates are less than 60 percent, or barely at break-even levels, and are much worse in the hardest-hit markets.

What's the Good News in the Real Estate Bust?

This is an optimistic book. The reader has a right to ask why I am so obviously pleased at the coming debacle in the real estate industry. The reason, of course, is that a major shift away from real estate investment will be a central element in the American transition back to a high-productivity manufacturing economy.

As I'm sure I've made clear, I believe the real estate boom of the past two decades was excessive. But the excesses occurred primarily at the end of the cycle—office buildings are perhaps the best example. Cyclical excesses are probably an integral part of a private enterprise system. But it would be wrong to characterize the massive concentration of resources in real estate over the past twenty years as a waste. The violent demographic transitions that were underway *required* massive investments in real estate, and the real estate and financial industries responded with vigor and verve.

But that cycle of investment is now over for a long time. Investors, including home buyers, who have taken on substantial debt in the hope of big capital gains will be hurt in the cyclical transition, just like the LBO buyers who plunged in at the peak of the market.

It is difficult to exaggerate the importance of a shift away from a real estate–intensive economy. A few statistics will provide some perspective. Total mortgage debt is now the same size as the federal debt, or about $2.7 *trillion*. In the 1980s, during a consumption boom and a relative slowdown in real estate activity, mortgage debt still grew roughly four times as fast as consumer debt. Real estate and construction activity contribute about as much to the economy as the entire service sector, about seven times as much as agriculture and about ten times as much as major industries such as chemicals.

There is no precise way to measure the impact that twenty years of fevered real estate activity has had on personal savings and on productivity-enhancing investment in manufacturing and other basic industries. But it clearly has been profound. The sheer scale of the numbers I've cited in this chapter demonstrates that.

The inevitable shift away from a real estate–intensive economy will have effects equally profound. Personal savings will rise as housing absorbs a lower share of growing incomes. Mortgage debt will slowly drop as the baby boomers stay put and start paying off their mortgages. The shift of surplus income away from real estate and into bank accounts and stocks and bonds will unlock vast resources for productive industrial investment.

The transition will undoubtedly be painful for key real estate–dependent sectors of the economy. The savings and loan debacle is only the first of several to come. Problems at the FHA may be on the same scale. Some investors and some homeowners will see their equity values disappear as their housing investments fail to keep pace with the general economy.

But the pain of the transition will be amply cushioned by the positive effects in the rest of the economy. The reduced strain on the credit markets will help lower interest rates, just as the imperatives of global industrial competition cause an acceleration in the pace of business investment.

The tidal shift of assets away from real estate is just one more element in the emerging Schumpeterian picture of a global industrial boom. With our housing and commercial space needs taken care of for a decade or more, savings will rise, interest rates will fall, and the pace of industrial investment will continue to quicken, all helping to increase the competitiveness of American industry and American workers in the fierce struggle for global industrial supremacy.

SUMMING UP

Economists have spilled much ink lamenting the differences between America's economic performance in the 1970s and 1980s and the performance of countries such as Japan and Germany—particularly as regards the lower American savings rates and low rates of American productivity growth. But they have, to a great degree, neglected the fact that America really *was* different. Because of a unique confluence of demographic events in the postwar era, America alone experienced a "baby boom," a spike in births producing a generation roughly 50 percent larger than normal.

Despite the energy, flair, and color that a burgeoning population of young people transmit to a society, they are a drain on resources. For most of the first three decades or so of life, people consume more than they produce. As babies, children, and students, they exact a considerable expenditure of public and private resources; as young workers, they lower productivity and average skill levels; and as young householders, they are typically in debt—consuming more than they save, taking more than they contribute.

But America has survived the baby boomers' years of dependency. The members of that same cohort are maturing into their forties and, soon, their fifties—years of stability and productivity, when they become net contributors to society rather than the other way around. For the next twenty years, the population profile in America will be much like those of Japan and Germany for the past twenty. And the impact will be felt with the force of that same 50-percent excess in numbers that has marked every one of the baby boomers' generational transitions. But this time that impact will be almost wholly benign. Almost all the crucial variables—savings, worker productivity, social discipline—will turn in the right direction.

One key economic sector that will suffer from the sudden onset of stability will be real estate, particularly in the residential market. The advent of the baby boomers and a number of other coincident demographic developments drove an unprecedented twenty-year American housing boom. Housing speculation produced such attractive returns for so long that it siphoned off a substantial portion of American household wealth, with serious negative effects for industrial investment.

That boom is over as well. And while the flattening out of home prices will come as a shock to homeowners hoping to make a killing on real estate, the consequent shift of resources back into savings accounts, stocks, and bonds, will be just what the doctor ordered for America's, and the world's, industrial progress.

Assimilating the baby boomers has been one of the great social, economic, and political challenges of the postwar period. It is a challenge that we have managed to surmount, if in somewhat tatterdemalion fashion. We are now in a position to begin to reap the benefits of an older, more experienced, more stable population—one able to meet the new challenges posed by the global drive toward high-efficiency economic performance. The profound demographic transition under way in the United States is just one more sign of the massive converging forces signaling that a Schumpeterian phase-change is under way, that the economy is moving from a period of dislocation and disruption to a period of prolonged growth and prosperity.

III

GOVERNMENTS

6

DISAPPEARING DEFICITS

For at least the last six or seven years, America's federal budget deficits have been the world's economic bogeyman. Scratch almost any banker, economist, stock broker, editorial writer, or Congressman and the response is automatic: Federal budget deficits cause high inflation and high interest rates, are at the root of the high American trade deficit, and have converted America into the "world's largest net debtor."

Amazingly enough, none of those statements is true. Government budget deficits have never had the ill effects everyone seems to think they do. And it is simply not true that the United States is the "world's largest net debtor."

More important for the argument in this book, government borrowing in almost all the industrialized countries, including the United States, is shrinking so fast that forward-thinking portfolio managers are genuinely worried about finding enough high-quality bonds for their portfolios. The shrinking volume of government borrowing—the shrinkage is already quite rapid—is one more powerful force that will be driving down interest rates over the next decade, freeing up borrowing capacity for private industry, and speeding the pace of industrial investment. Couple that with the shift of personal income and savings away from real estate assets and the global price competition in the goods markets, and you can see how all the deep, underlying trends are pointing in the same direction—low inflation, low interest rates, and a continued investment boom.

But there has been such a hue and cry raised about America's federal deficit and "international debt," and so much misinformation and confusion, that it is almost impossible to talk sensibly about the trend toward lower government borrowing without first devoting a few pages to those issues.

America's Federal Budget Deficit

A federal budget deficit is the gap between the money the federal government takes in as taxes and what it lays out in spending. If the federal government spends more than its tax receipts, it must borrow the difference, which it does by issuing treasury bonds and notes—essentially just IOUs carrying fixed rates of interest. Conventional economic theory treats government borrowing as neither a good thing nor a bad thing in itself. If the economy is in recession, government deficits and borrowing are normally a good thing. By spending more than it takes in as taxes, the government is *increasing* the nation's overall spending and giving a boost to economic activity. The huge deficits the government ran up during World War II, for instance, put to flight the last lingering vestiges of the Depression.

But if the economy is *already* growing rapidly, conventional theory points to a long string of evil consequences that follow upon continued government borrowing. The borrowing will use up personal savings, leaving insufficient money for business investment. As business competes to borrow the savings that are left, lenders will charge more for the available funds, so interest rates will rise. The extra government spending will also increase personal consumption, but since business investment will be lagging, production will not keep pace. There will be a goods shortage, and that will cause prices to rise, accelerating inflation. At the same time, foreigners will make up some of the lost production, causing a trade deficit.

The conventional theory of budget deficits fits neatly with Keynesian mathematical models. It's a simple, clean piece of analysis that is easy to understand and gives fairly precise guidance to economic policymakers. The only problem, once again, is that it doesn't comport very well with what happens in the real world.

In the first place, much of the gloom-and-doom school of deficit analysis manages to overlook the crucial relation between a given budget deficit and the size of the underlying economy. A $100-billion deficit will have five times the impact on a $1-trillion economy as on a $5-trillion economy. Charting changes in budget deficits without reference to changes in the size of the economy is a gross misrepresentation, and the recent deficits, in fact, become much less frightening when they are expressed as a percentage of GNP.

There is also a basic confusion between *federal* deficits and *government* deficits. All other countries combine the surpluses and deficits at the national and local levels before reporting their government deficit or surplus. Only the United States presents the federal surplus/deficit number as if it were the only one that mattered. In recent years in the United States, state and local surpluses have been quite large, despite all the publicity about state tax shortfalls. Tax surpluses at the state and local levels offset the economic effect of federal deficits in the same way that increased federal taxes would.

The charts on the following pages show how the federal budget "crisis" tends to disappear when it is looked at sensibly. The top line shows the apparent rapid growth in the federal deficit—it looks as if it is skyrocketing out of control. The second chart shows the same deficit as a percentage of GNP, and suddenly the problem gets much smaller. The third graph, which is really the only one that matters, shows the *combined* state, local, and federal surplus and deficits as a percentage of GNP, and suddenly the deficit record in the 1980s becomes very unremarkable. You can also see that the total government deficit has been dropping rapidly over the past several years. I will have more to say about that later in the chapter.

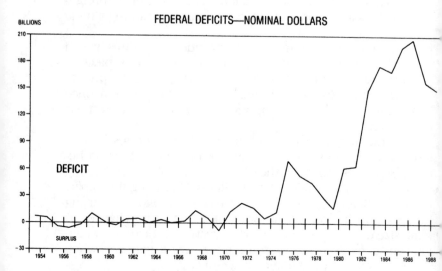

When the Federal deficit is expressed in nominal dollars, i.e. without adjusting for inflation or the size of the economy, it appears so big that it almost soars off the chart.

Source: U.S. Dept. of Commerce

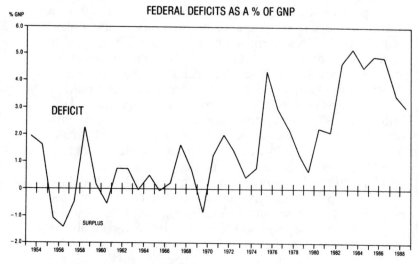

But, if Federal deficits are expressed as a percent of GNP, the increase during the 1980s becomes much less steep.

Source: U.S. Dept. of Commerce

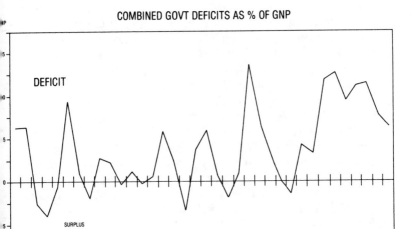

And when all levels of government are included—i.e. Federal, State, and Local—it turns out that the 1980s deficits, while large, are not extraordinary. The present level of deficit has occurred several times within recent history, including the conservative 1950s.

But the exaggerated size of the deficit is only part of the story. When Dwight Eisenhower ran big deficits in the 1950s, he was *buying* things such as tanks or roads. But only about a third of the modern federal budget actually purchases goods and services. The remaining two-thirds are *transfer* payments of one form or another, including interest payments. Transfer payments don't buy anything or produce anything; they merely shuffle money. The government takes money from one group of people and gives it to another group of people. The GNP isn't changed at all.

The largest transfer payments are those paid through the Social Security Trust Fund—about $223 billion in 1988— although there are many others, including federal and military pensions and welfare payments. There is no way to measure their economic impact. The people the money was taken from would have spent some of it and saved some of it. The people it is given to likewise spend some of it and save some of it. Moving the money from one set of owners to another un- doubtedly changes the total amounts that are spent and saved, but there is no way to know by how much or even in what direction, although there are economists with strong views on all sides of the issue. (The only sure thing, as Milton Friedman points out, is that the size of government increases in order to manage all that shuffling of money around the economy.)

The impact of federal interest payments is even more ambiguous. Currently, *all* of the federal budget deficit can be attributed to interest payments. Interest payments on the federal debt run about $150 billion, substantially more than the current deficits. Recall that I said that when government spending is higher than its tax receipts, it borrows the difference by selling treasury notes and bonds. The buyers of those IOUs, for the most part, are pension funds, banks, and other financial institutions, and they hold the lion's share of federal debt.

Since the interest payments on the federal debt account for the entire deficit, that means that when the government needs to pay interest, it borrows the money it needs by selling more treasury paper. The buyers, of course, are the same financial institutions that hold the debt in the first place. In short, the government sells bonds to pension funds and banks, then pays the proceeds back to them in the form of interest. (About $25 billion is paid to foreigners, who own about 15 percent of the federal debt, but that is a tiny amount in a $5-trillion economy.) Whatever the economic impact of such financial churning, it is far too small even to be measured.

There are a number of other problems with the conventional ways of thinking about federal budget deficits. Peter L. Bernstein and Robert Heilbroner have analyzed most of them in an elegant little book published in 1989 called *The Debt and the Deficit: False Alarms/Real Possibilities*. A couple bear mentioning here. The way we add raw interest payments to the deficit overstates the true impact on the economy. A borrower who pays 5 percent interest during a time of 5 percent inflation is not giving anything extra back to his lenders. About half the federal interest bill actually pays only for the loss of purchasing power due to inflation and constitutes no change in wealth one way or the other—that is, it has none of the inflationary or savings-reducing effects that conventional analysis attributes to budget deficits.

Finally, there is the issue of capital spending. When a business borrows to build a new factory, it doesn't deduct the cost of the factory from its sales revenues for the year—if it did it would probably show a huge loss. Instead, it "depreciates" the building; that is, it makes a regular deduction from earnings each year *over the expected life of the building.* The government doesn't keep its books like a business. If it spends money on a new highway, it shows the total expense in the same year, instead of depreciating the highway over its useful life.

As several maverick economists, including Bernstein and Heilbroner, have pointed out, if the federal government made reasonable adjustments for capital spending and the inflationary component of interest payments, there is a good argument that the total government accounts haven't been running a deficit *at all* during most of the 1980s.

One more illustration, much in the news during the last year, demonstrates the ambiguities that surround the issue of budget deficits. Because the government insured deposits in savings and loan banks—the "thrifts"—it must pay off the depositors of the hundreds of bankrupt thrifts around the country. Part of the bill, some $50 billion, will be met by selling bonds. The White House, with its eye on the apparent size of the deficit, wanted that borrowing "off the balance sheet"—that is, it didn't want to count it in the deficit. Congress, perhaps partly to embarrass the administration, insisted that it be counted. A compromise was finally reached, so part will be counted and part won't be.

The issue, in fact, was a complicated one and illustrates how difficult it is to know what should count toward the deficit and what shouldn't. The Congressional Budget Office, the nonpartisan analytical arm of the Congress, suggested that the savings and loan bonds should more logically *not* be counted in the deficit. Their reasoning was as follows: Most of the thrifts were insolvent because their real estate portfolios had gone sour—they had overlent in places like Houston and Tulsa where the 1970s real estate bubble went bust. But those economic losses have *already* happened. The real economic losses, that is, are the vacant office buildings throughout the Southwest, the lost construction jobs, the developers whose equity has been wiped out. Local real estate prices have pretty well incorporated those losses, and canny real estate investors, in fact, are already "bottom fishing" for attractive opportunities in Houston and other Southwestern cities.

Considering that the savings and loan losses have already happened, the Congressional Budget Office reasoned, selling bonds to make good the thrift depositors has no economic impact one way or the other. It merely shifts money from one set of savers—the bond buyers—to another set of savers—the thrift depositors. The *interest* the government pays on those bonds *is* a real cost, of course, but that will be spread over thirty years and will have little impact by itself. And it *will* be counted in future budget deficits.

I use the savings and loan example, of course, not to argue one way or the other about the proper budgetary treatment of those bonds but merely to point out how hard it is to know what is a budget deficit and what isn't. With such an enormous amount of uncertainty, it is hardly surprising that the deceptively neat economic models that are supposed to predict the impact of federal budget deficits on the economy fail miserably.

For example, a basic truism of the conventional analysis is that federal budget deficits increase inflation and raise interest rates. I summarized earlier why that is supposed to be so— presumably, budget deficits sop up savings, so the competition for the available funds raises interest rates. At the same time, the shortfall in investment—because of the difficulty of borrowing to finance new plants and equipment—will create goods shortages, driving up prices and inflation.

These basic relations, which are at the heart of the mainstream analysis of budget deficits have almost *never* been true. For the past ten years, in fact, the relation has been almost precisely the *opposite* of the conventional wisdom. When deficits rose, inflation and interest rates dropped. And the uptick in inflation and interest rates in 1988, of course, came when the deficit was finally dropping.

I don't intend to argue, of course, that federal budget deficits lower inflation and interest rates. The relationship most of the time is probably random. The real economy is just too complicated to capture in a simple model and too complicated for the government to fine-tune by manipulating a single variable like the federal budget deficit.

Similar reasoning applies to the argument that budget deficits cause trade deficits. During the 1980s, in fact, the trade deficit *did* go up at the same time as our budget deficit. It is the only one of the conventional wisdom's predictions that came true at all over the period. But again, the relationship is probably just accidental. In the first place, for forty years prior to the 1980s, there has *never* been a consistent relationship between budget deficits and trade deficits. The coincidence in the 1980s is a one-time event. I'll look at trade issues in detail in Chapter 7.

Finally, data from other countries show no relation at all between budget deficits and trade deficits. Great Britain has been running strong budget *surpluses* for the past several years. Much to the surprise of the conventional analysts, Great Britain's trade deficit has soared during that time. The most sensible conclusion is that the relation between budget and trade deficits, like that between budget deficits and inflation and interest rates, is probably random.

Perhaps I should say at this point that, on the whole, I believe it is better for governments *not* to run budget deficits because of the moral hazard involved. It is much easier for politicians to borrow than to raise taxes. If the government must live within its tax receipts, then the unwillingness of the electorate to pay higher taxes will act as a powerful curb on the natural instinct of government agencies to expand. However, the point of this discussion is not to argue one way or the other about the merits of deficit spending, merely to show how little substance there is in the conventional gloom-and-doom school of deficit analysis.

What about the future? There can be almost no doubt that, sometime around 1995 or so, the current federal budget deficits will disappear. The reason will not be a sudden attack of thriftiness in the federal government. It is simply that, as we have seen, the rate of worker retirement is slowing down at the same time that the baby boomers are moving into their high-earning working years. The result will be that social security tax receipts will be much higher than social security payments for about twenty years, so the total government cash account will swing hugely into surplus. Some of the surplus projections are absurdly high—a much-quoted projection by the Social Security Administration foresees a $12-*trillion* surplus by 2010.

I find it inconceivable that the taxpayers or the Congress would ever allow such a surplus to accumulate, but it seems clear that the pressures in federal budget management will be shifting from managing spending overruns to worrying about trust fund overaccumulations. A number of skeptics have argued that the excess social security collections aren't "really" surpluses, because they will be needed to fund benefits thirty years from now. And they point out that even the huge accumulations projected by the Social Security Administration will still not be enough to fund social security benefits between 2020 and 2030, the peak retirement years for the baby boomers.

But the *reasons* for running a surplus have nothing to do with its economic impact. A surplus is a surplus, even if all the money will be needed twenty years later. And with regard to the impending social security "crisis" in 2030, that is something like predicting World War II in 1900. Shifts in lifestyles, earnings patterns, and savings arrangements over the next forty years, whatever they are, are likely to swamp all the careful forty-year projections that analysts are busying themselves with. Several decades of strong global economic growth is the best way to ensure that there is either a sufficient social security surplus or sufficient borrowing capacity to pay for the retirement benefits of the baby boomers thirty or forty years from now.

International Debt and Trade Deficits

If measurement problems make it difficult to have a sensible discussion of the impact of budget deficits, they almost preclude any reasonable consideration of America's international financial position. To begin with, that staple of editorial jeremiads, that America has become the "world's largest net debtor" with more than $500 billion in net foreign debt, is flatly untrue.

The "largest net debtor" rhetoric stems from a misunderstanding of the Commerce Department's international balance sheet accounts—the misunderstanding is so blatant that sometimes I believe it must be intentional. To begin with, consider how a company keeps its balance sheet. Customarily, the left side of the balance sheet lists all of the company's "assets"—its cash in the bank, its inventory, its plant and equipment. The right side of the balance sheet lists its "liabilities." One kind of liability is debt—payments the company is obligated to make according to some defined schedule.

The second kind of liability is called *equity*. The difference between a company's assets and its debts will be equity. Equity is the portion of all the company's assets owned outright by the shareholders, assuming all debt has been paid off. Equity is obviously not the same as debt at all. But it is listed on the liability side of the balance sheet because when the company winds up its affairs and pays off all its debts, what's left over is distributed to the shareholders. So the equity represents a kind of claim by outsiders—the shareholders—on the company's assets.

The Commerce Department follows a broadly similar practice in trying to construct a balance sheet for the country with respect to the rest of the world. On the left side of the balance sheet, it lists all foreign assets owned by Americans— by the government, private corporations, and individuals. On the right side of the balance sheet it lists all assets in the United States owned by foreigners. The idea is that foreign assets owned by Americans are a kind of claim on the rest of the world, and the assets in America owned by foreigners are a kind of claim on America.

The first point, of course, is that only some of the claims on our international balance sheet are in the form of "debt." A treasury bond held by a foreign central bank is properly a debt. We must eventually redeem it according to a predetermined schedule. But the hotels in Honolulu that are owned by Japanese hotel chains are not "debts" at all. They are much more like equity. Because they are a form of equity in America, the Commerce Department properly lists them on the "liability" side of the balance sheet.

If a shareholder doesn't wish to own his shares any longer, he has no right to insist that the company buy them back. He has to find someone else to buy them, and he may very well take a loss in the process. Just so, if Japanese investors wish to get out of their Hawaiian hotel investments, they have no claim to present to the American government or to American citizens. All they can do is hope to find a buyer for their hotels, and if there are no eager takers, they will have to keep lowering their asking price and ultimately take a loss on their investment. Obviously, an equity holder has a major stake in the health of his investment. If the Hawaiian economy deteriorates substantially, the Japanese investors will take a loss on their hotels. That is the basic difference between debt and equity. A debt holder cares only about getting his debt paid back. An equity holder makes money only if the enterprise in which he owns equity is successful.

In fact, there is a strong argument that the United States is better off when foreigners have a large equity stake in the country. After the OPEC oil crisis in the 1970s, for example, Saudi Arabia made very large equity investments—in real estate and in such businesses as refineries and service station chains. Even if Saudi Arabia had the power to manipulate oil prices, which, as I shall show later, I don't believe it has, it would have to be careful about precipitating another crisis because its very large American investments would suffer.

The "largest international debtor" rhetoric stems from simply adding up both sides of the Commerce Department's balance sheet accounts and comparing the difference. At the end of 1988, Americans held $1.3 trillion worth of assets abroad, and foreigners owned $1.8 trillion of assets in the United States. About $525 billion of the foreign holdings were equity-type investments. Another $600 billion represents the American assets of foreign banks. Foreign governments held $325 billion of U.S. currency and government securities. (Foreign governments need large dollar balances for trade purposes—about 70 percent of world trade is conducted in dollars. It is not obvious when foreign government holdings become "excessive.") The remaining assets are mostly private holdings of corporate and government bonds. Lumping all of these various claims into a single monolithic "debt" number is a gross misrepresentation of highly complex reality.

But the misrepresentation goes deeper than that. Oddly

enough, although the Commerce Department's accounts show America in a very large net liability position since about 1985, through most of the 1980s, Americans earned about $20 billion a year *more* on their foreign assets than foreigners did on their American assets, and at present the inflow and outflow of earnings are almost precisely equal.

How to square the earnings record with the official net liability position, let alone the "largest net debtor" rhetoric? The answer, again, lies with accounting conventions and measuring problems. The Commerce Department, following normal conservative business accounting principles, generally values assets at their *purchase price*. Since the big American overseas investment drive came in the 1950s and 1960s, American overseas assets tend to have a much lower "book value" than the assets purchased by foreigners in the 1980s. The same conservative accounting logic causes the department to value monetary gold, an "asset," at $42.22 an ounce, roughly a tenth of its market value. Asset *pricing* conventions, that is, make the balance sheet accounts utterly meaningless as a measure of American "indebtedness." The more directly relevant earnings figures, on the other hand, imply that America may even have been a *creditor* nation throughout most of the 1980s, including the peak years of the "largest net debtor" hysteria.

The gloom-and-doom school of analysis sometimes resorts to a more sophisticated argument. Even if much of the "debt" is really in the form of equity, they contend, in future years that equity will entail a continuing drain of profits and dividends overseas, leaching away America's wealth. The argument, once again, is wrong, this time on two counts.

First of all, on a practical level, foreign investors do not typically take their profits and dividends back home. They reinvest them to keep their foreign factories or their foreign hotels competitive. I have already described the foreign investment patterns of companies like IBM and Sony. If anything, the Japanese companies have shown a tendency to invest even *more* than their acquisitions earn. Bridgestone, the Japanese company that purchased Firestone Tire, almost immediately announced a billion-dollar investment program in its North American operations. American companies, with a long record of overseas investment, have always behaved in exactly the same way: They consistently reinvest half to two-thirds of their overseas earnings in their host countries.

But the argument is wrong on a theoretical level as well. Americans are just as able to judge investment values as foreigners. In recent years, Japanese investors in particular have been willing to pay much higher prices for certain investments, such as hotels and real estate, than Americans are willing to pay. By paying a higher price, they are implicitly accepting a much lower return on their investment than Americans are willing to accept. Above a certain price, that is, Americans judge that they will be better off making an alternative investment. In economic terms, if a foreigner is willing to pay more for a hotel than Americans think its future earnings justify, Americans will be better off selling it. Even if *every* penny of profit is repatriated to the foreigner's country, Americans are behaving rationally by taking the high selling price and investing in assets that they believe will return higher profits over the long run. One party or the other may be wrong in judging the future worth of the investment, of course, but that's what investing is all about.

Twenty-five years ago, the American overseas investment drive met the same complaints about selling off national "patrimonies" that are heard in America today, and they were just as ill-founded. Apart from the loss of the long French lunch hour—it didn't fit American standards of business efficiency—Europe has clearly prospered as a result. The continued globalization of industry and markets means that all industrialized countries will become much more economically entangled than ever before—everyone will own assets in everyone else's country. Pointing to the rising volume of foreign assets in America as a problem of "American debt" is simply false. More accurately, it is a measure of the growing stake the rest of the industrialized countries have in America's continued economic health, just as America, at least since World War II, has had a major stake in strong economic performance in the rest of the world.

The Looming Shortage of Government Bonds

The recent alarm over budget deficits is one of the best illustrations I can think of for the general rule that the conventional wisdom is usually not only wrong but, more often than not, is *totally* wrong. The real problem facing the world's financial markets over the next decade will not be how to absorb a mountain of government IOUs, as the alarmists are insisting. The real problem will be precisely the opposite. The problem will be *finding* enough government debt to satisfy the financial markets' appetites.

Let's take a look at how incredibly fast the supply of government debt will be shrinking. Governments borrow, as we have seen, when their spending requirements outrun their tax receipts. When governments are running deficits, they are net sellers of their own bonds and are increasing their national debt. But when governments collect more taxes than they spend, they redeem more bonds than they issue, and the supply of bonds available in the open market begins to contract.

We have already seen how rapidly, as a percent of GNP, the total deficits of the American government have been shrinking—from roughly 5 percent of GNP in 1986 to less than 2 percent in 1988. But deficits are shrinking even faster in the rest of the world. The Organization for Economic Cooperation and Development—the OECD, the economic watchdog of the major industrialized nations—reported no fewer than seven members running budget surpluses in 1988. Great Britain, long one of the big deficit countries, has been running a surplus for several years and was expected to buy back $23 billion worth of debt in 1989. *The Economist* magazine projects that at the current trend of debt retirement, Great Britain's entire national debt will be wiped out by the end of the century.

West Germany was running deficits of about 2.5 percent of GNP in 1983—bigger, relatively speaking, than America's current deficit—and is expected to be in surplus by 1991 or 1992. Japan had a 5-percent deficit in 1983 and is just on the verge of moving into surplus. France's deficit is trending down below 1.5 percent of GNP, while Australia, Denmark, Sweden, and New Zealand are all headed toward surpluses in the near future. Just as important, the bonds being retired generally carry much higher interest rates than the new ones being issued. Japan, for instance, is now retiring government debt issued at 8 percent or more in the early 1980s and replacing it with paper carrying coupons well under 5 percent. The same is true, relatively speaking, in almost every other country.

All of that is genuinely good news. Even if one is skeptical, as I am, about the impact of government debt on interest rates, it seems that if the *whole world* reduces its government borrowing drastically, interest rates sooner or later must fall. Coupled with the shift of investment away from housing, as we saw in the last chapter, the drop in government borrowing should vastly increase the pool of capital available for business investment. The simultaneous shift away from government borrowing and away from massive investment in residential real estate is another one of those Schumpeterian phase changes, the kind of fundamental reordering of the economic system that will have profound and far-reaching effects.

In fact, the interest rate impact of a global reduction in government borrowing is likely to be much more dramatic than conventional analysis suggests. Standard models don't take into account the degree to which modern financial markets *need* substantial amounts of government debt for their continued smooth operations.

I will give three simplified examples of how modern financial markets have come to rely on government debt as a basic component of standard investment portfolios.

There is more than $2.3 trillion invested by private and public pension funds to secure worker retirement benefits. Financial specialists refer to pension investing as an "asset and liability matching problem." The assets are the cash currently in hand and under the control of the pension fund investment managers. The liabilities are the future retirement payments that must be made to retiring workers. Those future liabilities, of course, can't be known precisely, because they will depend partly on the age at which workers choose to retire, but actuarial experts can estimate the size and the timing of the liabilities with a reasonable degree of accuracy.

The pension investing problem, then, is how to invest the pension fund assets so there will always be enough cash in the kitty to pay out the retirement benefits as they start to fall due. The investing techniques used are known as *immunization* strategies. I'll explain them in more detail in the profile of BEA Associates following this chapter. Suffice it to say here that immunization strategies normally require that a very high proportion of an investment portfolio be kept in government bonds. As a consequence, both pension fund assets and their bond holdings are growing faster than new government debt issuance and will continue to do so as the deficit keeps on shrinking. The demand for government bonds, that is, will continue to grow faster than the supply.

A second example of the importance of government bonds in modern investing is the insurance industry. Essentially, the business of insurance is an asset and liability–matching problem, just as with pension funds. The difference is that insurance assets come from the regular flows of premium income. The liabilities are the insurance benefits paid out upon an accident, a death, or some other insured-against event. The insurance company's objective is to invest its premium income so it always has sufficient cash to meet its liabilities and pay expenses—with, one hopes, something left over as profit. And just as in pension funds, immunization logic pervades much of insurance investment thinking. Government bonds are an extremely important component of insurance portfolios, and there is no prospect that the industry's demand for bonds will shrink when the supply does.

Finally, Wall Street's new "rocket scientist" computer-and-mathematics whizzes have invented all kinds of "synthetic" instruments and "synthetic" portfolios in recent years to meet particular investing needs. Many of them involve the use of government bonds, because of their ready availability, the wide range of maturities, and the "depth" of the market—that is, it's always possible to find a buyer or a seller for government bonds, which is not true for many other investment instruments. By combining government bonds and new types of instruments such as "index options," a funds manager can create a portfolio that mimics almost any group of stocks but is cheaper to create and trade and is somewhat less volatile than a comparable portfolio of the stocks themselves. Once again, trends in the financial markets have created a steady appetite for government bonds.

The simple point of all three examples is that modern investing technique depends very heavily on a ready supply of government debt. But the growth of government debt in the United States has already fallen below the rate of growth in GNP. In many other countries, the supply of government debt is already shrinking in absolute terms. As our social security surpluses build up over the next decade, both the new supply of American government debt and the absolute level of debt in the market will shrink quite quickly.

The conventional wisdom is still obsessed with American "deficits" and "international debt." As I have attempted to show in this chapter, I believe those have been trumped-up concerns for some time. The real problem, over the next decade or so, will be in finding *enough* high-quality debt instruments to satisfy the needs of financial markets. Insurance companies, in particular, are likely to have a very difficult time. Since they became accustomed to a limitless supply of high-return government bonds in the 1970s, insurance companies have generally underpriced their policies, expecting to be bailed out by the high interest earnings on their portfolios. The 1990s will bring some rude shocks to insurance company executives, as the trickle of red ink on underpriced policies turns into a flood.

For most of us, the shrinking availability of bonds will be an unmitigated boon. As bonds become "scarcer than hen's teeth," as one Wall Street trader has put it, the price of government bonds will rise sharply. That is another way of saying that interest rates must fall, and fall sharply. (Many people find that relation confusing. Take a simplified example: I own a bond that pays interest of $10 a year forever. If prevailing interest rates are 10 percent, I could sell the bond for $100. But if prevailing interest rates were only 5 percent, I could sell the bond for *$200*—the $10 interest payment is 5 percent of $200. Therefore, the price of my bond goes up as interest rates come down and vice-versa.)

It will be a self-reinforcing cycle. We have already seen that the entire annual American budget deficit consists of interest payments. Falling rates will, by themselves, reduce the deficit and therefore the necessity of issuing more bonds, which will in turn help reduce rates, and so on.

Couple the worldwide shift toward a shrinking supply of government bonds with the massive impending shift of American assets away from real estate that I discussed in the last chapter, and the demographic-related shifts in savings both in America and in Japan, and the pressures building for a huge, permanent downward shift in interest rates become truly enormous.

It is just one more example of the fundamental reordering of the economy that is under way and one more factor that is ensuring the coming of a global boom.

BEA Associates

Mark Arnold typifies the new breed of portfolio managers who have taken over Wall Street in the 1980s.

Fifteen or twenty years ago, portfolio managers—professionals who invest large amounts of other people's money—were basically stock pickers. Some were "technicians," who tracked each day's fluctuations in the market averages for clues as to what might happen tomorrow. Most were "value" players who searched for stocks that seemed to be priced lower than their companies' prospects justified. They pored through company reports and government economic data and kept their ears cocked to the gossip at Wall Street's favorite watering holes.

The big-name portfolio managers were all in stocks. There were relatively few bond managers, and they weren't paid very well. Bonds were boring.

The business of portfolio management has been radically transformed by the arrival of applied mathematicians like Mark Arnold and the advent of readily accessible high-speed computers. The new rigorously quantitative methods of portfolio management have permeated every aspect of the money management business but may have had their greatest impact in bond management.

Arnold is slim, blond, bespectacled, a boyish-looking 37. His English accent is quiet and precise. He trained in pure mathematics at the University of London and did graduate work at the University of Michigan. After working several years in England, first as an actuary, then as a bond salesman, he joined BEA Associates and is now a director of the company responsible for its bond management strategies.

"Markets are fun when they are inefficient or a little chaotic," Arnold says with a small smile. "That's when you have real profit opportunities. And for a long time now there have been plenty of opportunities in government securities."

The profitable chaos stems directly from the huge increase in the supply of securities issued by the U.S. Treasury to finance the federal budget deficits that began to spiral endlessly upward after 1975. Total federal debt—that is, the cumulative value of the securities issued by the U.S. Treasury and still outstanding—grew gently from $382 billion in 1970 to $544 billion in 1975.

Federal debt then accelerated past the $1 trillion mark in 1981, hit $2 trillion sometime during 1986, and is now about $2.7 trillion.

Treasury securities (called "bills," "notes," or "bonds" depending on their maturities) are just IOUs promising to pay back with interest money borrowed from the public. There is no possibility that the government won't pay the money back—if it is short of cash when the payment day arrives, it can always print some more.

The question for investors, of course, is not whether they will be paid back, but how much the money will be worth when they finally get it. If the government is consistently forced to print more money to meet its obligations, the value of money will decline—in other words, there will be inflation. Investors will therefore demand higher interest rates to compensate them for the loss of their loan's purchasing power. In extreme cases, as in present-day Brazil and Argentina, the government's ready recourse to the printing press has elevated inflation and interest rates to the 1,000 percent-plus levels.

"What makes treasury securities so important," says Arnold, "is that they are pure interest rates. A treasury *is* the interest rate. With a bond issued by a corporation, there are several kinds of risk. There is liquidity risk. That is, if you want to sell the bond, will anyone want to buy it? That can't happen in treasuries, because the market is so broad and deep. There is 'event' risk—something goes wrong with the airline industry that hurts all of its bonds. Then there is company risk—the company that issued the bonds has too much debt and can't pay its bonds off. But in treasuries, the only risk is the interest rate."

When Arnold talks about interest rate risk, he is referring to the relation between a bond's principal value and the prevailing rate of interest. An investor gets *two* kinds of returns from a bond. One is the interest payment at the stated rate. The other is the possibility of a capital gain or loss. For example, if I buy a $1,000 five-year treasury note that pays 8 percent interest, I will collect the interest every six months while I own the note and will get my $1,000 back when the note matures.

But what if the market interest rate on treasury notes rises to 8.5 percent while I own my security? In effect, I'm losing money on my investment, because my $1,000 could be earning 8.5 percent instead of just 8 percent. If I want to sell the note to another investor, I won't be able to get the full $1,000 for it. The investor will pay me a *discounted* price, that is, a price just enough less than $1,000 so that his capital gain when he redeems the note will exactly make up for the difference between the 8 percent interest my note pays and the 8.5 percent the market tells him he has a right to expect.

Calculating the discount involves a lot of tedious arithmetic. (The lost interest has to be compounded for each day remaining on the security.) But if, for instance, my note has three and a half years to go when I want to sell it, the buyer can look up on a bond table or ask his computer, and he will find that a discount of $14.87 will exactly make up the difference between the market rate of 8.5 percent and the 8-percent rate the note actually pays. So he will offer me only $985.13 for the note and I will suffer a capital loss of 1.487 percent. On the other hand, of course, if interest rates *fall,* I will deserve a premium for my note since it pays a higher-than-market rate of interest.

The "interest rate risk" that Mark Arnold talks about, then, is the loss in potential capital value suffered by a portfolio of bonds as interest rates fluctuate. The interest rate risk is much greater the longer the term of the bond. It's easy to see why that is so. If I buy a thirty-day treasury bill at 7 percent for $100, for instance, the government will pay my $100 back in only a month's time, plus a month's worth of interest at 7 percent, which is about fifty-eight cents. Since the cash interest paid on a short-term bill is so small to begin with, a move of interest rates up or down a bit isn't going to affect the value of my investment very much.

But if I buy a thirty-year bond, the interest payments over the life of that bond will add up to a much bigger number than the principal repayment thirty years from now. So if interest rates go to 8.5 percent, a buyer of a thirty-year bond that pays only 8 percent interest will insist on a substantial discount—in fact, $54—so his capital gain at the end of the thirty years will make up for the lost interest. Interest rates, that is, rose only half a point, but my bond instantly lost more than 5 percent of its value. Long-term securities, then, are much more volatile than short-term securities: Their market value will fluctuate much more dramatically when interest rates move up or down.

BEA's clients are mostly pension funds. Companies such as Ford, General Motors, and Unisys as well as state and local governments set aside money each year so they will be able to pay the contracted retirement benefits for their workers. They contract with portfolio managers like BEA to invest their pension fund assets—the better return they earn, the less money the company needs to set aside to fund future benefits. American pension fund assets exceed $2.3 trillion. BEA has about $9 billion under management, and the average account size is in the $100 to $200 million range.

Arnold's job is far more complicated than just finding bonds that pay the highest rate of interest. "My objective is to *eliminate* interest rate risk on my client's investments," he says. The technique he uses, at its simplest level, is called "immunization." That is, he starts by looking at his client's liabilities. If it is a pension fund, what is the profile of its projected future stream of pension payments?

"Every pension program," he says, "can be reduced to a stream of future cash flows to be paid by the company. And any bond portfolio is also a set of cash flows, of interest payments and principal repayments. A client can either give me his actual future projected payouts from the pension fund or he can give me a proxy in the form of a broad market index, like the Shearson-Lehman Hutton Government and Corporate Bond Index [a broad sample of outstanding bonds]. Either one can be reduced to a set of cash flows. And once I have that, I can go about setting up a portfolio that meets the client's needs."

When Arnold talks about eliminating interest rate risk, he means that he will construct a bond portfolio in such a way that its value will move *in the same way* as the value of the client's liabilities as interest rates rise and fall.

From Arnold's perspective, his client's stream of future pension liabilities is a portfolio just like a bond portfolio. And the pension liabilities have a current market price just as a bond portfolio does. Insurance companies stand ready to take the pension liabilities off a company's hands for a price. Ford, in other words, instead of continuing to fund its pension liabilities, could simply pay a lump sum to an insurance company to assume all responsibility for paying those pension liabilities as they became due. As the market rate of interest goes up, the lump sum payment needed to divest the liability goes down. (The reason is that the insurance company would invest the lump sum at a higher rate of return and so could cover more of the future liabilities out of interest earnings.)

Modern bond management builds on the fact that *both* the assets and liabilities will fluctuate in value with interest rate movements. The client therefore can be protected from interest rate risk by guaranteeing that the fluctuations in the assets and liabilities are always exactly the same. That is called immunization. If Arnold can *match* the stream of cash flows in his bond portfolio with the stream of liabilities in his client's pension program, then he will have succeeded in immunizing his client. No matter what happens to interest rates, and no matter how the market value of the bond portfolio fluctuates, his client will be protected, because the present value of his future liabilities will be moving exactly in lock step.

It is the deep market in treasury securities and modern computer power that makes portfolio management techniques like immunization possible. There are an uncountable number of combinations of available treasury securities that provide cash flows to match any particular pension fund's future liabilities. Arnold uses a mathematical technique he calls "multiple liability immunization" to pick the optimum combination.

The basic mathematics, known as optimization algorithms, is a variant of the solution to the famous "traveling salesman" problem. (Assume a traveling salesman has to visit a number of cities. What sequence of cities will produce the shortest possible route? Once the number of cities exceeds a very small number, the required calculations quickly become enormous.) Without the high speed of modern computers and theoretical advances in computerized algorithms, the calculations that Arnold carries out routinely for each of his clients would simply be impossible.

"Once I've optimized a treasury portfolio for a client," says Arnold, "then I can start to apply my own judgment to add further value. The easiest thing to do, of course, would be to leave the portfolio fully invested in treasuries, but I can usually find better buys than that. We typically end up with about 55 percent of a portfolio in treasuries, about 10 to 15 percent in various mortgage-backed obligations' and the rest in corporates.

"Nobody in the bond market is stupid. But certain players have tastes and patterns of buying that create market inefficiencies. We try to take advantage of them to improve our portfolios. For instance, municipal bond funds always advertise how high their current return is. It's the high current return you see in the newspaper ads that draws in consumers. And the fund managers get paid based on the volume of funds they attract. Therefore they don't pay attention to total return; that's not what they are paid to do. That creates opportunities for us."

Arnold points out that the highest-paying municipals usually have call provisions. If interest rates drop, the borrower has a right to pay off the bond at its face value, cutting off the opportunity to make a big capital gain. But since retail municipal bond fund managers are striving for the highest current yield they will pay somewhat more for bonds with call provisions than a total return calculation would justify. Arnold's computers are constantly tracking the small deviations from true market values and pinpointing the tiny windfall opportunities that distinguishes good portfolio performance from the merely mediocre.

Clearly, Arnold's whole approach to bond management is organized around a ready availability of treasury securities. If there were suddenly a shortage of government bonds, as Roland Leuschel of Banque Bruxelles and several other economists have recently suggested, the results, he says, would be "momentous." Or as he put it in a recent interview with *Institutional Investor:* "In the '70s and '80s, governments were financed massively through the bond markets. We've had enormous interest rates, and it's been very easy for fund managers to buy government bonds. I mean, we're just used to more and more supply. And I think it will require a completely different mentality to deal with the situation when the supply isn't there.

"I still find it hard to conceive of," muses Arnold. *"Somebody* will step up to the mark. Maybe the Japanese will start issuing bonds again. Maybe it will be Russian bonds. Who knows? But we might be seeing a fundamental change. Interest rates have risen since World War II. I don't claim to be a global economist, but it seems that rates have risen because almost all governments adopted inflation as their basic economic policy. Inflation is really just a surreptitious tax—a tax on assets. Voters liked more government spending, so governments borrowed, printed money, and essentially paid off their debts by inflating them away. In the last few years there are signs that inflation is no longer a good vote-winner. Politicians are talking about zero inflation, a return to hard money. If that's really what's happening, rates will drop very far and very fast. These kinds of changes can happen very quickly. It won't really hurt our business," says Arnold. "Companies will still have to fund their pension plans. In fact, they will have to invest even more money because returns will be lower.

"The real problem," he concludes ruefully, "is that if the supply of bonds shrinks, the market will start getting very efficient. There just won't be the opportunities to make money we've seen over the past few years. There's just no fun in efficient markets." His face takes on an expression of distaste. "Bonds will be boring."

7

OF BARRIERS AND FORTRESSES

The Trade Tangle

The continuing American trade deficit is one of those "economic imbalances" that so alarms conventional analysts. Trade politics, in fact, have come to dominate much of our foreign relations, particularly with Japan but to almost as great a degree with Western Europe.

I do not believe that the trade deficit is a particularly important problem. I think that much of the conventional analyses, and the political slogans they have inspired, are simply wrong. I do worry, however, that our more ham-handed responses to the *perceived* problem of the trade deficit may actually create some serious economic dislocations. In this first section, however, I will try to present a summary of the key data bearing on the trade problem to help the reader understand how complicated the issues are. I've already declared my policy biases, but I will try to present the data as fairly as I can, before I look at some of their implications.

Throughout most of the postwar period, the rest of the world bought more goods and services from the United States than the United States bought from the rest of the world. The ongoing American surplus was recycled back into the world economy, at first largely in the form of government grants and loans (like the Marshall Plan and various military-assistance and foreign-aid programs) and later more frequently in the form of bank loans or direct investment—that is, overseas American earnings were used to purchase foreign factories, office buildings, or other assets. General Charles de Gaulle, the nationalistic French leader, became almost apoplectic in the mid-1960s over the American "expropriation of French industry."

The inflow and outflow of payments to the rest of the world are usually grouped into several categories. The most basic is the "merchandise" or "goods" balance, which measures imports and exports of cars, consumer goods, oil, food, and the like. Next comes the "services balance," which includes payments for banking, insurance, tourism, or other services like advertising, as well as interest, dividends, and capital gains on foreign investments. Finally, the broadest measure of all is the "current account balance," which adds unilateral transfers, like government aid programs, to the data for goods and services.

The United States first began to run merchandise deficits in the 1970s, primarily because of the suddenly rising bill for oil imports. But throughout most of the 1970s, the broadest trade measure, the current account, stayed roughly in balance. Surging agricultural exports, particularly to the Soviet Union, earnings on the spreading network of American financial services, and a boom in manufactured exports to Latin America offset the imports of oil. There were deficits in some years and surpluses in others.

The last current account surplus was in 1981, a year fairly typical of the 1970s pattern. There was a big merchandise trade deficit of $28 billion, driven by a huge $74 billion net outlay for oil imports. There was also a small, but growing, manufacturing deficit with Japan that was more than offset by manufacturing surpluses with Europe and Latin America. American overseas financial and services earnings were still enough to pay for the merchandise deficit and produce a small $7 billion overall surplus on the current account.

The trade picture came unglued starting in 1983. The current account flipped from surplus in 1981 to a deficit of $9 billion in 1982, then plunged to a *$107* billion deficit in 1984, climbing to $141 billion in 1986 and $144 billion in 1987. Since then, the deficit has moderated somewhat but was still $127 billion in 1988 and about $61 billion for the first half of 1989. All of these data are in current dollars. Taking account for inflation, the first-half 1989 deficit represents a decrease of about 20 percent from the 1987 peak.

The graphic below shows what happened to the trade picture between 1980 and 1988, the last full year for which data are available. America was still running a services balance in 1988, although it had narrowed somewhat since 1980. At the same time, there was enormous *improvement* in the oil account, of about $41 billion, because of the steady drop in oil prices through the 1980s. (America still ran a big $34 billion oil deficit in 1988, but that was down from 1981's $75 billion deficit.) There was a big $33 billion deterioration in the capital goods account, primarily because of machine tool imports, but that was substantially offset by a $27 billion improvement in the industrial supplies account—items such as steel. Industrial supplies were still in deficit, but the deficit had shrunk substantially.

But the biggest swings came in cars and consumer goods. The automotive deficit swung from $11 billion in 1980 to $55 billion in 1988, a $44 billion change, while the consumer goods deficit soared from $18 billion to $72 billion, a $54 billion swing. Put in simplest terms, the entire $100 billion deterioration in the merchandise trade account since 1980 was caused by increased imports of cars and consumer goods. There were a number of other ups and downs, of course, but against these two items they all pale into insignificance.

To put the changes in a geographic context, the trade deficit with Japan grew by about $42 billion between 1980 and 1988 (a $5 billion improvement over 1987), almost all of it in cars. But the swing with Europe was almost as great, from a surplus of $26 billion in 1980 to a deficit of $16 billion in 1988—which was a sharp improvement over the $27 billion

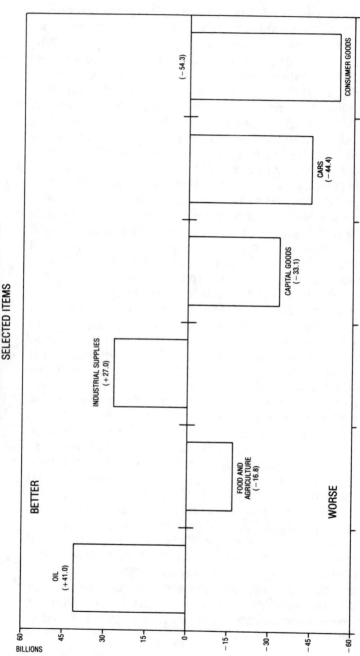

SWINGS IN THE TRADE BALANCE: 1980–1988
SELECTED ITEMS

BETTER

OIL
(+41.0)

INDUSTRIAL SUPPLIES
(+27.0)

FOOD AND
AGRICULTURE
(−16.8)

CAPITAL GOODS
(−33.1)

CARS
(−44.4)

CONSUMER GOODS
(−54.3)

WORSE

BILLIONS
60
45
30
15
0
−15
−30
−45
−60

The oil trade deficit improved sharply in the 1980s, while swings in industrial supplies and capital goods trade roughly balanced. But the deficit in cars and consumer goods worsened by almost $100 billion.

Source: U.S. Dept. of Commerce

deficit in 1987. Almost all of the European deficit is with West Germany. There was also a $10 billion deterioration in the trade account with Latin America, primarily because of the withdrawal of bank financing for Latin American imports. The trade account with the OPEC countries, of course, improved substantially as oil prices dropped.

A number of analysts have suggested that it is unfair to single out cars and consumer goods as the source of the explosion in the trade deficit. They correctly point out that more than half of American imports are industrial supplies and capital goods. That's true, but rising imports of industrial supplies and capital goods have been more or less offset by strong increases in capital goods and industrial supplies *exports*. Lumping them together, America imported about $224 billion of capital goods and industrial supplies in 1988 and exported about $201 billion. The figures for 1980 were $164 billion in imports against $147 billion in exports. The overall balance is almost identical, although there have been lots of ups and downs in individual items.

The concentration of the trade deficit in cars and consumer goods makes it an easy target for political intervention. Just as important, the deficit with Japan has yielded only grudgingly to standard macroeconomic remedies, such as the lower dollar. (By contrast, the falling dollar has resulted in a relatively rapid decline in the deficit with Europe, which accounts for most of the improvement over the past couple of years.) Little wonder that there has been such an outburst of "Japan-bashing" from the Congress, labor unions, and lobbyists for a more aggressive American trade policy. But before discussing the possibilities and pitfalls of political intervention, we should examine briefly some of the conventional explanations for America's ballooning trade deficit.

Why a Trade Deficit?

There are almost as many explanations for the American trade deficit as there are schools of economists. Most of the explanations have some grain of truth, but even taken together, they are not very satisfactory. Here are a few of the most frequently cited causes.

The American Budget Deficit. The theory is simple. Trade deficits arise when a country buys more goods than it produces. A budget deficit puts more spending power in people's hands than the government takes out in taxes, and the extra spending power naturally finds its way overseas.

But the link between budget and trade deficits is not nearly so simple as that. For one thing, except for in the 1980s, American budget and trade deficits have almost never tracked each other. To cite an overseas example, over the past five years, England's trade and budget accounts have moved in precisely the opposite directions. England now has a rapidly growing budget *surplus* and a rapidly growing trade *deficit* at the same time.

The Low American Savings Rate. Fifteen years or so ago, Americans saved about 8 to 9 percent of their incomes. Now they save about 4 to 5 percent. That extra jolt of spending, the reasoning goes, naturally washed into overseas markets.

I believe there is some truth to the savings argument, but it doesn't explain enough. If low savings caused the trade deficit in cars, for example, we would expect to see Americans depleting their savings to buy more cars, with the excess coming from overseas. But that's not what happened. Most of the reduction in savings was siphoned off into real estate, as I showed in Chapter 5. American car sales stayed roughly constant in the 1980s, but Americans *switched* to foreign cars, so Detroit lost market share. It's harder to blame that on a low savings rate.

High American Growth Rates. The recession in 1981–82 was worldwide, and America recovered faster than most other countries. European growth rates were practically flat until almost 1986, and most of Latin America suffered negative growth rates. Countries with depressed consumption sold their surplus production into America's roaring economy but didn't provide much of a market in return.

Growth-rate differentials are also clearly part of the story. And they are a reasonable explanation of the growing deficit with Europe. West Germany, for instance, had very little growth during most of the 1980s, and West German unemployment soared above 10 percent, an extraordinarily high rate in a country accustomed to unemployment in the 1 to 2 percent range. (Because West Germany had a trade surplus and a low inflation rate during the 1980s, we have a tendency to cite it as an economic success, ignoring its painfully high unemployment rate.) But differential growth rates are no explanation for the steadily worsening deficit with Japan or the other East Asian "tiger" economies, because they all grew even faster than America during the 1980s.

The High Dollar. Japanese exporters to America get paid in yen, not dollars. When an American pays dollars for a Japanese car, a bank converts those dollars to yen before sending the payment to the exporter. When the dollar rises in value against the yen, it takes fewer dollars to pay the yen price that the Japanese exporter wants. By the same token, it takes more yen for a Japanese *im*porter to pay the dollar price that an American wants. So a rising dollar makes it easier for Americans to buy foreign goods and harder for foreigners to buy American goods.

The dollar rose dramatically through most of the 1980s and clearly helped feed the American trade deficit. The problem is that there are no convincing explanations for the dollar's amazing strength through most of the 1980s. In any case, by 1989 the dollar had descended to a level most economists thought was either about right or slightly undervalued. And while that brought some improvement in the trade deficit, it wasn't anything to get excited about.

Unfair Trading Practices. Since the standard economic arguments are so unsatisfactory, it is natural to assume that someone isn't playing by the rules. In fact, most countries, the United States included, engage in one form or another of unfair trade practices. America, for instance, spends tens of billions of taxpayers' dollars each year to keep foreign agricultural produce out of the United States and to subsidize farm exports. The United States has been a massive force for free trade for most of the past half century, but by any fair count, the array of American export subsidies and import barriers is about as imposing as in most other industrialized countries.

Japan requires special comment in this regard, but I will reserve that until later in the chapter. Suffice it to say for the moment that if trade barriers caused the sudden huge swing in the trade deficit, we would expect to see a sharp upsurge in protectionism in other countries during the 1980s. But, on the whole, that did not happen. Protectionism in most other countries *decreased* during the same years that the American trade deficit has been rising.

All of the conventional explanations for the American trade deficit, as I said, contain some element of truth, but even taken together, they are too easily shot through with holes. The deficit with Japan, in particular, seems impervious to conventional economic explanation. Part of the problem, I believe, is that the analyses are much too narrowly focused. Concentrating on the trade deficit is like watching the swishing of an elephant's tail as he walks through your garden. The swishing tail might knock over a few things on its own, but it's hardly the most important thing going on. At this point, I should like to step back from the trade numbers a bit and put the entire problem into a somewhat broader perspective.

Foreign Trade Versus Foreign Sales

The overseas branches and affiliates of American companies had over $1 *trillion* of sales in 1987, the last year for which data are available. (The data throughout this section exclude banking, because of the obvious measurement problems.) Total overseas employment was in excess of six million workers, and total profits were in excess of $61 billion (or about the same as the trade deficit in the first half of 1989.) About half the sales, or more than $500 billion were from manufacturing companies.

American companies overseas are significant exporters. If overseas American companies are included, America's share of world exports is actually slightly higher than it was twenty years ago. More than half the trade deficit each year is accounted for by imports from *American* companies. Up to 40 percent of our imports from places like Taiwan, Hong Kong, and Singapore come from American companies. Some products are imported and exported several times. Many Chrysler engines, for example, are cast and machined in America, exported for further assembly to Mexico, then reimported for final assembly in America.

It's important to grasp the scale of American overseas operations. American company overseas sales in 1987 were four times bigger than American exports and seven times bigger than the 1987 trade deficit. The $1 trillion in 1987 overseas sales was more than 20 percent of American GNP for that year (although overseas sales are not counted, of course, in GNP statistics).

In striking contrast, just a few years ago, total Japanese overseas sales, overwhelmingly consisted of products made in Japan and shipped to the outside world. American overseas sales overwhelmingly consist of products made and marketed in overseas markets by global companies. Major European enterprises—BP, Shell, Philips, Ciba-Geigy, Thomson—have long followed the same pattern.

Kenichi Ohmae, in fact, has argued that Japan has a "trade deficit" with the United States if the comparison is broadened to include all American company sales in Japan, whether imported or locally produced, against all Japanese company sales in America. The data to allow such a comparison are inherently foggy, and I don't think they support Ohmae's claim. But there can be no question that the perceived "trade balance" between Japan and the United States is substantially altered by including such major American presences in Japan as McDonald's, Coca-Cola, IBM, and Texas Instruments. I believe the balance is still in Japan's favor, however, since the American overseas presence is still heavily concentrated in Europe and Latin America—a legacy of multinational expansion programs of the 1960s—although it is building rapidly in Japan and the rest of Asia.

As I have argued at some length in the first part of this book, I believe there can be little doubt that the American and European pattern of global companies—production and marketing in local markets throughout the world—is the one that all global companies are evolving toward. The most global of the Japanese companies—the Sonys, the Hondas, the FANUCs, the Komatsus, etc.—have explicitly adopted aggressive programs of establishing local manufacturing, marketing, and research and development centers in all their major markets, either on their own or through varieties of partnerships, joint ventures, and strategic alliances. Most other Japanese companies are rapidly following their lead. By 1988

Japanese sales from overseas branches had climbed sharply to $450 billion, or about the same size as Japanese exports, still a much smaller ratio than for American companies, but a substantial change in a very short period of time.

The Trade Deficit in Context

Putting the trade deficit in the context of American company global operations, I believe, allows us to get a more useful perspective on the meaning, the causes, and the importance of the trade deficit.

In the first place, the volume of American exports is not a good gauge of American industrial competitiveness. Except for commodities like farm produce or timber, which obviously must be exported, putting goods on a ship is one of the least effective and economical ways of penetrating a local market. Concentrating on "increasing exports" as a self-contained policy goal is not only ill-informed, but likely to be counterproductive or even dangerous. It is utterly feckless to adopt macroeconomic policies with potentially enormous and unpredictable consequences, such as "driving down the value of the dollar," solely for the sake of increasing exports. But successions of Washington policy makers have been prone to do exactly that.

I believe it *is* significant, however, when a component of *imports* undergoes a sudden radical change. The sharp increase in oil imports and oil prices in the 1970s was a thumping reminder that we had become energy wastrels. As soon as the government stopped trying to manage the price of oil to protect people from the consequences of the price change, we adapted to the new realities remarkably quickly and effectively.

As is clear from the data in this chapter, the suddenly ballooning trade deficits in the 1980s were caused by massive imports of cars and consumer goods. Most kinds of imports increased, of course, but in areas such as capital goods and industrial supplies, the relation between total imports and exports stayed roughly the same, although there were lots of ups and downs in individual items.

And imports of cars and consumer goods increased for the most part because Americans *switched* from local to foreign suppliers, particularly Japanese suppliers. And it is obvious why they switched. American manufacturing, resting on the laurels of its global triumphs of the 1950s and 1960s, was badly out of date. But since the early 1980s companies have been adapting to the brave new world of high-productivity manufacturing, quite quickly, and on the whole quite effectively. There is still considerable room for improvement and major battles yet to be fought. But the direction is unmistakable. I will attempt to assess the present competitive position of American companies, particularly with respect to Japan, in Chapter 9.

What about the conventional explanations—budget deficits, savings rates, currency policies, and so forth? Did they have any impact? Who knows? They probably had some effect, but no one can measure how much, and they were never the main issues. If America had lower social security or defense spending in the early 1980s, or higher taxes, for instance, and lower budget deficits, Japanese car makers would *still* have beaten the pants off American manufacturers, and Americans still would have switched to Japanese cars in droves. That switch to foreign cars and consumer goods, is at the root of the entire surge in imports and the entire "trade deficit" in the 1980s.

Couldn't we have simply prohibited the import of foreign cars and consumer goods? That would have been absolutely the worst thing to do. As Jim Henderson of Cummins put it forcefully: No company in a protected market is ever competitive globally. France and England protected their car and computer markets for years, and sooner or later, most of their major companies either went bankrupt or are still eking out a starveling existence on government handouts.

If we had protected our markets, or, to be more accurate, protected them much more aggressively than we did, our manufacturers for the most part would still be in the same dire straits that they were in at the end of the 1970s. The productivity revolution we have seen just wouldn't have happened. Just as important, Americans would have lost the benefit of some very high-quality cars and consumer goods at excellent prices—not to mention some very high-quality capital items like computer-controlled machine tools, that are playing a major role in restoring our industrial competitiveness. The profile at the end of this chapter explores some of the costs of protectionism in more detail.

At this point, I think we can step back and put the trade picture into some common-sense context.

A trade deficit of $120 billion, or less than a tenth of American overseas sales (both exports and sales from overseas branches), is hardly an economic catastrophe. In the context of an increasingly integrated $12 trillion American-Japanese-European industrialized economy, it is a minor imbalance, about 1 percent, that in no way justifies the hysteria, the fevered attention to each month's (highly unreliable) trade report, or the outburst of economic nationalism that seems to have gripped the Congress.

It is absurd to focus the entire brunt of macroeconomic policy—federal spending policy, tax policy, interest rate management, currency policy—on "reducing the trade deficit." There are excellent reasons, in my view, for reducing the federal budget deficit. There are excellent reasons for seeking a stable, realistically aligned, international value for the dollar. The Federal Reserve has to help manage interest rates down over the longer term without reigniting inflation. And so on. But to place all of these policies at the service of an artificial construct like the "trade deficit" makes no sense at all.

Looked at closely, the trade deficit tells us that American manufacturing stayed stuck in the 1960s, while Japanese manufacturers burst ahead and defined the competitive conditions for the 1980s and the 1990s. The Japanese, as I shall suggest in Chapter 9, are not, on the whole, more competitive and productive than Americans. But they are superb manufacturers who have defined wholly new standards for competing in fast-moving consumer-oriented goods markets. So Americans in the 1980s began to buy their cars and many consumer durables from the Japanese. Since Japanese companies were only beginning the process of globalizing their businesses, the switch to Japanese goods showed up as a trade deficit.

Over time, for what it is worth, I expect the trade deficit to decline. In the first place, American manufacturing is much more competitive than it was in the early 1980s. More important, as companies globalize, products will be manufactured in local markets rather than being carried around the world in boats. As global companies emerge to dominate major industries, the concept of "national" surpluses and deficits will have increasingly less meaning. As Sony continues to Americanize its American operations and Europeanize its European operations, for instance, its Japanese origins will gradually fade away as a contentious issue, just as Ford's American origins do not seem to make British Fords any less British.

Paradoxically, as industries globalize, trade flows will become smoother and smoother. Currency misalignments are one of the major obstacles to international business transactions. Planning purchases in yen- or dollar-denominated goods is very difficult if one doesn't know what the yen or the dollar will be worth a month from now. Experiments with both managed exchange rates and freely floating currencies over the past twenty years have been disappointing, to say the least. But as Steve Nagourney has suggested, stable currency relations must *follow* the globalization of the goods markets, not the other way around. That is to say, as production technology, productivity, and production-cost structures in the industrialized countries gradually converge, *price* differences will gradually disappear. Currency values will be able to converge and stabilize once real costs and prices do. When the sourcing of industrial products and services becomes truly global, a truly integrated global financial market will also be possible, and trade channels will finally flow completely unobstructed.

But for the immediate future, a key problem will be the role of racism in working out America's and Europe's ongoing economic relations with Japan. The Japanese are more alien to most Americans than Europeans are. If J. Arthur Rank, or some other British movie studio, bought a failing American studio, I imagine it would have been reported in the business press as an utterly routine event—rather like recent British purchases of American advertising agencies. But look at the uproar that greeted Sony's purchase of Columbia Pictures! It was out of all proportion to the event, particularly since Columbia's shareholders, in my view, were grossly overcompensated for their stock. (They received about 350 times earnings!)

The flap over Mitsubishi's purchase of an interest in Rockefeller Center was similarly absurd. A reporter at *The New York Times* wrote that "another vital piece of American landscape" had been snapped up by the Japanese—as if Mitsubishi were going to move Rockefeller Center to Japan or turn it into a red-light district for visiting businessmen. Once again, a cash-rich Japanese company seems to have overpaid, in this case for a somewhat cloudy interest. No one in the United States, on the other hand, ever thought it worthy of comment when, as at the start of the decade, most of the office real estate surrounding the Imperial Palace Gardens in the center of Tokyo was owned by American companies.

The undercurrent of racism in Japanese-Western relations should be a matter of serious concern. When it comes to the Japanese, Europeans are even more xenophobic than Americans are. Japanese society itself, of course, is deeply racist with a strong tinge of nationalistic paranoia, as evidenced by the Japanese bestseller, *The Japan That Can Say 'No',* co-authored by Sony's Chairman, Akio Morita and Shintaro Ishihara, a former Cabinet member. (Much of what Morita says is actually quite reasonable; but Ishihara talks in right-wing, militaristic tones reminiscent of the 1930s.) Racism is the kind of unreasoning emotion that, far more than the "deficits" or "imbalances" that so worry conventional forecasters, could slow or utterly derail the powerful momentum toward broad-based global growth.

Despite the rancor of some recent Japanese-Western exchanges, my impression is that, at the working levels, the societies are rapidly getting used to each other—another instance of events outrunning the conventional political wisdom. I expect attitudes to improve markedly over the next five years or so. A sign of the times is the kanji characters on the back of business cards that are the newest status symbol among American investment bankers. Partly because of fear of protectionism, Japanese companies are globalizing at a breakneck pace and proving, in the main, to be good employers, decent corporate citizens, and cooperative business partners. By the same token, both Japanese and Western companies seem increasingly aware of the opportunities from blending the talents and technologies of East and West.

The Japanese themselves will bear a major responsibility

for stabilizing East-West economic relationships. For all their impressive industrial skills, the Japanese do not yet operate an open, modern economy. Although incomes in Tokyo are nominally almost twice as high as incomes in New York, they buy only about half as much. Anyone who has traveled in Japan knows how shockingly high basic prices are. The "47th Street Photo phenomenon" is legendary. Japanese tourists mob New York electronic goods stores, snapping up items like Sony camcorders at much lower prices than they can get them at home.

The reason is not that Sony or other Japanese companies are "dumping" items in America below cost—many of them, anyway, are now made in America. The reason is that the Japanese distribution system is hopelessly inefficient and out-dated. But the system is protected by a combination of business special interests and the ruling gerontocracy of the Liberal Democratic Party. Japanese goods are fairly priced in America; they are not fairly priced in Japan, and the people being wronged are not Americans but the Japanese.

The answer, of course, is not to raise prices in America but to lower them in Japan. The American government should continue to insist on reducing Japanese barriers to competition. But increasing American barriers in response helps no one; in particular, it doesn't help American consumers or, in the medium term at least, American companies.

Canada Bets on Free Trade

The Columbia River rises high on the forbidding Western slopes of the Canadian Rockies in the province of British Columbia. As the glaciers retreat each spring, the melting snow and ice swell Lake Columbia at the river's source. The river strains at its banks, then crashes through hundreds of miles of craggy Canadian forests into the rugged backcountry of Washington, before joining with the Snake and making a wide turn to West, where, now broad and smooth after a thousand-mile journey, it glides past Portland, Oregon, on to its destination in the Pacific.

The Columbia River represents one of the world's greatest reserves of hydroelectric power—a cheap, reliable, and ever renewed source of electrical energy, without any of the problems of acid rain, or radioactive waste, or carbon emissions that plague most other energy-producing industries. Most of the early hydroelectric power development along the Columbia was American. The famous Grand Coulee Dam, north of Spokane, Washington, is the largest single source of hydroelectric power in the United States. Until the 1970s, even most of the Canadian development, such as the huge Hugh Keenleyside and Duncan dams, were built with American money.

With the manufacturing boom in the United States in the 1980s, and the prospects for continued strong growth through the 1990s, energy usage is rising. As a result, there have been the first bubblings of concern that American power supplies may not be adequate for the coming decade of development. After grossly overestimating future energy demands in the 1970s, most major utilities stopped investing in new capacity in the 1980s. At the same time, one hundred nuclear power plants scheduled to come on line in the 1990s were either scrapped or, as in the cases of Seabrook in New Hampshire and Shoreham in Long Island, New York, were supinely mothballed.

Few Americans realize that Canada is the largest single exporter of energy to the United States by a wide margin. Its oil exports alone to the United States are greater than those of any other national supplier, including Saudi Arabia. Canada's position as America's leading energy supplier is buttressed by its enormous reserves of hydroelectric power, natural gas, oil, and coal. But until

162

early 1989, energy trade between the United States and Canada, while growing steadily, tended to be balky and unreliable and was conducted in an atmosphere of mutual suspicion. The watershed event was the signing of the Free Trade Agreement between the two countries that will create, over the next ten years, virtually a North American Common Market.

With successive Republican administrations in Washington ideologically predisposed toward free trade and preoccupied by the trade disputes with Asia, the Free Trade Agreement was never controversial in America. But because of the vast difference in the size of the two economies, Canadians necessarily viewed the prospect of free trade with the United States to be as much a threat as an opportunity.

Canada is America's biggest and least acknowledged trading partner. Despite all the attention in America to trade policy toward Japan or Germany, the bilateral trade volume between the United States and Canada is the largest in the world. Automotive exports to America account for 7 percent of Canadian GNP—but since the companies have American names, they are not controversial. Exports as a percentage of GNP are about two and a half times higher in Canada than in Japan, and three-quarters of them go to America. For all its small size, Canada absorbs almost a quarter of American exports.

With such an enormous stake in the bilateral business relation with America, and with such an unequal power position, it took unusual vision, patience, and persistence for Canadian statesmen to push the Free Trade Agreement to completion. Although most business organizations and economic analysts supported the agreement, there were widespread worries, particularly among smaller businesses, and most Canadian unions were actively opposed. But overriding the objections was the frank recognition that economic success in the 1990s will require meeting world-class competitive standards. With a skilled and well-educated labor force and vast natural resources, Canada should be one of the success stories of the 1990s. The booming trade in energy illustrates both how much damage can be wreaked by government attempts at economic micromanagement and the opportunities that are available in competitive markets.

Canadian-American energy regulation during the last two decades is one of the great horror stories of modern bureaucracy. When the United States suffered energy shortages during the Arab embargo of the early 1970s, Canada temporarily cut oil exports to America, then followed up with a series of unilateral actions and ''energy policies'' that attempted, among other things, to eliminate all energy exports to the United States by the early 1980s and to eliminate American investment in the Canadian energy sector. Throughout most of the period, government policy veered between imposing heavy taxes and other discriminatory pricing regulations on energy exports to the United States and offering volume discounts to Americans as surpluses mounted.

American policy was every bit as provocative and, if anything, even more bizarre. Price controls that artificially cheapened domestic natural gas effectively barred Canadian exports. Canadian refiners were denied access to convenient Alaskan oil. British Columbian hydroelectricity was prohibited from selling into California (during a time of energy shortages!). The government flip-flopped almost daily on building a trans-Canadian natural gas pipeline from Alaska. The pro-coal policies of the 1970s punished Canada with acid rain. Energy import taxes and discriminatory Superfund taxes disadvantaged Canadian petroleum. And so on.

Such a sorry record of wrongheaded meddling, it is tempting to believe, must have been guided by some malign intelligence bent on dragging down the competitiveness and productivity of both the Canadian and American economies. Would that it were so—the meddler could be driven to the North Woods and quietly disposed of. The banal and much more depressing truth is that almost all of the interventions were well-meaning errors by intelligent and public-spirited people. In a complex modern economy, the iron law of unintended consequences reigns.

Free trade in energy is giving an enormous boost to the energy sector of the Canadian economy. B.C. Hydro, the utility that controls the hydroelectric resources of Canadian sections of the Columbia, has laid out an aggressive twenty-year plan for adding more than a billion watts of generating capacity, which will still amount to only about a tenth of its readily available potential resources. In the middle of the continent, Manitoba Hydro is building a huge new complex to service the American Midwest, and in the East, Hydro Quebec has signed a long-term power agreement with the New England Power Pool (an organization of New England utilities) to supply a grand total of 33 trillion watt hours of electricity through 1996, with programmed increases of 7 trillion watt hours a year through 2000.

Natural gas exports should grow even more rapidly. Natural gas prices have been depressed for some years because of the gas "bubble" in the United States. The burst of oil drilling activity in America in the late 1970s and early 1980s uncovered vast reserves of natural gas, which have taken almost ten years to work off. With prices showing signs of firming, gas exports from Canada have doubled in the last three years. Growth should continue to be strong, because natural gas is the most environmentally benign of fossil fuels. As big new fields come on line—a recent discovery in Alberta is the largest in twenty years—the only limiting factor is pipeline capacity. Natural gas pipeline investment in Canada is rising sharply but is probably still too low to meet future American demand.

Energy trade between the United States and Canada is a clear "win-win" proposition for both countries. The Free Trade Agreement assures Americans continued supplies on a fair-share basis should there be a future energy crunch. The flow of revenue and investment into Canada will build wealth and fuel growth.

There are still problems. The remnants of the Trudeau government's "National Energy Policy" that limits American investment in Canadian energy is a major reason for the prolonged natural gas pipeline bottleneck. American coal miners are vociferously protesting the prospect of American coal-burning utilities switching to natural gas. (The consumer cost of sticking with coal, according to a U.S. Department of Energy calculation, would be about $115,000 per job saved per year, leaving aside the costs of acid rain.) The nationalistic Council of Canada worries that the treaty assures America of too large a share of Canadian energy. American unions have protested that, since the Canadian hydro companies are owned by their provincial governments, they enjoy unfair taxpayer subsidies. (But that's hardly America's problem. At some point, presumably, Canadian taxpayers will wake up to the idiocy of picking up part of the tab for American power costs.)

Energy, of course, is not the only Canadian industrial sector benefiting from freer trade. As soon as the agreement was signed, Sam Ajmera, a Bombay-born bagel baker in Toronto, bought a bagel-making machine that will allow him to ship a million bagels a day to New York and New England. Before the agreement, import duties shut him out of the American market entirely. Du Pont Canada has doubled its planned capital-spending program to take advantage of the prospect for increased U.S. sales. The Canada Malting Company has expanded its operations to America, making it the largest brewery supplier in the world. The expansion wouldn't have been possible before the Free Trade Agreement facilitated the rationalization of production between Canadian and American plants. A textile manufacturer in Ontario is building a new factory because duty-free cotton from America makes his yarns much more competitive on world markets.

But some Canadians are getting hurt. The loss of protection invariably means restructurings. Whirlpool and Gillette both announced plant shutdowns shortly after the agreement was signed—with free trade, they could supply Canada more efficiently from their American plants. Canadian fish processors can no longer demand that American fishermen process their Canadian catch in Canadian plants. Because global competitive standards are forcing higher productivity worldwide, the new factories being built in the wake of the agreement will generate far fewer jobs than older factories used to. Unions worry that the generous social benefits enjoyed by Canadian workers may fall to American levels.

Free trade is a two-edged sword. Greater competition and lower costs, over the long run, spur efficiency, productivity, and the creation of wealth. The declining standards of work and quality that inevitably accompany protectionism impoverish nations. England in the 1970s is the classic experiment. But the disciplines of free competition are harsh ones, and the burdens fall unevenly, both as between industrial sectors and social groups and over time. It has taken enormous courage for Canadians to push on into the brave new world of global competition. It will take still more for them to stay the course.

There are encouraging signs in the United States as well that businesspeople, despite all the uproar over Japanese trade policy, are beginning to take the commitment to free trade seriously. The unexpected battle over extending the "voluntary" restraints on imported steel during the summer of 1989 was an important straw in the wind.

Under pressure from industry lobbyists, the Reagan administration's commitment to free trade flagged noticeably through the mid-1980s. The "voluntary restraints" on steel imports—really just steel import quotas—were established in 1984 for five years, essentially freezing the American market share of nineteen countries and the European Economic Community. Countries viewed as having engaged in particularly unfair trading practices, or "dumping"—selling below production cost—were subjected to tonnage limitations as well. The voluntary restraints were only the latest in twenty years of steel import regulation.

The steel import restraints looked as though they were becoming a permanent piece of the American economic landscape. When Democrats challenged George Bush's commitment to continued protectionism during the 1988 campaign, he quickly promised to extend the quotas when they come up for renewal in the fall of 1989. The decision was widely viewed as an uncontroversial one, a simple case of good politics overriding economic theory.

No one had counted on strong objections from the Coalition of American Steel Using Manufacturers—for one thing, it didn't exist in 1988. The coalition was organized by Caterpillar, the big construction equipment manufacturer from Peoria, Illinois. William Lane, Caterpillar's director of governmental affairs, says, "We thought it was time to speak up. Steel is our most important raw material. The quotas raised our costs and made it much harder to meet foreign competition. Worse than that, because of the quotas, some classes of steel were simply unavailable in America, at any price. We thought we'd be more effective if ten or twenty other companies joined us, so we started making phone calls. To our amazement, in a couple of weeks we had three hundred companies signed on, and more requests to join were coming in every day." (Ironically, the country's largest steel user, General Motors, was a leading anti-quota enthusiast. GM's cars, of course, are still protected by import quotas that served as the original model for the steel industry's quota system.)

The coalition's case was thuddingly simple. Heavy steel-using manufacturers employed twenty-five times as many workers as the steel producers. They accounted for 44 percent of American exports and the lion's share of industrial investment. Twenty years of protectionism had resulted in steel costs to American manufacturers 25 percent higher, on average, than Japanese or German steel costs. Because of quota-induced shortages, steel prices had risen 15 percent on average in 1987 and 1988, and as much as 30 to 40 percent in specific short-supply products. The total cost to American steel users in 1988 alone was at least $6.5 billion. The steel quotas had saved possibly 17,000 jobs in American steel mills, but had caused some 52,000 workers in other sectors of the economy to *lose* their jobs. Whatever the benefit to the steel industry's profit line, the qouta system was destroying American manufacturing competitiveness.

No one was defending unfair trade practices; but as Lane pointed out to Congress, there were ample provisions in existing law to deal with "dumping" or similar offenses. The coalition's assault appeared to catch the steel industry entirely by surprise. Local newspapers in manufacturing areas took up the cry, and the campaign to extend quotas to other countries and impose controls for five more years quickly collapsed. Bush had promised an extension, and he finally approved a watered-down version of the original quotas for only two-and-a-half more years—with the clear understanding that the steel industry would be on its own from that point. (The steel industry was in a mild state of shock after the quota-extension battle. Several executives I spoke to simply refused any comment. "These guys [the coalition] are our best customers," said one. "We just can't afford to be at odds with them publicly like that. The fight's over. We got a little further relief. We'd just rather not talk about it anymore.")

The steel users' coalition highlights the unintended consequences of broadside attempts to manage trade for the benefit of particular industries or particular interest groups. The earlier imposition of auto-import restraints is still haunting the American automotive industry. The auto import quotas fixed Japanese company shares of the U.S. auto market and removed incentives for price competition. Since the Japanese could produce much more efficiently than the American companies in the early 1980s, the agreement effectively set a price floor, locking in very high Japanese profits. Characteristically, the Japanese companies reinvested the windfall in their companies, financing their move into the high-value, most highly profitable segments of the luxury car market, areas where the American companies had thought they were invulnerable.

Rubbing salt in the wounds, the Japanese manufacturers rapidly expanded their production in America, insulating themselves from currency fluctuations. (Local production, sensibly enough, is not covered by import quotas.) Far from protecting their markets, that is, the Big Three have seen the loss of the most profitable luxury segments of their businesses and the invasion of a host of high-productivity Japanese manufacturers, with an arguable claim to be turning out cars as "American" as any the Big Three make. The contrast with the Cummins Engine (see pp. TK) strategy could not be more striking. Cummins eschewed government help and chose to fight it out with Komatsu on the basis of price and quality alone. The company shed rivers of red ink in the process but ended up a leaner, much more efficient competitor, in firm control of its home market. By seeking government protection, on the other hand, the automobile companies merely postponed the day of reckoning, were accomplices in the inflation of Japanese profits, and are entering the 1990s with considerable self-doubt about their ability to keep up the struggle.

Foolish and self-defeating as the steel and auto import quotas were, the DRAM agreement pushed through Washington by the Semiconductor Industry Association in 1985 marks the high point in modern protectionist folly. American companies pioneered integrated circuit technology in the 1960s—with the American government financing almost all of the research and development and buying up almost all of the early production. DRAMs (for "Dynamic Random Access Memory" chips) are the basic memory chips in almost all computer and consumer electronic product applications. The Japanese began applying their formidable manufacturing skills to DRAMs in the 1970s, and were emerging as world-class competitors by the end of the decade.

Memory chips offer one of the most dramatic examples of price-performance improvements in industrial history. When the 1k or one-kilobit, chip (a chip that could store 1000 "bits," or on-off states) was introduced commercially in 1972, it cost about $10, on a production base of about 5 million chips a year. The 1k chip quickly gave way to the 4k chip, and by 1978, more than 100 million 4k devices were being turned out at a cost of about fifty cents a kilobit. The 64k chip was launched in 1981 and the 256k chip in 1983. By 1985, six Japanese firms were among the top ten world semiconductor manufacturers and had driven the price of the 256k DRAM down to less than one cent a kilobit, a thousandfold price reduction in less than fifteen years.

American chip manufacturers had lost $2 billion trying to keep pace, and, like the steel and auto manufacturers, came clamoring to Washington about chip "dumping." American trade negotiators quickly reached an agreement with the Japanese companies to keep their prices at a level where American companies could make a profit. The Japanese companies accepted the proposal with alacrity, indeed, with gratitude and relief. The American trade negotiators did not know—although arguably they should have—that the semiconductor agreement had saved the Japanese companies from a collective act of *hara-kiri.* The Japanese companies had installed capacity totaling some two-and-a-half times world demand and were engaged in an internecine competitive bloodbath. Their collective losses were double the American industry's. An *American* proposal to *raise* the prices charged for chips sold into the *American* market looked like bounty from a benign Buddha.

Immediately following the semiconductor agreement, DRAM prices in the United States tripled, and the American companies exited the fray anyway—most were never much interested in commodity chip production. The American computer industry lost a critical competitive edge when it suddenly had to pay much more for its chips, and Japanese financial statements flipped from crushing losses to soaring profits—from some $4 billion in red ink to $3 billion in the black in two years. As in the auto industry, those windfall profits were reinvested in production facilities, and the Japanese led the way into 1-megabit (one million bits) DRAM production in 1987. A clearer case of interventionist wrongheadedness would be hard to find.

The Canadian example should be an object lesson for Americans. Canada has a much smaller and weaker industrial base than the United States. Yet it has the confidence and the foresight to pursue free trade with its powerful neighbor rather than risk the debilitating comforts of protectionism. The history of interventionist trade policy in America has time and again demonstrated the wisdom of that course.

8

MARX AND LENIN MEET ADAM SMITH

The Coming of "Market Communism"

Soviet citizen Valery Gorokhov made a most unusual proposal to his bosses in Moscow in the fall of 1989. Gorokhov is the chief executive of the state-owned Moscow Experimental Plant (catering services), which produces machinery to make ice cream and cottage cheese and bottling equipment for brandy and soft drinks. The enterprising executive, together with the seven hundred employees at the plant, proposed nothing less than a leveraged buyout of their company.

Like many Western businessmen and employee groups, Gorokhov and his workers would borrow the money, although from a state-owned bank, and pay off the loan with the profits from the business. Gorokhov, indeed, hoped to diversify away from food-related machinery into microwave ovens, perhaps with a Western joint venture partner. The proposed deal would work much like the recent aborted pilot-led buyout of United Air Lines or employee takeovers of other American companies like Avis or Weirton Steel—the company's stock would be allocated to the employees and they would share in the profits. One of the attractions of the deal in Moscow, apparently, is that the employee-ownership wrinkle lends it a proper socialist flavor. If the deal goes forward, there are others waiting in the wings.

Mr. Gorokhov's proposed buyout is one of the first fruits of the fairly timid Soviet business reform laws passed in 1987 and 1988. His factory was one of the first to be leased under rules that allow the enterprise to retain part of the profits after paying the rent. Prior to the leasing rules, all profits were turned back to Moscow. As Adam Smith would have predicted a couple hundred years ago, under the old system most companies, including Mr. Gorokhov's, didn't show a profit; bosses can always find something to spend money on if the alternative is to give it away. Miraculously, as soon as the leasing rules permitted part of the profits to stay home, Gorokhov's factory started to make money—enough, it seems, to buy the whole business.

The economic reform movements under way in Eastern Europe and the Soviet Union are a sea change. (As I've been writing this chapter, events have been moving so rapidly that the foreign policy experts are gape-jawed. A statement that the Cold War was ending usually met with sharp skepticism in, say, September of 1989. By mid-November, the end of the Cold War was regarded as all but an accomplished fact.) The essential premise of the Cold War was that a militarized, aggressive, unified bloc of nations was committed to the expansion of Communist ideology and the state-directed system of Communist economic management wherever possible, most particularly in Europe. While the Communist world is still highly militarized, it has not been very aggressive in recent years, although that could easily change. But it is clearly no longer unified and, most important, there has been an unmistakable admission that the Communist system has failed.

Communism has always had the characteristics of a religious movement, but it is an *economic* religion. It is not likely that very many Soviet leaders really believed in Communism. (Like Stalin, most of them believed in *power.*) But it was the promise of economic liberation through Communism that gave the system its legitimacy and dynamism. Who can forget Khrushchev's boasts that "we will bury you"—he meant economically—or his claim that Kennedy's grandchildren would live under Communism. In the 1950s and the 1960s, a good portion of American intellectuals genuinely believed that Khrushchev was right. They were not pro-Communist, of course, but they feared that a state-directed system had inherent advantages over the more disorderly economic processes in the West. They were convinced that so long as the struggle was posed in primarily economic terms, the Western countries were fated to lose the Cold War.

Whatever the doubts of twenty or thirty years ago, the economic contest, such as it was, is conclusively over. The state-directed system that Lenin built may have made some minimum sense in the 1920s, when the priority was to build hydroelectric dams and cement plants, although the point is certainly arguable. But in the fast-moving world of the late twentieth century, central bureaucratic direction, particularly of the stolidly suspicious Russian variety, simply doesn't work.

Soviet leader Mikhail Gorbachev has expressly recognized the failure of the old Communist orthodoxy. But his attempts at reform appear unduly cautious when compared to the much more freewheeling changes under way in Eastern Europe. As this is being written in the winter of 1989, the new Solidarity prime minister in Poland, Tadeusz Mazowiecki, is installing a largely non-Communist government with almost no opposition from the Communist benches in the parliament. His economic ministers have promised to create "a normal market economy of the Western kind," complete with private companies, commercial banks, stock markets, and an unemployment compensation system to smooth the transition to efficient enterprises. The new industry minister, Tadeusz Syryjcsyk, professes to be a disciple of Milton Friedman, no less.

Events in the rest of Eastern Europe are moving with breathtaking speed. This book is going to press during the violent revolution in Romania. East German Communist leaders have been thrown in jail by the citizens. The Berlin Wall, long the symbol of the Cold War, is now a museum piece. There is a new non-Communist government in Czechoslovakia. The Baltic states are voting out one-party rule. The question of the leading role of the Communist Party has been raised openly even in the Supreme Soviet.

All of these currents of reform, of course, could be snuffed out at any moment, although repression becomes harder with each passing day. Witness the brutal speed with which the Chinese autocrats put down the democracy movement in Tiananmen Square. Rumors continually circulate of a conservative coup against Gorbachev, a prospect that becomes all the more plausible the longer the half-measures adopted so far fail to bring results. But whatever the setbacks, there is no question that this year, or next, or five years from now, reform will have to come. Few people in the West even realize what deep trouble the Soviet Union is in.

An Economic Basket Case

One of the problems of interpreting Soviet economic data is that the numbers are so unreliable. The official growth rates in the 1980s have been in the 1 to 2 percent range, much slower than in the United States or Japan and a huge fall from the bullish 5 to 10 percent rates of the 1950s and 1960s, when the Soviets were first emerging as a relatively modern economy. But the official growth rates, low as they are, are probably grossly overstated, and a number of analysts believe that the Soviets have actually been *losing* ground over the past several years.

The biggest problem is the huge drain of military expenditure. Gorbachev himself has admitted a budget deficit of about 15 percent of GNP, enormously bigger than any among other industrialized countries, and the military machine claims somewhere between 13 to 17 percent of all Soviet output. Indeed, some analysts believe that military spending absorbs almost a third of Soviet wealth.

In any case, the evidence of resource misallocation is everywhere. From the available data, it appears that the replacement rate of Soviet capital equipment for the last fifteen years has been considerably less than half that in the United States and, of course, much slower than in Japan or Western Europe. The bellwether Soviet steel industry is notoriously obsolete, with more than half of its mills using the old open-hearth methods, which have virtually disappeared in the West. Oil production is trending down and getting much more expensive, since most of the available reserves lie under the forbidding Siberian permafrost. A forced-draft effort to replace fossil fuels with nuclear power came a cropper with the disaster at Chernobyl.

The shortfall of investment in infrastructure is even greater than in basic industries. Astoundingly, in 1981 the state of Texas had more miles of paved roads than the entire Soviet Union, and total Soviet concrete and asphalt highway miles had actually *declined* by 5 percent since 1965—in a country that spans eleven time zones. Both France and West Germany have more telephones than the Soviet Union. America and Japan each produce more cars in a single year than the total Soviet stock. The United States has six times as many trucks and buses as the Soviets. And because of the lack of normal transportation facilities—truck parks, repair shops, service stations, parts distribution centers, telephone dispatching networks—the snarls and bottlenecks in the transportation system are worse than a bare statistical comparison would suggest.

The lack of a modern infrastructure means that much of the reported Soviet production is simply wasted. The Soviets are the world's largest producers of chemical fertilizers, but they admit themselves that about a third of each year's output is lost because of a lack of storage and handling facilities. In a country desperately striving to become self-sufficient in agriculture, some 20 to 25 percent of the annual harvest is allowed to spoil each year because of the lack of a proper refrigeration, storage, and transport system.

The level of productivity is appalling for a supposedly advanced country. Workers quip, "They pretend to pay us and we pretend to work." The labor force is 30 percent larger than America's but produces only half the output. The situation on the farms is a scandal. There are 30 million farm workers in the Soviet Union, compared to only 3 million in America, but the country still can't feed itself. Simply throwing money at the problem hasn't worked. Agriculture consumes 27 percent of total domestic investment, but there is little to show for it.

The machine tool inventory is twice as high as in America, but industrial production is only two-thirds as much. Steel production is 50 percent higher than in America or Japan, but steel shortages still plague the economy. Obviously, the system is using too much steel, or too much machinery, or the machine tools and the steel are of poor quality—or, most likely, all of the above.

Bad as the situation in basic industries and agriculture may be, the Soviets are even further behind in the new electronic and opto-electronic technologies that are driving so much of current industrial innovation in the West. The United States has some twenty-five times more computers than the Soviet Union. Some analysts have questioned whether it is even *possible* for the Soviets to develop a computer-literate society. The paranoid addiction to secrecy makes the kind of computer telephone networks that spread computer programs in the West almost inconceivable. This is a society that still closely controls its *copying* machines.

The centers of technological innovation in the West have been small-scale entrepreneurial ventures like those populating California's Silicon Valley and Route 128 in Massachusetts. There is nothing remotely comparable in the Soviet Union, and it is hard to see how the rigid Soviet resource allocation system can ever substitute.

Gorbachev has thrown himself into the reform task with a flair and energy not seen since Khrushchev and with considerably more consistency and focus. But it is hard to see how he can succeed, at least in the short term. The half-hearted reforms adopted so far have probably just made things worse. (It is impossible to have market prices at the retail level and state-managed prices at the wholesale level, but that's more or less what Gorbachev has been trying to do.) The conservative opposition in the Communist Party is apparently still very strong, and, most important, it's not clear that the common people really have their hearts in reform. Life in the Soviet Union is certainly drab, but the kind of cradle-to-grave security Russians are used to may be hard to give up.

But regardless of the near-term outcomes in the Soviet Union and in Eastern Europe, the curtain has been stripped away, and the reality behind the myth of Soviet Communism, like the Wizard of Oz, stands small and shivering before the world. Soviet military power is still formidable, but Communism's claim to be an economic and political rival of the West has been completely scotched. In that sense, the Cold War is definitely over.

As the Soviets and the Eastern European nations struggle to come to grips with the new economic realities, the threat of war in Central Europe will gradually recede. It is already very low. And, in particular, as the Soviets gradually shift resources away from the military to the rest of the economy, there will be a correspondingly gradual, but substantial, reallocation of resources in the West, particularly in the United States. Coming on top of all the other positive trends I have been discussing, the economic impact could be profound.

American Military Spending and the Soviet Threat

The United States devotes about 6 percent of its GNP to the military. Military spending absorbs just under a third of all federal spending and is about twice as much as the annual federal budget deficit in recent years. Put another way, it absorbs each year the financial equivalent of about three years' worth of American economic growth. American military spending is about twice as much as Europe, with roughly the same level of wealth, spends in its own defense. It is far more than the Japanese spend.

By far the greatest part of the military budget is organized around the defense of Western Europe against a Soviet attack. Although highly publicized programs such as Ronald Reagan's "Star Wars" defense system and controversial new long-range nuclear missiles like the MX get most of the attention, they account for only about 10 percent of the total budget. The lion's share of the spending, by far, is devoted to the maintenance and supply of conventional arms—primarily on supporting and equipping the soldiers, sailors, and pilots who would confront the Soviet armies in a replay of World War II in Europe.

The American forces obviously dedicated to the defense of Europe are the 300,000 troops already stationed there. In addition, there are pre-positioned supplies for two more divisions that are maintained on the North American continent but that would be airlifted to Europe at the first sign of hostilities. But just counting the forces specifically dedicated to the defense of Western Europe understates the European orientation of the American military budget.

The most expensive military program of all, for example, is the U.S. Navy's aircraft carrier program. It is not usually considered a "European" program. But the only justification offered by the navy for pursuing the present hyper-expensive policy of very large carriers, with their enormously expensive accompanying air defense systems, is that they will be necessary to attack Soviet naval bases as part of a conventional war in Europe. Take away the preoccupation with Europe, and the navy will still need carriers, but much smaller, less expensive, ones, and far fewer of them.

The long-term obligation of absorbing most of the costs of European defense was certainly not contemplated by the architects of American foreign policy at the close of World War II. They had originally planned to get American troops off the continent as soon as possible but prolonged their presence in the face of Stalin's aggressive moves in the late 1940s. The ruling assumption, however, was always that the Americans would withdraw once Europeans could handle their own defense.

The complexities of the current American commitment to European defense really date from the Kennedy administration. During the Eisenhower years, American strategic policy was called "massive retaliation." If the Soviets attacked Europe, the Americans promised a nuclear bombing of the Soviet homeland. Former president Kennedy and his defense secretary, Robert McNamara, partly because the Soviets were acquiring nuclear missiles of their own, adopted a new policy of "flexible response." If the Soviets attacked Europe with conventional forces, the first reaction would be with conventional forces alone. The Americans would maintain central control of nuclear forces and use them only if they saw fit.

The problem with the new policy was that the Europeans didn't believe it. It looked like a convenient way to keep the next war far from America. The compromise was that the United States retained a major military presence on the continent so it could both maintain control over the command decisions and at the time reassure Europeans that an attack on Europe was an attack on America.

The war scenario expected by most American defense planners was a surprise Soviet *blitzkrieg* assault, using tank armies, much as Hitler did in 1941, to break through NATO defense lines in central Germany. The prospect of Soviet tank attacks in Europe was always faintly implausible. It's never been clear what the Soviets would gain from an attack in Europe that would be worth the risk of an all-out American nuclear response. But it becomes more and more far-fetched as the years go by. Certainly, if the Europeans believed that an attack was at all likely, they would spend more on defense than they do. Instructively, most of the intra-alliance disputes over the past few years have revolved around European complaints about the continued presence of the American military bases.

Any Soviet attack scenario would have to assume the heartfelt cooperation of the Warsaw Pact armies supplied by Poland, Hungary, Czechoslovakia, East Germany, Bulgaria, and Rumania. In the present state of affairs, the Soviets can't even be sure whose *side* the satellites would be on. In addition, the high state of readiness apparently achieved by Soviet forces in the late 1970s cannot be maintained as Gorbachev attempts to shift resources to the consumer and industrial sectors of the economy. Gorbachev has already enunciated a new troop deployment policy that, he promises, will significantly reduce the threat of rapid-strike war.

Most American defense commentators seem to have despaired of the possibility of making major cuts in military spending because of the difficulty of drawing up truly comprehensive arms control agreements with the Soviet Union. My own research for a history of the arms race (published in 1988) convinced me that no arms control agreement has ever had much impact on arms spending. The only agreement that had any effect *at all,* I am convinced, was the 1963 nuclear test ban agreement. After the SALT I agreement in 1972, for instance, the Soviets vastly expanded their missile forces. "Cheating" had little to do with it: It is almost impossible to negotiate an agreement that isn't full of holes. And after SALT II, although both sides claimed to abide by the treaty—even though it was never ratified in America—both sides, particularly the Americans, still managed massive expansions in their forces.

Does that mean that we can never reduce arms spending? Or never reduce the military tensions of the Cold War? Not at all. It simply means that the military component of the Cold War will probably end without any grand agreement. There comes a point when the idea of a shooting war starts to look ridiculous. France and Germany fought a series of savage wars on the European continent with clocklike regularity for 150 years. And the French had little confidence that the Germans would stay subdued even at the end of World War II.

But by the middle of the 1950s or so, the idea of a war between France and West Germany became unthinkable. Both sides by that time had extensively rebuilt their military capabilities and disposed of genuinely formidable forces, but suddenly neither found the other's forces the least bit threatening. There was no grand proclamation to that effect, no comprehensive agreement to eliminate the threat of military action against each other. It just became unthinkable.

John Mueller, who argues on these lines in a brilliant book called *Retreat from Doomsday,* points out that Canada and the United States fought regular skirmishes against each other for many years and maintained military installations on their mutual border until late in the nineteenth century. Then at some point it just began to seem silly. There was no disarmament agreement between the United States and Canada. Over a period of years, the two countries just quietly reduced, and finally eliminated, their military preparations for an intra-American war.

Not only is it possible to reduce arms spending without comprehensive arms agreements but also, I suspect, that may be the *only* way to get it done. Comprehensive agreements draw too much attention, attract too much political flak, and pull too many special interests out of their hiding places.

There is precedent, in fact, for substantial arms reductions on both the Soviet and American sides in the absence of arms agreements. Khrushchev made very large cuts in the Soviet military establishment to help finance his economic programs. Between 1955 and 1958, he cut the military by about 2 million men—a cut probably in the 40-percent range. It drew little attention in the West, partly because the West was bemused by its own demonology and partly because Khrushchev took pains not to advertise it. Much of his fabrications about Soviet missile prowess, it seems in retrospect, were for the purpose of disguising, both from the West and from his own marshals, how much the Soviet force posture had deteriorated.

Richard Nixon, not generally remembered for his pacific instincts, is the American counter-example. He cut American defense spending, in constant-dollar terms, by about 50 percent from the 1968 Vietnam war peak and by 20 percent from the spending base before the Vietnam-related buildup began. The manpower cut was about 1.3 million from the Vietnam peak and about 500,000 from the pre-Vietnam base. Spending comparisons actually understate how much of a cut Nixon made. America shifted to an all-volunteer military force in 1970. In the course of just a few years, that necessitated military pay raises of about 75 percent, but Nixon still managed to cut spending overall. Like Khrushchev, Nixon got relatively little credit for the cuts, partly because he took pains not to publicize them in order to maintain his pro-military voting constituency.

Neither the Khrushchev nor the Nixon arms reduction policies could be maintained, because both sides weren't prepared to reciprocate. The Soviets eventually had to respond to Kennedy's massive defense buildup in the early 1960s. Nixon was caught napping in the face of the equally enormous Soviet buildup during the Brezhnev years.

The difference in the 1990s, one hopes, is that it may be the first time in the history of the Cold War that *both sides* have a substantial and publicly conceded interest in reducing arms spending—the Soviets to finance their reconstruction, and the Americans to reduce the impact of, or at least the criticisms of, their budget deficits.

My own projection is that American military spending will be reduced by at least a third in constant-dollar terms through the first half of the 1990s. That would leave it still somewhat higher than its low point in about 1977, or just before Jimmy Carter started a military rebuilding program. And it would still be higher, as a share of GNP, than in any other Western country at the present time. That level of reduction, which I think is modest, will save $100 billion a year in federal spending.

Skeptics will argue that a reduction of this magnitude can't be carried out in an orderly way. They are absolutely right. All previous cutbacks in military spending—Khrushchev's cutbacks in the 1950s or the American cutbacks after World War II, after the Korean war, or during the Nixon years—were disorderly in the extreme. They were uneven and wasteful, at least partly in order to disguise the magnitude of the cutbacks from pro-military critics. But they happened anyway and will happen again.

Seymour Melman, among others, has recently pointed out the fragility of so-called peace dividends. The country had expected such a windfall after the Vietnam war wound down. Lyndon Johnson had even made explicit plans to invest heavily in the nation's infrastructure—roads, bridges, and the like. But the peace dividend, Melman suggests, never materialized and the infrastructure investment never happened.

Melman is right that peace dividends are fragile, and that we under-invested in infrastructure in the 1970s. But he is wrong about the peace dividend. It was enormous, and we spent it—except not on infrastructure. A few numbers will show where the peace dividend actually went: In 1970, the federal government spent about $82 billion on defense and $75 billion on human resources—social security payments, Medicare, Medicaid, welfare, food stamps, Head Start programs, and the like. In 1976, the federal government spent $90 billion on defense (because of the rapid inflation in the early 1970s, that represented about a 27-percent reduction in actual buying power) and spent *$203 billion* on human resources.

Although he rarely gets either credit or blame for it, Richard Nixon raised American social spending more than any president in history—far more, for instance, than Lyndon Johnson's "Great Society" programs did. And a great part of the new social spending was financed by very sharp cutbacks in defense—cutbacks, that is, of roughly the same order of magnitude as the ones I am projecting here. Whether so much of the peace dividend should have been devoted to raising social welfare benefits is a separate issue of no particular relevance for my argument here. The point is that there is plenty of precedent for peace dividends. The question comes down to how the money is allocated.

Certainly there are plenty of pressures building for new federal spending programs, and there is no doubt that perceived spending needs will rise faster than the ability of any peace dividend to keep pace. But there also seems to be quite a different attitude toward federal spending in the 1990s than there was in the 1970s. Some part of the peace dividend will be absorbed in new spending programs. And some of it should be—Melman is right that our infrastructure is falling into a disgraceful state of disrepair. At the same time, the pressure to reduce budget deficits without a major tax increase is just too great to allow all the savings to be siphoned away in new spending programs. Reduced military spending, therefore, will accelerate the trends—which I have already described—toward reduced levels of public borrowing and lower interest rates throughout the industrialized world.

Adjusting to a Lower Arms Budget

Critics of American military spending often sound as though military spending is a total economic waste. That is not the case. As I will attempt to show in the next chapter, the United States is the world's leader in high technology. And that technological leadership stems, in great part, from the continued investment in military research and development.

The integrated circuit, today's microchip, was invented in a private research laboratory. (Actually in two. Texas Instruments and Fairchild independently filed patents at about the same time.) But the first chips were so expensive that there were no feasible commercial applications.

In the early 1960s, after production methods had been developed to make chips in salable volumes, the American military and space programs were the world's only customers. In effect, the military was the industry's nursemaid. It funded much of the early research and development of a promising new invention. And it was a friendly and cooperative customer, buying in volumes that edged the fledgling industry up the "learning curve," until the point was reached where the industry could produce large volumes of chips at reasonable costs.

In a real sense, the military's nursing of the microchip industry made the eventual proliferation of high-speed computers possible and laid the basis for the long American dominance of the computer industry. American critics—or admirers—of Japanese industrial policy often forget the major role played by the American government, through the U.S. Defense Department, in creating and fostering the development of American high-technology industry.

The microchip industry is just the outstanding example of an industry that was nursed from its embryo to commercial independence by the American military. There are many others. The military was virtually the only customer for the supercomputer industry in its early years. It was virtually the only customer for fiber optics through most of the 1970s and brought that industry to production volumes that made commercial applications feasible.

The rapidly growing opto-electronics industry, including new applications of all sorts for lasers—which are now common in the most mundane applications—was nursed to commercial viability by military spending. For all the criticisms of the new B-2 Stealth bomber, the pursuit of a radar-invulnerable outer skin has fostered a vast leap forward in composite materials—combinations of metals, plastics, and ceramics—that are already beginning to show up in cars and civilian airplanes. (The B-2, in fact, is an enormously expensive plane of dubious military value. But if the entire program were killed, the money would not have been wasted. Indeed, killing it outright would probably be the most cost-effective step.)

Americans criticize the European subsidies for Airbus Industrie, the government-subsidized European entry in the large commercial jet manufacturing industry. But the American civilian airframe industry reached critical mass primarily through its military order book and has always been cushioned through hard times by its extensive military business. The contract for a new generation of large military jet transports, the C5A, was expressly awarded to Lockheed in the hope of keeping the company competitive in civilian planes. (Boeing offered to convert 747s at a much lower cost. The thought of asking Airbus Industrie to bid never even occurred to anyone.)

Overall, the level of government support for research and development is higher in the United States than in any other country, measured either in total spending or as a share of GNP. (Government support for R and D is twice that in Japan as a percent of GNP, and four times higher in absolute dollars.) And most of it is filtered through the military. Military spending is the primary basis for the American leadership in high technology today.

I will have more to say about the quality of American technology in the next chapter. But the defense-oriented subsidies of American industry do have one decidedly negative impact. At least as compared to Japan, America is much more proficient in basic research on new technologies than it is in achieving commercial application of those technologies. (The point is not nearly so obvious in comparison to Europe.)

As a consequence, America has unmatched high-end machining, for example—missile gyroscopes and submarine propeller blades must be finished to exquisitely precise standards—but has been thoroughly outclassed in mid-technology machining for, say, automobiles or VCRs. Few of the technologies that Japan has developed to support its commanding lead in high-definition televisions, for example, are at the leading edge of science.

Robert Reich of Harvard University, among others, has argued that the defense emphasis of American research actually retards the process of commercial applications. GE-FANUC's Bob Collins concurs. He says, "We keep on making the same mistake. All of the federal attempts to boost industrial technologies still have a strong military influence. It's the bread-and-butter technologies where we're lagging, not the military technologies."

Overall, I believe the trend toward a lower defense base will help the American economy. The transition will not be completely painless. Scientists and engineers accustomed to working on exotic military or space applications will not convert overnight into commercial manufacturing engineers. (The facile assumption that, without the "drain" of defense spending, all those scientists would be designing better compact disc players has the ring of wishful thinking.)

But competitive pressures are pushing inexorably toward a greater commitment to industrial research and development, particularly in manufacturing and other product-related technologies. Lower defense spending, lower budget deficits, lower interest rates, and a greater pool of trained scientists and engineers available to industry will all help support and reinforce that trend.

The transition to lower defense spending will be eased by the economic opening in Eastern Europe. In contrast to the Soviet Union, or to other underdeveloped countries, the peoples of East Germany, Poland, Hungary, and Czechoslovakia have long and proud histories as developed, economically advanced nations. They have been cruelly oppressed for the past forty years, but it is reasonable to expect that they will bounce back quickly once the restrictions are removed. Adding another center of dynamic growth to the world economy will be just one more element feeding into the virtuous economic cycle that is emerging for the 1990s.

As I said in the Introduction, there are so many positive forces massing to drive the Schumpeterian economic "phase change" that we will see in the 1990s, that there is a great margin for error before the positive impetus could be reversed. In that sense, the impending shift away from a military bias in the American economy and the new opportunities in Eastern Europe are icing on the cake.

SUMMING UP

Much of Part III was devoted to dispelling phantoms. The American budget deficit is not about to bring the world to its knees. Aside from the moral hazard that persistent deficits pose for spending-prone politicians, it is difficult to point definitively to any ill effects from recent deficits. And, in any case, American government deficits—state, local, and federal—are declining rapidly as a percent of GNP, as are government deficits in the rest of the industrialized world. In the medium term, the problem facing financial markets will not be too much government debt but a possible *shortage* of government bonds.

Nor is America's international debt the paralyzing problem it is usually touted to be. In the first place, much of what we call debt isn't debt at all. Further, accounting conventions seriously distort the ledgers and make net American liabilities to foreigners appear much larger than they actually are. Indeed, based on actual asset returns, it is not clear that America was in a net liability position *at all* during the 1980s.

Similarly, viewed in the context of American industry's strong overseas position, the trade deficit becomes a much less daunting problem. Japanese international sales are still primarily in the form of exports. American business's international sales, which are much greater than Japan's, are overwhelmingly from decentralized manufacturing and marketing locations. The one shows up in trade data, the other doesn't.

That said, there can be little doubt of the origins of the 1980s trade deficit with Japan. Cutting through all the macro-

186

economic jargon and protectionist rhetoric, the fact is that Americans switched to Japanese cars and consumer hardware in the 1980s because they were better products that offered higher quality, better choices, and lower prices. That is still a challenge that American industry must meet. Despite rapid strides by American companies, the battle is by no means over.

But as Japanese companies globalize, following the path American companies took thirty years ago, and major companies continue to coalesce in strategic alliances, it will be harder and harder to remember what the trade wars were really about. Americans, and Japanese and Europeans, will buy high-quality cars from local factories managed by consortia of companies owned by shareholders scattered throughout the world. Trade will become more and more an intracompany affair and the obsessive charting of surpluses and deficits will gradually fade away from the financial headlines.

Finally, the rapidly moving events in Eastern Europe and in the Soviet Union, for the first time in more than four decades, hold forth the prospect of really ending the Cold War. A sudden drop in military spending will work hardship on certain defense-dependent sectors of the economy. But, like the shift away from real estate investment we saw in Chapter 5, the transition costs will be amply repaid by the freeing up of wealth and talent for the mainstream economy. When I started working on this book, the spectacular political realignments in Eastern Europe, with the added prospect of brand-new markets for Western goods and technology, were nowhere in sight. It is, as I have said, icing on the cake.

IV

AMERICA IN THE GLOBAL ECONOMY

9

CAN AMERICA COMPETE?

Much of what I have written so far suggests that the United States is regaining its competitive edge. But in this chapter, I should like to address the question directly. How competitive is America? Is Japan inevitably pulling further and further ahead? What should governments do or not do to advance their national competitiveness? Although my comments will be directed at the United States, and specifically at the evolving competition between America and Japan, to a substantial degree, many of them could apply to Canadian and European worries about Japan as well.

Putting Competitiveness into Perspective

The competitiveness debate in the United States too often becomes an exercise in wistful nostalgia, a hearkening back to a lost golden age, situated somewhere in the middle of the 1950s, when America was indisputably "Number One." It is the wrong way to pose the problem. America *succeeding* in a

191

global economy is not the same as America regaining its postwar position as the *capo da capi* of the industrial world, the imperious proclaimer and disposer of the postwar years. That role is gone forever and no one should wish it otherwise.

Building a peaceful coalition of prosperous industrial powers stretching from Europe through North America to East Asia was the explicit objective of the great generation of statesmen who directed American affairs at the end of the war—the Marshalls, the Achesons, the Kennans, the Bohlens. The measure of their success is that, as of the late 1980s, the income of urban adults in the major industrialized countries is practically uniform. The success of the liberal, market-based democracies has been so overriding that all the oppressive twentieth-century ideologies, from Fascism to Communism, are being put to flight far more effectively than would have been possible through force of arms. Never before has such a grand policy objective been so expressly adopted, so point-edly pursued, and so unambiguously attained. To seize upon that success as an index of American "decline" is simply to miss the point.

But even the relative decline, inevitable though it may have been, has not been nearly so precipitate as our gloomier pundits claim. The world-thumping success of Japanese com-panies in high-visibility consumer products and other com-plex manufacturing operations obscures how staggeringly unproductive much of the rest of the Japanese economy actually is. Productivity comparisons almost always focus on comparing rates of *change* rather than absolute levels of output per worker. It's much easier to compare rates of change because it doesn't involve sorting out currency effects or the different product mix from one country to another. But there have been a number of studies comparing absolute levels of output per worker—the most recent one I've seen was completed by the British Treasury in 1988. In general, they show that real output per American worker is still the highest in the world by a wide margin and about *50 percent higher* than that in Japan. Since the Japanese work longer hours than almost anyone else, their performance shortfall on an hourly basis is even worse. Overall Japanese output per worker is on par with England's and lags well behind West Germany's.

Japan's output lag stems from the gross inefficiency of its services and distribution sectors and most of its white-collar operations. Shearson Lehman Hutton's Steve Nagourney, for example, reports that most of the major Japanese banks have different overnight money rates at their city branches because they lack the computer power for interbranch rate coordination. The ratio of wholesale to retail sales, an important measure of how long it takes goods to percolate through to final consumers, is about double that in America. One reason for the "47th Street Photo Phenomenon"—the fact that Japanese electronic products are much cheaper in New York than in Tokyo—is that the big manufacturers run their own distribution outlets: the discount chains that offer lots of consumer choices in America and Europe are still practically unknown in Japan. According to a recent survey by *The Wall Street Journal*, almost all the major Japanese financial institutions transact most of their business by hand. The personal computer is only beginning to make inroads into Japanese business, and most machines are still only single-function devices, such as word processors—the pattern of office automation that prevailed in the United States around 1982 or so.

Japan's recent emergence as the "world's richest country" is mostly an artifact of exchange rates. *The Economist* reports that although average incomes in Tokyo are nominally twice as high as in New York, they buy only about half as much. Food is extremely expensive, partly because of agricultural protectionism and partly because there are no world-class Japanese food-processing and distribution companies. Switzerland's Nestlé is the biggest food company in the world; most of the other top global players are American. According to Nomura Securities, Kraft can import cheese to Japan and sell it for about half the price charged by local companies, which, of course, are clamoring for import protection.

The Japanese pharmaceutical market is the second largest in the world, but, again, there are no world-class companies and few exports; American and European companies have recently grabbed about 20 percent of the local market. The largest Japanese chemical company, Asahi Chemical, would barely make the list of top-ten American companies. Japan does not export chemicals, a solid export earner in America. The Japanese construction industry is notoriously fragmented, inefficient, and mobster-ridden. It is also politically powerful and has managed, by and large, to exclude much more capable American companies from bidding on massive public projects.

Peter Drucker, a longtime student of the Japanese economy, estimates that actual unemployment in Japan is much higher than the officially reported 1 to 2 percent, possibly even higher than in the United States. The figures are kept low by gross overstaffing in government and other service operations and by forcing workers in their mid-fifties into early "retirement" on meager pensions. It is not clear how much longer the lifetime employment system can be maintained. Drucker reports that as much as a third of the Japanese steel industry work force is probably superfluous, and the Japanese National Railway is reportedly pondering laying off as much as a quarter of its employees. I'll have more to say on these issues later in the chapter.

One industry that is a good litmus test of the competitiveness race between America and Japan is the computer industry. It is the one industry that everyone agrees will be a vital component of success. The global data processing industry, defined as computers, software, peripheral devices like printers, and peripheral telecommunications equipment, now racks up $240 billion in annual sales. In the not-so-distant future, it will be the world's first trillion-dollar industry. Just as important, in contrast to most other products, computers are a tool—the key to success in a whole host of businesses, from banking to car manufacturing. Obviously, the state of the American-Japanese competition in data processing is the subject of much anxious concern on both sides of the Pacific. I'll attempt to sort out some of the facts of the present situation in the next section.

The Competition in Computers

According to Clyde Prestowitz, a former State Department expert on Japan and the author of the highly pessimistic *Trading Places,* the computer contest is already over. The

Japanese "are going to run away with it," says Prestowitz. "It's going to be another TV industry." The author George Gilder, on the other hand, argues that over the past several years, American industry has actually been widening an already large technological lead over Japan. Both men are exaggerating, but from my own reading of the data Gilder is more nearly right from Prestowitz.

First some data, with the proviso that the data problem in this area is a serious one. The data series, such as they are, are recent and unreliable. There are lots of counting problems. What's the line between a "computer" and a device used mostly for children's games? With components for the simplest PCs sourced all over the world, how does one assign value to the individual parts? And so forth.

The most complete set of available data is a compilation carried out by the publication *Datamation* for the global "computer industry." That is the source for the $240 billion figure I cited above. The data show that America controls about 62 percent, or $148 billion, of the total industry. Japanese sales are about a third as big: With about $53 billion in sales, Japanese companies account for about 22 percent of the industry.

The American position, then, is obviously very strong. But the pessimists point out how fast the Japanese share has been growing. In 1984, the American share of the industry was 79 percent and the Japanese share only 9 percent. The overall industry has been growing by about 15 percent per year, while American company sales have grown only about 10 percent annually, compared to a Japanese growth rate of 45 percent. At its simplest level, the pessimists' argument is of the "if this trend continues" variety. And at its simplest level, of course, that kind of argument is merely silly. Compound growth rates are always high when they begin from a small base. If Japanese sales keep growing at their present rate, all else equal, IBM, which now controls about a *quarter* of the global industry, will disappear in about 1993. That's not likely to happen.

To understand what *is* likely to happen, we need to look at the data in more detail. They show, for instance, that the Japanese have done extremely well in areas that require complex, high-technology manufacturing. Their most striking successes have been in semiconductors—particularly items like 1-megabit DRAMs, memory chips with a million transistors packed on a silicon chip less than an inch across. Totally automated Japanese factories are turning out DRAMs in tightly controlled nitrogen-free environments, with sub-micron (less than a millionth of a meter) manufacturing tolerances, and are achieving yields well in excess of 90 percent. As I mentioned in the discussion on trade policy on page 168, the opportunity to win a dominant market position in DRAMs was handed to the Japanese by foolish protective legislation in the United States, but it was a spectacular manufacturing achievement nevertheless. Over the past five years or so, the American share of the world semiconductor market has dropped from 65 percent to only about 35 percent, and the American share of DRAMs has dropped to only about 15 percent.

Semiconductor market-share data, however, contain an important distortion: They exclude IBM, the world's biggest maker and consumer of semiconductors. IBM manufactures virtually all of its own semiconductors, but they are excluded from market share comparisons because IBM does not sell its semiconductors to other companies. When companies like DEC and Apple claim that they are at the mercy of Japanese semiconductor manufacturers for vital supplies, it is only because IBM is not willing to sell to them, while Fujitsu, Hitachi, and NEC are. By all accounts, IBM's semiconductor manufacturing is as advanced as any in the world. In the fall of 1989, for instance, IBM announced that it had been producing 4-megabit DRAMs "in volume" for some time—well ahead, that is, of any Japanese company, which confers a major advantage in the development of the newest generation of high-capacity machines. Gilder contends that, allowing for currency fluctuations and counting IBM's output, American/Japanese semiconductor market shares haven't changed much. That may be an overstatement, but he is clearly correct that excluding IBM makes a very large difference in the data.

Two other areas where the Japanese are performing well are in high-end mainframes and supercomputers. Supercomputers, in fact, have long been something of a holy grail for the Japanese industry. Strongly prompted by MITI, the Japanese industry sees a clear opportunity to unseat Cray, a relatively small and poorly capitalized company, from its long position of supercomputer dominance. The onslaught of the Japanese in supercomputers has been the source of much American alarm in both government and certain industry circles. The federal government, in fact, recently took the extraordinary step of denying the Massachusetts Institute of Technology permission to buy a Fujitsu supercomputer for a federal research program, insisting that they buy a Cray, even though the Fujitsu was arguably better suited to the project.

The high-end mainframe computer, another area targeted by MITI, is one more example of superb Japanese manufacturing skills turning out outstanding machines. The biggest success has probably been Fujitsu's IBM clone, marketed through its American affiliate Amdahl, with better than 9 percent of the American mainframe market, up from 6 percent in 1988. Not surprisingly as well, the Japanese have gained a clear lead in most areas of manufacturing equipment, particularly in semiconductor manufacturing equipment. Finally, although the Japanese have had relatively little success in the world personal-computer market, their screen and battery technologies are quite good, and they have staked out an early lead in laptop computers.

As this recitation should make clear, the Japanese have been much more than slavish copiers of American designs—although there has been much of that, too, as in the Fujitsu mainframe. Much of their better technology, particularly in semiconductors and semiconductor manufacturing equipment, is homegrown. The Japanese were never far behind the United States in semiconductor technology even a decade or more ago. Certain major recent advances, such as CMOS technology (for complementary metal-oxide silicon) for chip construction, were developed first by the Japanese and later adopted as the standard in the United States.

All in all, that is a fairly impressive set of achievements. What is the other side to the story?

If the computer race were only about who could make the smallest chips with the highest rate of manufacturing yield or who could build the best mainframes, the American industry, with the possible exception of IBM, would have good cause for quiet panic. But there is much more to data processing than hardware.

America has a massive lead over Japan, variously estimated

to be in the range of four to five years, in system design and software. Gilder's central argument, for which there is a good deal of justification, is that over the past decade the key battleground for data processing supremacy has shifted abruptly away from hardware to system design and software— precisely the areas of the American industry's greatest strength. The shift is probably not a temporary one, since it is driven by certain immutable physical laws.

Nothing can move faster than a photon of light, a tiny packet of pure energy. It takes a photon a full nanosecond, a billionth of a second, to travel one foot. Electrons move considerably slower. There are transistors that can switch from "off" to "on" much faster than in a nanosecond, as much as a thousand times faster (i.e., in a "picosecond"). Obviously, if the business end of your computer is much bigger than a foot across, your machine is wasting enormous amounts of potentially productive time as electrons plod from one end of the machine to the other. Advanced systems designers now talk about "flight time" through a circuit—carefully tracking the physical distances electrons have to travel through a chip, trying to optimize performance along the shortest possible average path.

As machines get faster and faster, such physical constraints as the speed of an electron come to dominate performance. To a certain extent, they can be surmounted by sheer manufacturing virtuosity—making computers smaller and smaller. But then they run hotter and hotter, and at some point all those silicon components will turn back into sand. The Cray supercomputer is an example of a brute-force manufacturing solution. As a Dataquest analyst told me, "Seymour Cray is the world's greatest plumber. He can pack standard components closer than anyone in the world but still get the heat out so his machines can run when everyone else's would burn up."

But there are much more elegant solutions available. "Parallel processing," for example, is a software approach to the supercomputer problem that divides standard problems into parts that be processed simultaneously. American companies such as Thinking Machines, a small Massachusetts firm, have produced machines that rival the Cray for many supercomputer problems, using perfectly standard parts. The secret is in the software that controls how the computer approaches each separate task. A variety of other American companies, soon probably including IBM, offer similar products. The threat to the Cray, in fact, comes less from companies like Fujitsu than from companies such as Convex, Convergent Technologies, and the other entrants in the "mini-supercomputer" sweepstakes. Those are miniaturized powerhouses, much cheaper than a traditional supercomputer, that can perform at supercomputer levels for many standard supercomputer applications. At this point, the Japanese are not represented in mini-supercomputers at all.

In the final analysis, the Cray supercomputer that is the object of so much alarm and concern quite probably represents a dead-end technology. That is to say it is precisely the kind of technology that governments, both Japanese and American in this case, find it easy to understand and rally behind, with all kinds of pernicious effects, ranging from the diversion of crucial industry energy and intellectual resources to the mere waste of tax money.

Similar phenomena are also beginning to drive the semiconductor industry. There are physical limits, once again, to how many components can be packed on a chip. Once those limits are approached, as they are being at present, it becomes very difficult to make further gains in speed and power from manufacturing technology. The most advanced chips, the microprocessors, are thinking devices. The Intel 386 chip is a small computer that packs the power of the biggest IBM mainframes of a decade ago. The new 486 chip represents yet another quantum leap forward, and there are more powerful ones in the wings. While the manufacture of these chips is complex and demanding, it is not leading-edge technology. The secret of Intel's chips lies in their design, in the thinking processes that are embedded in their architecture. NEC's V-series chips are positioned as rivals to Intel. (Intel, in a bitterly contested, and finally indecisive lawsuit, maintained NEC's chips are a pirated design.) But they have made almost no serious inroads to date, and almost all Japanese personal computers use Intel, or Motorola, microprocessors.

It is a subject of hot debate in the industry whether the Intel microprocessors themselves represent a dead-end technology. Most of the power of a standard microprocessor is unused most of the time. "Reduced Instruction Set Computing," or RISC chips, greatly increase the speed and power of a microprocessor by using software to perform many of the little-used functions of the standard microprocessor. (I'll explain the RISC concept in more detail in the profile of LSI Logic following this chapter.) In this case, speed and power are obtained by simplifying rather than complicating the manufacturing problem.

By the same token, the standard arrays of microprocessors and memory chips that are the time-honored configuration of most computers are giving way to much smaller numbers of ASICs or "Application-Specific Integrated Circuits." ASICs are chips specifically designed for a particular function. Purpose-built chips can, obviously, maximize circuit design around a particular set of problems and so vastly increase processing efficency. ASICs were an impractical solution for most applications until just a few years ago. It took years to design a new chip, so system designers were forced to fall back on standard devices. American software-based design tools now make it possible to design and produce new chips in a matter of months or sometimes even weeks. Computers will still need standard DRAMs, of course, but as manufacturing technology converges—American factories can now match the Japanese in productivity and yields—the competitive advantage is clearly shifting from the company with the massive standard-chip factory to the company with the fastest and most sophisticated circuit-design software. And at the moment all of them are American companies.

Much the same type of trend can be seen in the mainframe industry. One reason it's hard to be excited about the Fujitsu mainframe is that mainframe sales have been flat or declining for a long time. Some analysts envision a not-so-distant future when mainframes have been completely replaced by networks of powerful microcomputers linked by new devices called "servers," dedicated to maximizing processing efficiency for each specific function—mathematics processing, file handling, data inquiry, etc. Configurations of powerful servers from Sun Microsystems, for example, decisively outperform most mainframes for computation-intensive applications, although conventional mainframes still are most suitable for repetitive transactional functions, like maintaining bank deposit records. All the server manufacturers, again, are American companies.

As computers continue to permeate office and factory operations, the very concept of a mainframe has an obsolescent smell to it. I'm speaking of the notion of the computer room as a kind a temple, remote from actual operations, maintained by a dedicated priesthood who mediate between the computer and ordinary mortals, interpreting requests and dispensing Delphic answers.

The direction of the argument is clear. The single-minded Japanese drive to excel at high-technology virtuosic manufacturing enterprises like DRAMs, supercomputers, and giant mainframes, may actually penalize them in the race for the next-generation technology, where the premium will be on flexibility, design, and accessibility.

In fact, I suspect the biggest threat to the powerful American position in software and software-related design tools is the growing American consciousness of its own superiority. Software is a $55 billion industry. About 70 percent of total sales, and virtually all sales of the most advanced programs, originate in America. The position is a self-reinforcing one. Systems designers prefer to work closely with software gurus as they design and vice-versa, so the best systems designers and best software writers inevitably gravitate to America. (There are no ethnic skills involved here; some of the best American designers are expatriate Japanese. In fact, a remarkably large number of the major innovators are recent immigrants from all points on the globe.) But the signs of arrogance are unmistakable. American companies are generally reluctant to write their programs in languages other than English and have been very slow to develop *kanji*-character-based systems for Asia. For the moment, the inaccessibility of so much American software has probably hindered other countries' development efforts, but such a strategy, whether conscious or not, like the unwillingness of American companies to make right-hand-drive cars for Japan, usually contains the seeds of its own destruction.

So which country is likely to win the next decade's race for computer supremacy? I have been discussing the "computer race" in terms of an American-Japanese rivalry, because that is the way the discussion is usually framed. But, frankly, I think it is a meaningless question. Beneath all the clarion calls to industrial warfare, the computer companies, large and small, are rapidly forming alliances and partnerships—IBM with Toshiba for screen technology, Hitachi with Texas Instruments on the 16-megabit DRAM, the big Japanese chip manufacturers with the American design houses, and so on. The powerhouse company in the mid-1990s will be the one that merges Japanese manufacturing skills with American design and software skills—envision a billion-dollar manufacturing plant turning out an infinite variety of ASICs from the drawing boards of a software "factory" in California. The value added in the two processes would probably be about equal.

I think such an outcome is inevitable. The major obstacles at the moment, I believe, are not business or technological problems but political ones. In the next two sections, I should like to comment briefly on the politicization of industrial policy that is taking place in America and on possible paths of development in Japan's relations with the rest of the world.

Japan in the Modern Economy

"Unsustainable trends," Herbert Stein usefully reminds us, "tend not to be sustained." As always, it is helpful to look at the "Japan problem" in a somewhat longer perspective. Japan, it is often forgotten, was a deficit nation for thirty-five years after the end of World War II, right into the early 1980s. The current leadership is still, to a much greater degree than in any other country, composed of men who came to power in the war's aftermath. A new leadership generation is waiting in the wings, but they have not yet made much of a visible impact.

There is no question that during its long climb back to a leading position among industrial nations, Japan has aggressively practiced what Peter Drucker has dubbed "adversarial trade." Its trade policies have been much like those adopted by other developing nations, like Brazil and India. Foreign investment was welcomed but subjected to stringent conditions. Technological investment in Japan was almost always saddled with the requirement of a local joint venture partner, local licensing of key technologies, and other restrictions. And there can be little question that Japan, anxious to achieve its own place in the technological firmament, has often been less than scrupulous in respecting both the letter and the spirit of licensing agreements. America, of course, whose entire post-war policy was oriented primarily around building its allies' economies, usually viewed such practices with a relatively indulgent eye.

The enforcement of all of these rules is the province of the semi-legendary Ministry of International Trade and Industry, or MITI. There are very close ties between government officials, particularly at MITI, and the executives of the major business "families," or *keiretsu*. Indeed, MITI officials almost always graduate into top jobs at the big companies. Policy directives, therefore, can be carried out with remarkable dispatch, and the success of the prescriptive Japanese approach to economic management is apparent for all to see. It is the close-knit, xenophobic, almost impenetrable character of the Japanese business, political, and social system that has been emphasized by scholars and journalists such as Chalmers Johnson, Karl van Wolferen, and most recently James Fallows.

All of this is true. But, once again, there is another story. The question is not whether Japan has behaved like a typical developing country in the past, but whether, now that it has achieved such spectacular economic success, it will begin to behave like a mature global power.

Let me suggest a different way to frame the question. Are the Japanese human? The optimistic view of the Japanese economy, one that foresees rapid and substantial change, is predicated on the simple assumption that the Japanese are beginning to enjoy being rich, are getting interested in consuming and leisure activities, are slowing down from their intense, compete-at-any-cost mentality.

One sign of the times is the suddenly booming interest in luxury cars in Japan. The big car companies are betting that Japanese car ownership may double over the next half decade or so, with a sharp shift in taste away from economical little boxes on wheels to conspicuously sporty models. Consider the Nissan Silvia, a new sports car available only in Japan. It is targeted at the "twenty-seven-year-old who takes his girlfriend out to dinner." Her father thinks he's too young. "Then he sees his car and changes his mind."

Bill Emmott, the business editor of *The Economist,* and a longtime resident of Japan, makes a powerful argument that the Japanese, at the end of the day, are pretty much like other people. His new book, *The Sun Also Sets,* is a helpful antidote for some of the gloomier views. To take just one example, Japanese overseas travel is growing so fast that it is actually recycling a very large portion of the country's overseas investment earnings. Consumption spending, as the Silvia example suggests, is already growing rapidly. A new generation of young adults, unscarred by the searing memories of postwar deprivations, are beginning to insist on the same amenities in housing, public services, and specialty food and other consumer items enjoyed in other rich nations. Since 1986, in fact, *all* of the growth in the Japanese economy has come from domestic consumption. Foreign trade has been a negative contributor, as the Japanese export surplus has been shrinking both in absolute and relative terms.

Charles Wolf of RAND has pointed out that Japanese government spending for public amenities is 50 percent lower, relative to GNP, than in the United States and half that in Europe. It is dissatisfaction with this state of affairs that is adding impetus to the sudden wave of support for Japan's tiny Socialist Party. Emmott foresees that a steadily Westernizing Japan will continue to be a formidable global competitor, of course, but as the leader of a block of yen-oriented industrial powers, much as West Germany is the leader of a *de facto* mark-oriented block of European powers, rather than as a world-conquering golden horde.

There is, in fact, an even more radical set of possibilities. According to the International Monetary Fund, "the impact of demographic change in Japan will be the most extreme" of any of the industrialized countries. The number of aged dependents will double starting about 1995, straining the most ungenerous pension system in the industrialized world. The sharp rise in dependency will come at a time when Japan's tradition of lifetime employment will be strained to the breaking point. Part of the incomparable speed and efficiency of big Japanese manufacturing companies comes from farming out most of the detailed production to small job-shop-oriented firms. Workers in those firms do not have anywhere near the same protections and benefits as the workers in the firms at the top of the industrial chain.

As wage costs rise in Japan and Japanese firms continue to adopt global production strategies, unemployment, particularly among older, less-skilled manufacturing workers, may be expected to increase sharply. On this view, the prospect is for, at best, sharply reduced private savings, sharply increased social spending and public deficits, and, overall, a substantially less competitive country. At worst, it recalls the specter of the violent clashes between small-business and big-business factions that characterized Japan in the 1920s and that were ultimately resolved by the local version of Fascism that prevailed until 1945.

No one should wish Japan ill. Its economic success has been a beacon light for all of Asia and increasingly for Latin America—and for that matter, Europe and the United States. The steady merger of the American and East Asian economies that I believe is inexorably taking place holds the promise of unparalleled economic progress. But we sometimes need reminding that the circumstances of nations can change very quickly. When America was at the height of its powers in 1965 or so, few people could have foreseen the "helpless, pitiable giant" it was to become barely a decade later.

My expectation is that Japan will handle its coming difficult transitions with the smoothness and skill that has become its trademark. As it grows more accustomed to its role as a mature power, and its major industries increasingly become citizens of, rather than exporters to, the rest of the globe, the adversarial frame of mind that has driven its rise to power will diminish. As a newer generation begins to relax and enjoy some of the fruits of their parents' labors, its economy will being to look rather more like those of the other advanced industrial powers, although enriched by a long tradition of thrift and careful workmanship. It will continue to be a center of advanced manufacturing for a long time to come but more often as part of global industrial alliances raising the standard of living for everybody.

A Word on "Industrial Policy"

As alarm about American competitiveness has spread over the past several years, there has been an upwelling of demands for an "industrial policy" of some form or another. The term "industrial policy" covers a multitude of measures—and a multitude of sins. At their worst, policy demands emanating from the general direction of research centers like the Massachusetts Institute of Technology and the American semiconductor and consumer electronics industries insist that the federal government restore American competitiveness by directing resources, including taxpayer resources, toward certain high-priority industries, which, not surprisingly, include semiconductors and consumer electronics. The most ambitious initiative has been the call for a billion-dollar federal subsidy for the development of high-definition television, or HDTV. As of this writing, the proposal seems dead—one hopes permanently so.

Why are such proposals such bad ideas? Let me count the ways.

In the first place, they tend to call for an uncritical replication of an institution like MITI in the United States. Even if MITI worked as effectively as some industrial policy advocates seem to think—which is certainly open to question—there is no reason to believe that Japanese policy mechanisms could be transplanted to America. There is nothing in America remotely comparable to the tight web of relationships that exists between the Japanese government and *keiretsu* executives. Industry targeting in America would inevitably collapse into a morass of Congressional log-rolling, expensive failures, and bitter recriminations.

Europe is the living example. Most of the continental governments have a long history of targeting and industrial initiatives. Great Britain poured money into its car companies until the industry's reflexes were so dulled by gorging on government subsidies that the car companies simply rolled over and died. None of the global car companies that will survive a decade from now is likely to be European, with the possible exception of a few niche players, such as Mercedes.

Semiconductor and computer initiatives proliferated throughout Europe in the 1970s; the result was a virtual takeover by the Americans as resources were dissipated on losers. It is the European example, not the Japanese, that requires close study by Americans.

Secondly, the reputation of MITI is probably vastly overblown. The Japanese government was distinctly unenthusiastic about the Japanese entering the automobile industry in the first place and later actively discouraged Honda from doing so. The industries in which the Japanese have rung up outstanding successes are the ones that play to their undeniable skills in organizing sophisticated manufacturing operations. In a number of others, their performance has been less than spectacular. In both cases, success and failure appear to be quite independent of MITI intervention.

In the mid-1970s, MITI identified seven industries as "strategic," that is, industries that would hold the key to success in the 1990s and that warranted all-out targeting in the best MITI industrial policy tradition. They were robots, semiconductors, mainframe computers, genetics and biotechnology, office automation, telecommunications, and pharmaceuticals. Only robotics and semiconductors have been clear-cut successes. Japanese prowess in big computers has grown rapidly, but they still are far from holding a leading position, and mainframe computers, in any case, increasingly look like a technological dead end. The office automation initiative has been a resounding failure, while progress in the remaining areas has been spotty and slow.

Significantly, the successful initiatives, robotics and semiconductors, played directly to Japanese strengths. Their booming consumer electronics industry was a voracious user of DRAMs, while consumer electronics and automotive factories were prime testing grounds for robots. Most of the other initiatives were pushing against the wind. Biotechnology, for instance, requires a powerful establishment in basic scientific research—the kind that exists in the American university complexes and is absent in Japan.

Finally, in addition to exaggerating MITI's successes, industrial policy advocates often exaggerate the resources MITI commands. In a recent story of the scare-mongering variety, *Business Week* called MITI "the sugar daddy to end all sugar daddies." After showering $200 million on a futile five-year effort to produce a self-programming computer, the magazine reported, the agency was plunging into its deep pockets and blowing $36 million on another try. *Thirty-six million dollars?!* By Pentagon standards, that is distinctly chump change. The money showered by the various American defense agencies on artificial intelligence, software standards, new programming languages and protocols, and related technologies runs well into the billions. America does not need to create new agencies to waste taxpayers' money.

The much-touted American HDTV initiative has been the most aggressive campaign launched by the industrial policy advocates to date. It very likely would have replicated the pattern of MITI failures rather than of its successes. HDTV is a fantastically complex technology that converts analogue over-the-air TV signals into a highly detailed digitized screen image. George Gilder argues, and in this case I believe he is absolutely right, that it is a dead-end technology, like the Cray supercomputer.

The American Bell System companies have repeatedly asked permission to carry cable-television pictures and have been repeatedly denied it on the grounds that it would decrease "competition." If that permission were granted, the Bell companies in the space of a few years would wire up American homes with fiber-optic cabling. High-definition digitized television pictures could then be transmitted directly over the telephone system far more cheaply and far more effectively with a much greater choice of channels than would be possible with any of the proposed HDTV technologies. (Japan, incidentally, lags the United States in fiber optics, which may be one of the reasons they have chosen the HDTV route that they have.) Spending money on HDTV will, if anything, simply retard the development of a truly competitive American alternative.

But if policies like the HDTV initiative are the path of folly, what would an effective American industrial policy look like? Let me propose some simple do's and don't.

- We should not waste time or taxpayers' money trying to distinguish winners from white elephants. The government has no place trying to play the stock market.

- We should be careful not to obstruct competition. The refusal to allow the Bell companies to carry television pictures does nothing for American competitiveness. It merely protects some *competitors*—in this case a generally motley and technologically retrograde grab bag of cable TV carriers.

- We should continue the recent welcome trend of encouraging industrial alliances and coalitions rather than attacking them in the name of "antitrust." Global competition is sufficiently fierce to wield an effective lash over the laggard or complacent company. Who can believe that our government spent hundreds of millions of dollars in the 1970s to break up IBM? Alliances like the U.S. Memories consortium among semiconductor companies—although it is off to a somewhat shaky start—may be essential for organizing the massive capital for the next generation of semiconductor plants. There should be no antitrust obstructions to such arrangements, but neither do they require taxpayers' money.

- We should understand that a competitive industrial structure is a prime source of national wealth. Recent legislative initiatives—mandating universal health coverage programs on small businesses and the like—should be regarded with great skepticism and caution. If the voters want social welfare programs, the government should buy the services and pay for them with taxes. Invisible taxes like mandated social expenditures on business are bad social policy and bad competitive policy.

- We should invest in the infrastructure that allows an industrial society to function—roads, bridges, airports, and, above all, the educational system.

- We should keept a vigilant eye for genuinely unfair trading practices on the part of other countries. (American pressure on the Japanese to open up their convoluted distribution system is, I think, entirely well-founded and is doing a great favor for ordinary Japanese consumers.) But we should turn a skeptical ear to the plaints of American companies for special protection or special favors.

American-based companies will do fine in the 1990s. What they need from government are merely the things that government is supposed to provide anyway. A reasonable degree of social order and public tranquility. A reasonable and predictable commercial contractual and regulatory environment. A stable and predictable currency regime. Social, tax, and environmental obligations that are reasonable on their face, reasonably contrived to achieve their objectives, and reasonably consistent with practice in other major industrial countries.

That is a deceptively simple list—a much taller order than it looks. If we can achieve all these things in the name of an "industrial policy," we would have grounds for being very optimistic indeed about the future course of American industry.

LSI Logic

A quiet revolution in the computer industry happened one afternoon in mid-1988 on Jen-Hsun Huang's work-station screen at LSI Logic's San Jose Design Center. For the previous nine months, Huang had been designing a new kind of personal computer—what eventually hit the market as the Sun Microsystem Sparcstation 1—the hottest, most powerful, most multifunctional computer ever made that could sit on the top of a desk and be sold at personal-computer prices.

But the revolution wasn't the machine; the revolution was embodied in the shifting colors dancing across Huang's screen. Huang and Sun's engineers had designed the working guts of the new computer entirely in software. The finished machine—the controllers, the microprocessor, the memory, all the labyrinthine circuitry that makes up nerve channels and synapses of an electronic computer—existed solely in the form of millions of magnetic blips inside Huang's work station.

On that afternoon, Huang had finished building the new machine in his computer and was about to turn it on to see if it worked. From his computer's memory, he called up the version of Unix software that would serve as the operating instructions for the new machine, and he "booted" it—he turned his metaphysical machine on.

"It worked perfectly the first time," says Huang. Each of the registers simulated on Huang's screen filled with data when it was supposed to fill, each of the millions of transistorized switches flipped in the sequence it was supposed to flip. "It was very slow, because it was pushing my computer to the limit," says Huang. "The real-life machine is much, much faster. But when we fabricated the chips for the real machine, we knew they would work exactly the way they were supposed to, because we'd already put them through all their paces."

The Sparcstation 1 is the first major industry product to be built entirely from the top down. Except for a memory chip—simply a passive storage device—there are no standard components in the Sparcstation 1. All the chips—the tiny silicon platforms with their intricately beautiful chiaroscuros of gates and paths and switches—were designed and built by LSI Logic to carry out precisely the functions targeted for the Sparcstation 1 in the most efficient and cost-effective way.

"Andy Bechtolshelm (one of the Sun's four co-founders) came to me one day and we sat down and specified the machine that was eventually to become the Sparcstation 1," recounts Huang. The requirements Bechtolsheim laid out were daunting. A sales price under $10,000. Ten MIPs performance. A "MIP" is a million instructions per second, a measure of computer processing speed; most 1985-vintage mainframe computers had processing speeds of about one MIP.) A small "footprint"—easy to fit on a desk. A plug that went into a conventional wall outlet. High-resolution graphics for engineering and scientific applications. A highly manufacturable machine, so production could be fully automated. That meant surface-mounted boards, and the minimum number of them—the final version has only a single board.

"Over the next nine months, we honed the specifications. For instance, Andy decided to add voice, and he was right." Huang turned to a real Sparcstation on his desk. "I'm sending a chip schematic to another design center, but I talk through the design concept embodied in the graphic. Tomorrow, another engineer will call up the schematic, and my voice will be stored in digitized form so he can listen to me talk it through if he wants. It requires an enormous amount of capacity, but once you have it, it's very hard to do without. It would take me hours to type in all I need to say."

As the design team polished the specifications, Huang entered the requirements into his computer. Sometimes he entered an actual schematic for a section of chip. Sometimes he merely specified a "behavioral description"—the machine should do such-and-such a task, and his computer translated that into a set of circuits.

"Before the Sparcstation," says Huang, "all personal computers were built from general-purpose chips—an Intel microprocessor, a Chips and Technology controller, etc., etc., dozens and dozens of chips. The system designer doesn't have access to the inner workings of most of those chips, so putting together a computer involves a lot of intuitive tweaking to get the performance you want. And you can never optimize configurations, or even predict potential error conditions, because you can't model them. That's why you often hear of a major bug showing up in a critical component like the microprocessor a year or so after it's been in the market. We took the opposite approach. Everything in the Sparcstation was designed specifically to carry out the functions we wanted in that machine."

The Sparcstation 1 was therefore the first "all-ASIC" work station or personal computer. ASIC stands for "Application-Specific Integrated Circuit." It is one of several root changes in the basic concepts of designing and building computers that is forcing an already turbulent industry through a continuous restructuring and calling into question most of the received wisdom about the requirements for competitive success.

To understand the concept of an ASIC, consider the problem of computerized image-processing. Image-processing is a key capability in the application of computer technology to manufacturing production, for example, as well as in many other areas. When a robot's eye is trying to pick out a specific shape or a CAD machine is twisting an image of a metal part to derive a stress pattern, they are performing extraordinarily computation-intensive tasks that in the very recent past would have defeated many of the largest computers.

To the computer, the visual data appear as a cloud of digitized bits, a swarm of on-off pulses. The computer applies mathematical algorithms, like Fourier transforms, to identify patterns in the cloud, then reinterprets those patterns into a visual display that is meaningful to humans. It is a capability that is of limited usefulness *unless* the computer can process images very fast. A robot can't take an hour to think about the next hole on a circuit board. A human engineer can't spend a day watching a slow-motion gavotte on his work-station screen.

The standard way of solving the image processing problem is to write the mathematical algorithms in software and run the operation with the general-purpose microprocessor in an off-the-shelf computer. The microprocessor is a series of circuits, switches, and other components that can handle almost *any* problem, provided the software, the program instructions written out in thousands of lines of code, specify each operation in absolute detail—precisely which switch to turn on or which gate to open at each stage of the operation. It was the marriage of the powerful general-purpose microprocessor with high-level programming languages that fueled the computer revolution of the past twenty years.

(High-level language programs called "compilers" do most of the grunt work for a programmer. The programmer writes "Add A and B," and the software embedded in the language package automatically translates that message into the dozens of detailed circuit-specific instructions that the computer needs. Before the invention of high-level languages the sheer complexity of programming placed a practical limit on the problems that could be readily tackled with a computer.)

An ASIC chip, by contrast, has the computing task embedded directly in its circuitry. If the required operation, for example, is to add A and B, multiply the total by C, and divide that result by D, the chip will be designed to carry out that mathematical process and no other. There will be four input sources, and whatever signal enters on the "A" source will be automatically added to one on the "B" source and so on. There will be no lines of written code, no extraneous circuits or gates to manage. The chip will be simpler to make and will perform its designated task much faster and more efficiently than a general-purpose chip possibly could. It is the difference between an electric can opener and the can-opening blade crammed into a Swiss Army knife.

LSI Logic, with roughly $550 million in sales projected for 1989, is the world's leading ASIC company. It is third worldwide in total ASIC sales, behind NEC and Fujitsu, but far ahead of its competition in designing and producing the most complex and sophisticated ASICs. (Japanese ASIC production is concentrated in "commodity," or less design-intensive ASICs.)

The lion's share of LSI Logic's revenues comes from manufacturing. The company has eight manufacturing centers around the world, all of them capable of sub-micron geometries. (The most advanced chips require circuitry at dimensions of less than a micron, or a millionth of a meter. Sub-micron manufacturing capability is the hallmark of world-class chip facilities, or "fabs.") LSI Logic is the only company in the world licensed to produce both the Sun and MIPS RISC chips, two of the hottest—and competing—microprocessors available (more about RISC chips below). But it is the *combination* of LSI Logic's design skills with its manufacturing capabilities that give it a competitive edge.

LSI Logic was founded in 1981 with $6 million in venture capital. The founder and present CEO is Wilfred Corrigan, the former CEO of Fairchild Semiconductor—the original Silicon Valley firm and the greenhouse for most of the spectacularly talented men and women who have made the "Valley," the mile after mile of industrial parkland between San Francisco and San Jose, the pulsating center of innovation in the world electronics industry.

Corrigan intended from the outset that his new firm would be a global company, or as the company likes to say, a "glocal" company—a global business with a strong local flavor in each major market. With limited capital, he accomplished that by enlisting minority equity partners. The company is organized in a holding company structure with a wholly owned American company and three majority-owned subsidiaries in Japan, Canada, and Europe. Each of the companies adheres to the LSI Logic business strategy but has concentrated in different end-market segments. The Japanese company caters primarily to consumer product and computer manufacturers, the American company to computer manufacturers, and to defense and aerospace customers, and the European and Canadian companies to telecommunication manufacturers—representing in each instance the leading edge of regional technological excellence. All the products, of course, are available in all markets, so the American subsidiary benefits from the Japanese company's consumer electronics prowess and so on.

Corrigan's second objective was to be the world's most advanced designer and manufacturer of ASIC chips. Jim Koford, a Fairchild veteran and one of the design gurus who built the software that accomplished the revolutionary doings on Huang's computer screen, tells the story: "I met with Wilf in 1980. He'd left Fairchild when it was bought by Schlumberger and his non-compete agreement had expired. He said, 'I think it's time for ASICs. Rob Walker has agreed to join. If I can get Ed Jones and Bill Jensen, are you ready for another try?' And, of course," says Koford, "we were the people you would have to have. I thought about it, and it was obvious that Wilf was right; it *was* time for ASICs, and so here we are."

Conceptually, ASICs are a throwback to the earliest days of computing. In the waning days of World War II, when geniuses like Alan Turing and John von Neumann were building the first modern computers—blinking arrays of vacuum tubes the size of a small gymnasium—each operation was hard-wired into a "bread board." Instead of writing out lines of coded instructions, the "programmer" painstakingly connected the wires and tubes into the circuits required to perform the desired computing operation.

The concept of written programming instructions that guided general-purpose circuits was a major breakthrough, although the mass development of software had to await the advent of higher-level languages, since the original programming languages were so difficult to learn. But even through the 1960s—the period that saw the birth of the modern mainframe with the IBM 360 series—a small group of designers including Jones, Walker, and Koford were convinced that special-purpose circuitry, with the key operations hard-wired right into the computer, would almost always run faster than general-purpose circuits.

The problem was that circuit design was getting extraordinarily complex. Even with fifty or a hundred gates on a circuit (modern chips have several hundred thousand gates), the number of possible interconnections quickly becomes staggering. Through the 1970s, as more and more circuits became etched on silicon, chip design times began to stretch into the years, with teams of engineers laboriously drafting schematics that phalanxes of women with pads on their knees laid out on huge plastic sheets on gym floors.

The solution, it was clear to the Joneses, Kofords and the Walkers of the world, was automated design. Just as high-level programming languages took much of the tedium out of writing program codes by automatically translating English-language statements into machine language, design software would translate design objectives into the optimum set of circuits. "The high-level language concept is even more powerful when applied to circuits," says Koford, "because it lets you do things like automated test pattern generation—you can develop mathematical algorithms to test your circuits under any conceivable operating condition, something you can't possibly do with a circuit you've laid out by hand."

Koford became fascinated with automated design while at Stanford, and he joined Fairchild in the mid-1960s to work on the problem. "We built what must have been the world's first CAD work station in the modern sense in 1966. It was a single-user machine, although much bigger than a desk, with a graphics capability—just a plotter at first—that would lay out schematics from a general problem statement. It did essentially what we do with our work stations now but at the time only for very small circuits. We were working to increase its power, although, to be honest, we were pretty naive about how much raw computing power it takes to design a circuit of any substantial size."

The announcement of the first Intel 8-bit microprocessor, the 8008, in 1973, essentially the same chip that powered the first PCs, quashed any interest in Koford's work. "ASIC work went into what we call the 'Dark Period,' " says Koford. "The new microprocessors and faster memories had so much power that it just didn't make sense to try to design special-purpose chips. You could always get the job done faster and cheaper with the general-purpose chips." The ASIC gurus that Corrigan brought back together to form LSI Logic scattered in the 1970s to teaching, to consulting, some to other fields. Koford went into data communications and forgot about his first-ever work station until Corrigan phoned him.

"We call 1980 the 'Reawakening,' " says Koford, smiling. The industry was undergoing a radical change once more. A whole series of parallel developments were pushing computer design back toward hard-wired circuitry. In the first place, the big computer manufacturers had commercial reasons for moving away from general-purpose chips. The more their most expensive machines depended on unique circuitry, the better protected they would be from commercial knock-offs.

Then there was the "glue logic" problem. "I had just begun to notice this about 1980," says Koford. "Microprocessor costs were coming down fast. But you'd open up a standard PC and you'd see the microprocessor that cost maybe $50, but it was surrounded by a couple dozen other chips that cost maybe $500 all together. When microprocessors were so expensive, you didn't think much about those other chips. But all of a sudden, the big cost savings would come from combining all the peripheral chips—what I call the 'glue logic,' because they tie the system together—into a single chip."

Then in 1980, Carver Mead and Lynn Conway published their textbook *Introduction to VLSI Systems*. "That was a truly landmark event," says Koford. Mead and Conway were evangelists of computer-aided chip design who had been waging a long guerrilla battle to give the topic academic respectability. "Their textbook introduced chip design into the academic mainstream," says Koford, "and then we began to get a stream of young people from the key university centers—Berkeley, Cal Tech, MIT, Stanford, Illinois—who understood and had an interest in what we were doing."

The remaining developments were all technical ones. New methods of building chips—many of them pioneered in Japan—made possible much higher circuit densities at much lower power requirements. "And then in just the last few years we've had these enormous increases in readily accessible raw computing power. The machines I was working with in 1982 to 1983, as far as I was concerned, were pretty much the same as the ones I was using in 1973—a little faster, a little less expensive, but in the same range. But the breakthroughs in the past few years have been phenomenal. In 1982, I was working on a $300,000 machine that ran at .9 to 1.0 MIPS. Now I'm using a $10,000 machine that runs at 12.5 MIPS."

To put the ASIC revolution into perspective: As chip manufacturing moves deeper into the world of sub-micron dimensions, the technology begins to encounter hard physical limits. Below 0.5 microns—currently the smallest practical circuit dimensions—it becomes almost impossible to keep circuit elements from interacting with each other, and each new small increment in circuit density becomes harder and harder to achieve and much more costly. The newest sub-micron X-ray lithography plants will cost at least $1 billion each. (X-ray lithography is a small-dimension etching methodology, replacing photo lithography, because X-rays can dig a narrower channel than light beams can.)

As the gains from sheer manufacturing virtuosity get tougher to eke out, the focus shifts back to design skills—how to get the maximum possible performance out of a given piece of silicon real estate. Design in the world of high-density circuitry is a software problem; rapid high-density design is beyond the capability of the best human engineering teams. The American lead in design software—considered to be very large by most observers—suddenly looms of central importance.

The RISC microprocessor is a good example of design leverage. Sun, MIPS (another Silicon Valley overnight sensation), IBM, and, belatedly, Intel are all manufacturing "reduced instruction set computing" microprocessors of radically different design that have begun to decisively outperform even the most advanced standard microprocessors, like the Intel 486. Like the advanced ASIC chips, the RISC is an elegant way around the physical barriers that are limiting advances in general-purpose chips. As it turns out, only about 20 percent of the circuits on a standard microprocessor receive intensive use. RISC designers simply moved the less frequently used operations off the chip into the computer's operating system software, opening up vast amounts of silicon "acreage" that permitted major improvements in speed, power, and performance. I used the word "simply" in the preceding sentence, but the RISC chip is a minor triumph of systems design.

Developments like RISC and ASIC chips, along with the standardization of the computer operating system Unix means, in Koford's words, "In theory, anyone can go into the computer business. If you have a good idea how to increase the speed or performance of a machine, you can design the chips with us, use the Unix operating system, and you're in business." Not surprisingly, there have been a host of new companies springing up selling small, remarkably powerful new machines—Apollo, Convex, Convergent Technologies, Stardent, MIPS. The Japanese have no presence in this market, except through stock purchases or manufacturing licenses.

At the moment, the emerging competitive structure of the computer industry is extremely fluid. The Japanese clearly have superb manufacturing skills, and the industry will be using their mass-produced, high-quality commodity DRAMs for many years to come. The Americans clearly have superb system design skills and have grabbed a clear lead in the most advanced new system technologies. (In response to criticisms of the practice of licensing the newer designs to Japanese companies, the usual response from the design-focused houses is that their competitive edge lies in the chips three or four generations ahead already on their CAD screens, not with yesterday's chips.)

The overall impression, in fact, is one of convergence. American manufacturing has improved—spokesmen for even the generally alarmist Semiconductor Industry Association concede that the manufacturing skills differential is rapidly disappearing. The Japanese companies are clearly chagrined by their inability to compete in software and in chip design and are redoubling their efforts. (There have been reports that Japan's concern about its shortage of software engineers has lately been turning to panic. The Japanese government estimates the current shortfall at about 50,000 software engineers, growing to as much as 900,000 by the year 2000.) As the bitterness of some of the present American-Japanese trade disputes moderate, the expectation must be for increasing resort to global strategic alliances, with both the American and Japanese partners leading from their strength.

Where will LSI Logic fit in the next generation of computer companies? "We've designed more advanced chips than anyone in the world," says Jim Koford. "Our leverage is mainly intellectual, but I think that will keep us around a long time."

10

WHAT COULD GO WRONG?

I have made the case that the 1990s will see a prolonged global economic boom, one that will be centered in the industrial countries but that will gradually capture more and more developing nations in its sweep. I have also made the argument that the United States, in particular, will be one of the prime beneficiaries of the boom. It's a bright picture, but it's time now to take a look at the pitfalls along the way. I want to begin, however, by looking at a variety of problems that are not directly relevant to my argument.

Some Real But Irrelevant Problems

I recently presented a much-abbreviated version of the arguments in this book in an article in *The Atlantic*. As one would expect, readers' mail was about evenly split between letters agreeing with the article and letters taking strong issue with it.

Now there are plenty of reasons to worry that my optimistic predictions may not come true, and I'll list most of them later in the chapter. What struck me about the negative mail, however, was that so many of the problems raised had very little to do with what I was saying.

To begin with, a global economic boom will *not* solve all of the world's problems. In the United States, for example, such difficult and complicated problems as race relations, drug addiction, and homelessness will continue to be with us. ("Homelessness" in America is not a simple housing problem. A very large proportion of the homeless are drug addicts, alcoholics, or mentally disturbed, or all of those things at the same time.) The terrifying social and economic gap between a largely black underclass and the rest of the country will still be there. These are all genuinely hard problems. At the moment, for example, social theorists are bitterly debating whether government aid, or what kinds of aid, makes underclass problems better or worse. I don't pretend to know the answer to any of those questions.

But I am quite sure of one thing: Whatever the problems are, it will be much, much easier to deal with them during a period of robust economic growth than during a prolonged economic crisis.

Much the same applies to some of the daunting problems of the Third World. In the best of times, for the foreseeable future, there will be poverty and misery in places like Ethiopia, the Sudan, Chad, and most of the rest of sub-Saharan Africa. Population growth in places like Bangladesh, Tanzania, Sri Lanka, the Muslim republics of the Soviet Union, and many other poor countries will continue to outrun the resources of those struggling economies. Once again, making a serious dent in poverty in the world's poorest countries may be beyond our resources and intelligence, but it will be much easier to do so during a period of economic boom than during a major world depression.

There is a stronger version of these arguments that one occasionally encounters. This is that social problems at home or in the Third World will actually *prevent* a global boom. At the risk of sounding callous, that is extremely unlikely. Despite their visibility in certain major older cities and their prominence in political discussion, America's "hardcore" underclass—in the sense of the completely alienated, the criminally inclined, the drug addicted—constitute a very small percentage of the population. The real problem, that is, is small enough both to offer hope that we can solve it or, if we don't, to ensure that it will be only a minor drag on the rest of society.

The same applies to the poorest countries of the Third World. Again, at the risk of sounding callous, all of Africa has a gross domestic product smaller than Great Britain's; all of Latin America has a gross domestic product smaller than West Germany's. With the exception of oil, which I'll discuss in the next section, there are, for all practical purposes, no resources in any of these areas that we really need or couldn't easily substitute for. Nor is the "Third World debt overhang" as much of a problem as it is sometimes touted to be. Much of it has long since been written off by the banks anyway.

A global economic boom, in fact, will offer many opportunities for much faster economic growth in the Third World. Countries like Thailand, a bitterly poor country just a decade or so ago, are beginning to replicate the economic miracles we have already seen in South Korea, Hong Kong, Taiwan, and Singapore. India is not that far behind. Latin American countries, such as Brazil and Mexico, could join them. Again, I don't pretend to know how to insure that that happens, although I am sure that a key requirement will be throwing off the yoke of their corrupt elites—whether of the military, left-wing, or right-wing varieties—that stifle the natural energies of their people. (One of the problems with the Third World debt is that so much of the lending—$150 billion, according to Morgan Guaranty Trust—was simply stolen by the elites and squirreled away in foreign private bank accounts.)

I am in no way belittling the gravity of our social problems at home or the social and economic problems in many countries abroad, and I am not pretending that the economic boom I foresee will solve them. But we need to separate issues of participation and distribution from the trends in the larger economy. Assuring that all sectors of American society have the education and competence to participate in the economy of the 1990s will be a major, and daunting, task for government in the next decade. I am neither pretending to know how to do that nor predicting that such problems will take care of themselves. My point is simply that we will be much better positioned to deal with such issues under conditions of rapid economic growth than while struggling along in a persistent state of economic crisis.

Some Non-Problems

Another despairing argument I frequently encounter is that the world is running out of natural resources. Oil and energy supplies are the most often cited. Under the pressure of a short period of global growth, the argument goes, we will rapidly deplete readily available energy supplies, increase our dependence on the OPEC cartel, and end up in precisely the dreadful situation we saw in the mid-1970s—energy prices and inflation spiraling upward while real economic activity spirals down.

The "running out of resources" argument is, bluntly, fashionable nonsense. If there has been any constant in energy supply forecasts, it has been the consistent tendency to underestimate available reserves. Between January 1987 and January 1988, for instance, the recoverable world oil reserves estimated by the *Oil and Gas Journal* rose from 697 billion barrels to 887 billion barrels. Between 1982 and 1986, OPEC increased its own reserve estimates from 466 billion barrels to 645 billion barrels. The World Energy Conference estimated that proven recoverable oil reserves rose 30 percent from 1987 through 1989. According to Cambridge Energy Research Associates, the years of available supply has stretched to more than forty-five years, up from just over twenty-eight years in 1979. The same is true for most other fuels. Coal reserves are up an astounding 80 percent in the past three years to more than a trillion tons. Natural gas reserves are doubling every ten years.

Some people still worry. Most of the reserve increases are outside the industrial countries. Could it be possible for a cartel of energy-producing countries to deny vital supplies to America, Western Europe, or Japan? In fact, absent genuinely foolish policy-making—which is always possible—that is highly unlikely. Oil is traded freely on world markets. Few of the producing countries have the resources or the self-discipline to maintain a truly effective cartel. (The 1973 and 1979 crises were caused more by speculation and hoarding in the developed countries than by supply management on the part of OPEC.) If the developed countries build oil reserves when supplies are cheap, as the United States has been doing, if not quite as aggressively as one might hope, we could easily outlast any attempt by the poorer producing countries to impose production cuts, and a cartel is only as strong as its weakest members. With a modicum of common sense, that is, and a modicum of policy flexibility, future oil production cartels should hold no terrors for the industrialized countries.

Much the same applies to most other natural resources. Indeed, as the industrial economy advances, natural resources become less and less important. The key element in the electronics industry, for instance, is silicon—that is, plain sand, one of the most abundant materials in the world. The raw material component of most advanced electronics products is usually only about 2 percent of sales cost. Chemicals, plastics, and exotic new "composite" materials, most of them made from readily available feedstocks like natural gas, are replacing iron, steel, and aluminum. Previous industrial revolutions were characterized by huge increases in the size and weight of products. Now the opposite is true. Products and plants, from cars to steel mills, are smaller, lighter, less resource- and energy-intensive.

But then we have the opposite worry—the fear that an *abundance* of energy resources will hasten the "greenhouse effect," or a catastrophic global warming. Or that the refuse of an industrial boom will choke us all on our own garbage, on the sulphur dioxides from our cars, on the toxins in our algae-strangled lakes. This, at least, is a more plausible worry. But, again, with the benefit of some sensible policy making, I think we will find that it is grossly exaggerated.

First of all, the science behind the predictions of a "greenhouse effect" is very shaky. Only about 3 to 4 percent of the carbon dioxide emissions going into the atmosphere comes from human sources, including all burning of fossil fuels and manmade catastrophes, such as rain-forest destruction. Human carbon sources are a tiny stream in a vast circulating ocean of atmospheric carbon dioxide that is dominated by plant respiration and decay and ocean absorption and evaporation.

The predictions of global warming depend crucially on mathematical models of how human carbon sources interact with the much larger natural circulatory engines. And the fact is not nearly enough is known about it to construct such models with any degree of accuracy. The human contributions are still so marginal that they are simply swamped by the statistical unknowns. Some of the models actually predict that increased carbon dioxide emissions will *cool* the world by increasing cloud cover and clouds' "albedo," or their action of reflecting sunlight away from the earth.

Even the data that first suggested a long-term warming trend have recently been called into question. The methods of measuring temperatures over the past hundred years have been quite variable, and many of them, it turns out, may have been quite unreliable—much turns on issues such as the heat-transmitting characteristics of the canvas buckets that were used to take ocean temperatures seventy-five years ago. The flap over "global warming," for the time being, in short, is grotesquely premature. Certainly there is as yet no case for diverting hundreds of billions of dollars to head off some hypothetical catastrophe coming fifty or a hundred years from now.

In any case, even if carbon emissions are a threat to the planet, the technology for reducing them is readily at hand. The "green" movement will have to stop wishful thinking about solar and wind power and face up to the attractiveness of pollution-free nuclear energy. (Much of the apparent cost disadvantages of nuclear energy stem from the planning and approval obstacles imposed by their politically astute opponents—the classic Catch-22.) With improvements in battery technology, it will be feasible to draw even much of our automotive power from nuclear sources. In twenty years or so, even more attractive alternatives, like hydrogen, should be available. England, after all, ran out of wood fuel three hundred years ago and survived nicely—in fact, it had an industrial revolution.

Most pollution threats, in fact, will come not from growth in the industrialized countries but from development in the so-called Third World. The forest burning in Brazil, the coal emissions in China and Poland, the poisonous air in Mexico City, all represent far more serious problems than any in the developed world. Heavy pollution tends to be a problem of the early stages of industrialization. The air in nineteenth-century Birmingham was much worse than it is today. Lake Erie was a sewer thirty years ago; now it has substantially recovered. Anyone who remembers Pittsburgh in the 1950s knows what a difference sensible pollution control measures can make in a wealthy society. Pollution, indeed, far from being the inevitable partner of industrial progress, tends to be *reduced* as industrial economies mature and free up resources to protect the environment.

The choice, in short, is not between economic progress and pollution. The situation is exactly the opposite. The faster the new industrializing countries modernize, and the wealthier they become, the sooner their pollution problems can be dealt with.

The destruction of the Amazonian rain forests ranks as a special case, not because of potential "greenhouse" dangers, but simply because of the thousands of species of plants and animals that are being irretrievably destroyed. But the answer is not moralistic finger-wagging from the developed countries. The American "opening of the West" was marked by a plundering of native peoples and resources at least as savage as that taking place in the Amazon. Nor do we have any moral right to insist that the Amazon countries forgo development for the sake of our zoos and botanical gardens.

The answer, if there is one, will have to lie with an orderly development program financed in substantial measure by the developed countries. If we wish to save the Amazon, in short, we will have to be prepared to pay for it. I have no doubt that some orderly solution is within our economic capabilities, particularly in view of the long-term prosperity that is on the horizon. But I doubt that the political will or competence exists—either in the developed or undeveloped countries—to engineer so happy a solution.

To return to the theme of this section: an adequate answer to the destruction of the Amazon may well be beyond our capabilities. But if a solution is at all possible, we are much more likely to find it during conditions of a global economic boom.

Some Real Pitfalls

None of the problems mentioned so far will obstruct a boom. They will not necessarily be solved by an economic boom, but they will become more amenable to solutions under conditions of rapid economic growth. But there are some genuine threats to the coming economic boom, most of them, fortunately, well within our present capacities to manage.

Probably the most dangerous obstacle to a new cycle of global growth, and the one most within our political control, is the economic nationalism brewing in the halls of Congress and the councils of Europe. I've already recounted the melancholy results of previous attempts at European protectionism: Its heavily protected national industries, for the most part, simply wasted away in their hothouse environments. And I've recounted some of the idiocies of recent American attempts at protectionism—policies that, for instance, radically boosted the profits of Japanese car manufacturers and Japanese semiconductor makers. The most hopeful sign, as I recounted in the story of Caterpillar and the fight against steel import restraints, is that American businessmen increasingly seem to recognize that protectionism is *against* their interests.

The path that Europe will take is not nearly so clear. Despite all the hoopla surrounding the magical date of 1992, when, supposedly, all of Europe will become one vast integrated, world-class economy, I don't anticipate that we will see much change. The closer the date draws, the more serious the infighting is becoming—over a monetary union, for example. More important, the end of the Berlin Wall–type restrictions makes the economic unification of the two Germanies very likely. The Europe of 1992 was drawn essentially along Cold War boundaries. The sudden awakening in Central Europe must throw all such calculations into confusion.

The importance of the 1992 date, in any case, lies more in its anticipation than in its actuality. There are already more than 14,000 civil servants in Brussels writing rules for the European Economic Community. Since the objective is a common set of economic rules, a Gresham's Law of rule-making inexorably presses the Brussels bureaucrats to adopt the worst of the currently available choices. It is, for example, very difficult to discharge an employee in Europe, but most difficult of all in Italy. One may expect to see the Italian job tenure regulations adopted in Brussels. West Germany has the most restrictive board membership requirements—dedicated board seats for union representatives are required for most companies. Predictably, over Margaret Thatcher's alarmed objections, Brussels is trying to impose similar requirements throughout the community. It is far easier, in short, to adopt the most limiting rule than to withstand the clamor of the special interests who would lose some small amount of protection under a more sensible regime.

The Brussels bureaucracy is fertile soil for protectionists of all sorts. As of this writing, free traders have managed to fight off a host of noxious trade rules—against American banks, or American television programs, or Japanese cars—but some of those victories still hang by a thread. (One recent trick is to adopt hortatory rules; that is, there are no formal prohibitions against American television programs, but stations have been strongly encouraged not to show them.) The human instinct to regulate, particularly amid the Cartesian traditions of Europe, dies hard. The victims, if the Brussels rule writers have their way, will be European companies, who could miss out on the next cycle of global growth just as, for example, they missed out on last decade's boom in the electronics industries.

The hopeful portent, paradoxically enough, is that the recent spate of antitrade legislation in Europe and the United States has been a shot of adrenaline for global markets—a rare instance of a fundamentally wrongheaded political intervention actually increasing economic efficiency. For example, the fear that Europe's 1992 rule makers will exclude non-Europeans has started a rush of American and Japanese firms to Europe. I've mentioned the battle over the British Blue-birds—they are Nissan cars manufactured in Great Britain.

The British finally carried their argument that the Bluebirds were British and so exempt from French import restraints against Japanese cars. There are now more than one hundred Japanese firms in England, compared to only one—YKK Zipper—in 1972. By the same token, America's direct investment in Europe in 1988 exceeded Japan's in the United States.

The economist Mancur Olson has argued that mature economies decline as special interests flourish: Each one demands some special protection at the expense of efficiency, until the economy as a whole grinds to a crawl. We have seen much of that in recent years—from unions and companies demanding special protections from foreign competition, regardless of the costs to consumers, to dairy farmers fighting the use of hormone supplements to increase their cows' milk production. I believe that the emetic dose of competitive medicine America and Europe received from East Asia in the early 1980s has regenerated our combative instincts, helped rehone our skills, and taught the lesson that protection or subsidies are no substitute for world-class businesses.

I suspect, in fact, that it may already be too late for the protectionists to do great damage. Political consensus tends to coalesce slowly, and even now the trade spats have an anachronistic air. The rapid move of global companies into local markets, the intricate network of partnerships, joint ventures, long-term supply arrangements, and cross-ownership within global industries makes a mockery of the instinct to throw up the ramparts. Vigilance will still be required, and there are many battles left to fight, but I think it is now the protectionists, for once, who are fighting the rear-guard action.

At the end of the day, I am less worried about the problems we can foresee, such as protectionist legislation, than about the ones that are impossible to predict. Let me give an example.

The political scientist Francis Fukuyama recently created a stir with his essay on the "end of history." Fukuyama's argument, stripped of its philosophical apparatus, was a throwback to that of the "end of ideology" theorists of a generation ago. For reasons similar to those I recounted in Chapter 8, Fukuyama foresees the world moving inevitably toward the Western model of market-oriented social democracy. In our technocratic, technological age, sweeping ideologies like Fascism and Communism have lost their power to seize men's minds. Moreover, fundamentalist religious fervor is now the province of only the most backward parts of the world, as in Iran or the southern provinces of the Soviet Union.

The task of modern governments, in Fukuyama's paradigm, will be limited to seeking efficient courses along carefully demarcated paths—how to raise up the disadvantaged remnants of society, for example, without destroying their self-respect or initiative. Difficult problems, to be sure, but narrow ones, with little of the flavor of the great ideological disputes of the past. Fukuyama presents his thesis with some regret. The emerging technocratic society, he fears, will be "boring."

Now *that* really worries me. It brings to mind John F. Kennedy's statement in 1962 that "there are no ideological problems left." The only problems facing government were "technical problems, administrative problems." No prize for prescience there. Over the next fifteen years or so, the country almost drowned in a tub of ideological ferment.

Could it happen again? Of course—although the considerably more advanced average age of the population in the industrial countries, compared to a generation ago, is grounds for hope that it won't. But in the final analysis, I suspect, if the global boom is derailed, it won't be because of trade battles, or energy shortages, or problems of the underclass at home or overseas, or for any of the reasons that gloomy pundits seem to enjoy so much dwelling upon. Instead it will be because of some kind of utterly unpredictable social turmoil in the developed countries, led no doubt by the best-off classes, and grounded in nothing more substantial than the obdurate human refusal to be bored.

And What If We Succeed?

The most interesting problems, in fact, may be those of success. Thirty years ago, John Kenneth Galbraith inveighed against the slothful market-fixing practices of the big national companies, the car companies and the steel companies. He was right, and the complacent giants got their comeuppance from the harsh competitive winds from East Asia in the 1970s and 1980s—Schumpeter's "perennial gale of creative destruction."

But what about a decade from now when a handful of global car companies, global computer companies, and global chemical companies have emerged from the pack to positions of true global dominance. Who will keep them in line? Competitors from Mars?

The standard Schumpeterian response is that global success will not mean the end of competition. As soon as the victorious car companies begin to relax, they will find that some other hungry giant has been envious of their share and has been working on an entirely new product made of new materials or with new principles of locomotion—whatever.

I'm not so sure. Maintaining some reasonable control over the new giants may be as challenging a task as we have ever faced. Even thinking about constructing a global Securities Exchange Commission or Federal Reserve or Federal Trade Commission boggles the mind.

But those are the problems of a still-distant future. And we stand to have a lot of fun in the process of getting to them. And when the problems of our global economic success do become pressing, fortunately, they will be issues for another author.

AN INVESTMENT STRATEGY FOR THE 1990s

Investing, in the broadest sense, is a question of choosing among possible futures. Let me sketch briefly a couple of wildly different economic scenarios just to illustrate how expectations of the future affect your investment decisions.

Ravi Batra, for example, predicts a massive global depression in the 1990s. In Batra's scenario, prices for all sorts of goods and commodities will *fall*. There will be a dramatic *de*flation of the kind we saw in the 1930s. (As I said at the beginning of the book, of course, I believe this type of forecast is dead wrong. I cite it here, again, just for the purposes of illustration.) If prices fall, obviously, the value of a cash dollar will rise—it will buy more things with each passing day. The proper investment strategy in a Batra depression scenario is to get out of things or pieces of things, like shares in companies, because their value will be falling, and get into cash, because its value will be rising.

In fact, people who entered the 1930s with lots of cash did very nicely indeed. The average return on a dollar in cash, in terms of increased buying power, which is all that really matters, was about 33 percent between 1929 and 1933. Of course, those returns were earned only by people who had real cash—at home in a sock—not a *claim* on cash, like a savings account passbook. Mere claims on cash often were worth nothing because the banks holding the cash failed. The ultraworrier, of course, who fears that the government will fall during a depression, won't even trust currency but will convert his dollars into gold.

The opposite scenario to Batra's, the kind that would be associated with, for instance, the Institute for International Economics in Washington, D.C., would be one of runaway *in*flation. (I think this scenario is dead wrong as well.) In an inflationary environment, the value of cash will *fall,* since a dollar will buy less and less with each passing day. During the peak inflationary years in the mid-1970s, a dollar kept in a sock at home was losing value by as much as 13 percent a year. Since money loses value so fast during high inflation, lenders need to charge higher interest rates. High rates are a heavy burden on business, so the value of bonds and stocks falls. And, for the most part, this is what happened in the 1970s. In real terms (that is, correcting for the effects of inflation), the stocks making up the Dow Jones Industrial Average declined in value by more than 80 percent between 1968 and 1982.

People who expect a high inflationary environment, therefore, will stay away from cash and financial assets, like stocks and bonds, and put their money into hard assets, like real estate. With prices rising everywhere, the logic goes, the prices of assets like real estate should at least keep pace with the price rises in the rest of the economy and, one hopes, even outpace them. And as we saw in Chapter 5, real estate produced very good returns throughout the 1970s. Gold is also a favored investment during times of high inflation, underlining its role as the traditional port in a storm during periods of great instability, whether the ill winds are inflationary ones or deflationary ones.

The main point from both of these examples is that investing during times of great instability is very hard. As the economy whipsaws from one extreme to the other, everyone's assets are perennially at risk. By contrast, during the stable environment of steady economic growth I foresee during the 1990s and beyond, investing will be comparatively easy, provided the investor is guided by good common sense and a basic understanding of how markets work.

In the rest of this chapter, I'll outline some basic principles for planning your finances during the coming global boom. The outlook, you'll recall from previous chapters, is for steady growth in the developed countries, probably averaging in the 3 percent range after inflation, although there will be much faster growth in newly industrializing countries like Thailand. I'm talking about averages here, of course. Growth rates in individual countries, as always, will fluctuate from year to year, and every country will have short recessions or low-growth spells once in a while to work out the imbalances that build up in every boom. The range of fluctuations, however, will not be wide, and the pauses will be short ones. There will be relatively low inflation. I think 3 percent, again, is a reasonable guess, although it may actually be considerably lower, down as low as 1 percent. Interest rates will be falling gently, settling down to a rate of about 2 to 3 percent above the base inflation rate on government paper. In the United States, the inflation in real estate values will end, savings will increase and will be shifted away from real estate into financial assets like stocks and bonds.

Some Basics of Investing

There are a couple of basic investing rules always to keep in mind. The first is the obvious point that in a well-functioning market, the higher the risk of an investment, the higher the reward. The second is that *volatility,* or the tendency of an asset to change in value over the short term, is a major form of risk. In much of this chapter, I will focus on the implications of this second rule.

The individual investor's problem is to earn as high a return as possible *at the level of risk* it is safe for him or her to absorb. The question is how do you figure out what your risk appetite should be? A useful way to approach that question is to think about risk in terms of volatility.

In general, the least volatile, and the lowest risk, investments are instruments like treasury bills. They are even less volatile than cash in a sock, because the interest rate they carry will usually make up for any loss of purchasing power due to inflation. They are very short-term investments—from thirty to ninety days—so there is little risk that inflation will change dramatically over their life. A reasonable return to expect on a treasury bill, then, is an interest rate pegged to compensate for inflation plus a small premium for the use of your money. In fact, over the past sixty years or so, treasury bills have returned on average a little more than 3 percent, roughly the rate of inflation plus a small premium. (For the past several years, the real return on bills has been quite high. That is because the Federal Reserve has been pushing up short-term interest rates to slow down the growth of the economy. That will not continue forever, of course.)

Stocks are at the opposite pole from treasury bills. Anyone who has watched the wild gyrations of the stock market in recent years knows that the value of stocks is very volatile over the short term. On October 19, 1987, the value of the Standard & Poor's 500 stocks dropped more than 20 percent. On October 13, 1989, the Standard & Poor's 500 stocks dropped 6 percent, with most of the drop in the last *hour*. Volatility is not the only risk in the stock market, of course. In theory, if the companies you own stock in become insolvent, you will lose your investment entirely. You cannot lose your investment in treasury bills, on the other hand, since the government can always print money to pay you back. As a practical matter, however, companies traded on the major exchanges do not become bankrupt overnight. The real risk is not that your stock investments will disappear, but that they will fluctuate dangerously in value.

Obviously, anyone with money in the stock market is substantially at risk from day to day. As a consequence, stocks may be expected to pay much higher rewards than treasury bills. And in fact they do. Over the past sixty years or so, stocks have returned, on average, counting dividends and capital gains, about 10 percent compounded annually, or about three times the returns paid by treasury bills over the same period. I will come back to this point.

Corporate bonds fall between treasury bills and stocks in

terms of risk and volatility. Their returns over the past sixty years, at about 4.4 percent, are actually closer to that of treasury bills. But the nature of the bond market has changed dramatically over the past decade, and I will reserve my comments on bonds till a later section. I should like now to look more closely at investing in stocks as a case of managing the quintessential risky investment.

❚ Making Money in Stocks

There are several ways of thinking abour risk in the stock market. One way is to distinguish between "systematic" risk and "unsystematic" risk. Systematic risk is risk that will affect almost every single stock. If there is a sudden spike in the inflation rate, for instance, prices for almost all stocks will usually fall. (There are always a few contrary investments in bad times—gold stocks, for instance.) If I am right in my forecast for the 1990s, the returns from investing in a broad portfolio of stocks—that is, accepting systematic risk—will be quite good.

"Unsystematic" risk is the risk that applies to an individual company. Companies fail even in good times. In fact, the volume of business failures often *increases* in good times, because capital is readily available and more people with bright ideas are starting businesses. Even if the economy is booming along quite nicely, if people don't like my new mouse trap, my business will fail. If you own stock in just one company, then you will be making a double bet. You will be betting that the company whose stock you own will be a success *and* you will be betting that business conditions as a whole will not be so adverse that they will drag down even good companies. You will be accepting both the systematic risk that applies to the market as a whole and the risk that your company won't do as well as you'd hoped—the unsystematic risk.

In general, then, it will be true that the fewer stocks you own, the more volatile and the more risky your portfolio will be. (There are always a few stocks, such as utilities, that are usually less volatile than the market as a whole, but one can never be sure they will continue to behave that way over the short term.) So it is safe to say that the more kinds of stocks you own, the closer your stock portfolio will approximate the market averages. It is possible, in fact it is easy, for professionals with the aid of computers to construct portfolios that will follow the overall market's performance almost to the penny. Such portfolios are called "indexed" portfolios. The closer a portfolio of stocks follows the overall market, the less unsystematic risk there is.

There is a different kind of volatility, and a different kind of risk, associated with the *length of time* you hold a portfolio. Unlike treasury bills, the stock market as a whole is very volatile from day to day. Most observers believe, in fact, that volatility has increased in recent years, as the string of "Black Mondays" and "Black Fridays" seem to attest. One reason for this is the use of computers by professional fund managers to generate very large volumes of trades.

Over the last decade, the markets have introduced a variety of new "derivative" instruments, such as "index options," that were supposed to help professional traders reduce the risk in their portfolios. Computer-oriented trading professionals have discovered ways to take advantage of tiny price changes in the derivative instruments compared to stocks to make large amounts of money by buying and selling huge amounts of stocks and derivative instruments at the same time. Such investment strategies are called "program trading." When the program traders enter the market in force, they will buy or sell millions of shares of stocks, and prices will gyrate wildly up or down for reasons that have nothing to do with the value of the underlying companies. If the small investor is on the wrong side of program-generated price swings, he will get murdered.

But now recall what I said about the stock market's performance over the long term—that consistent 10 percent annual rate of compound growth. The fact is that risk in the stock market diminishes greatly the longer you hold your shares. All of those wild day-to-day price swings tend to even out over time. Any randomly selected stock portfolio that was held for a full year at any time over the past sixty years was likely to lose value about one time in three. If the portfolio was held for five years, the chances of losses dropped to only one in nine. If it was held for ten years, the odds dropped to less than one in twenty-five.

To summarize, the average returns in the stock market overcompensate the long-term investor, for actual risk in the broad market over the long-term is quite modest. But they *under*compensate the short-term investor because the chances of losing money over, say, any given month are quite high.

Is it possible, then, to "beat" the market? No, it is not possible to beat it, but it is possible to invest to take advantage of the return structure built into it. The simple way is (1) to invest in a widely *diversified* portfolio of stocks to eliminate "unsystematic" risk, and (2) to invest over the long term—any money you are putting into the market you should plan to leave there for at least five years. I will come back to this point.

Should you worry about picking the right stocks? A few more facts about the market, and you will be able to answer that one yourself. Some fifteen years or so ago almost all stocks were owned and traded by individuals—ordinary people like you and me. Since then there has been a great rise in the share of stocks held by pension funds and other financial institutions, including mutual funds. Today, about 40 percent of all shares outstanding are held by institutions, but *90* percent of the trading is done by institutions. Let's consider what that means.

Before the markets came to be dominated by institutions, the professional portfolio manager had a substantial edge over the amateur. He could spend his whole day studying company reports, talking to other professionals, sniffing the winds from Washington. Since most buying and selling was done by individuals, often on the basis of little more than tips from Uncle Joe, it was reasonable to expect that, on average, the professional would come out on top. It's similar to the way professional poker players make money. If a top player sits down at a five-hand table of strangers, he will pick out the other good player in a couple of minutes—I'm told there's never more than one—then the two of them will proceed systematically to fleece the other three.

But now that the stock market is dominated by institutions, there are no more amateurs at the poker table. Every time a professional fund manager decides to buy a stock, some other professional fund manager has decided to sell it. Since the stock will either go up or down, one of them has obviously guessed wrong. (There are exceptions to this general statement, but they are not important here.) Since one professional will have guessed wrong and one will have guessed right on almost every stock transaction, one would expect, therefore, that, on average, professional fund managers would produce returns at about the average for the overall market.

In fact, they do worse than that. Professional managers tend to trade more than individuals, because, after all, buying and selling stocks is their *job*. So the cost of trading pulls their overall performance down. Add the fees that they charge, and their performance gets worse yet. As of 1989, professional managers as a group had failed to match market average returns in nine of the past fifteen years. For the first eleven months of 1989, almost 80 percent of professional stock managers failed to beat the Standard & Poor 500 index. Some managers beat the market every year, of course, but there is usually quite a different set of winners and losers each year. On average, and for obvious reasons, professional managers do somewhat less well than the "dartboard method," or simply picking a good selection of stocks at random. The point is, you can't beat the market by betting on individual stocks. You make money by investing in the widest portfolio possible. You want to invest in the *whole market*, not individual companies.

The rules for investing in stocks, then, are quite simple:

• Never put money into the stock market that you might need at any time in the next five years. If you are forced to sell stocks for medical bills or college tuition or some other emergency, you may find yourself selling during a downswing and end up taking a beating. In general, you shouldn't be buying stocks until you have at least one year's after-tax income in the bank, in a money market fund, in treasury bills, or in some other interest-paying cashlike investment. The amount of savings you need, however, will depend on your age, on whether you have children, or on how stable your job is. But in making those judgments, it's best to be conservative.

• Invest in a broadly diversified mutual fund or, better yet, several of them. (Check the fees and fee structures carefully;

they're often very complicated. "No load" funds are always much cheaper than funds that charge heavy up-front fees. Since you intend to leave your money there, you won't mind fees that are weighted toward charges for withdrawals.) My own preference is for fully indexed funds—that is, funds expressly designed to match a broad market average. They're usually the cheapest by far, they don't require a lot of high-priced stock-picking talent, and the risk over the long term is very low.

• Don't panic. The only people who took a loss on 1987's "Black Monday" (when stocks dropped more than 500 points) were the people who sold out. Just a few months later, the market was perking along quite nicely once again. Remember, you are in the market for the long term. If you have a broadly diversified portfolio, you needn't even bother reading the financial pages.

• Invest consistently. One of the best methods is so-called dollar-averaging—that is, investing a specific percentage of your salary each month. It's called dollar-averaging because sometimes you'll be buying when the market is high and sometimes you'll be buying when it is low. But on average you'll do just as well as if you tried to pick and choose when to enter and leave the market.

The next decade will be a very good time to be in stocks. You can protect your net worth and earn very good year-after-year returns if you follow the simple rules I've outlined here. Make your money work *with* the logic of the market, rather than trying to beat it at its own game.

One final word about the stock market is probably appropriate here. Although the decade of the 1990s will be good for investors, it will not be kind to Wall Street. I've mentioned the shift to computerized stock management at several points in this chapter. The fact is, after a decade of forced-draft growth to keep pace with the financial revolutions of the 1980s, Wall Street has become one of the most overstaffed, overpaid, and inefficient operations since Louis XIV's court at Versailles. As computerized efficiency begins to work its magic on Wall Street, as it is in most other service industries, a lot of high-paid jobs will disappear. Seen through Wall Street's eyes, this will look like an economic catastrophe. For the rest of us, it will be no such thing. It will be just one more step along the road to a true high-productivity society, the only source of real—as opposed to illusory—wealth.

What About Bonds and Other Instruments?

Bonds are much more complicated instruments than stocks. A bond's capital value will fluctuate with interest rates. In general, as interest rates rise, the capital value of a bond will fall; as interest rates fall, the capital value of a bond will rise. The longer the term of a bond, the more drastically its capital value will shift as interest rates change. For a bond with a short life, such as a treasury bill, the changes in capital value will be negligible. For a long-lived bond, the swings in capital value can be quite severe.

Investors in bonds also must be careful of "call provisions." Many bonds provide that the issuer (the institution that borrowed money by selling the bond) can "call" the bond at some stated price at prespecified times. What that means is that if interest rates fall, the issuer will be entitled to buy the bond back, usually at the original price, and the investor will lose the expected increase in capital value. (Many investors in municipal bonds or federal agency bonds, who think they are racking up big capital gains when rates drop, are shocked to see their gains disappear when their holdings are called.)

The attractiveness of bonds for some investors is that they often move in the opposite direction from stocks. Bonds therefore provide a rough "hedge" against the ups and downs in the stock market. Since you shouldn't be in the stock market anyway unless you are prepared to leave money there for a long time, hedging against temporary ups and downs shouldn't be a major concern.

For the average investor, a mutual fund–type portfolio of medium-term bonds (say, one to five years)—either governments or high-grade corporates—will pay somewhat higher returns than money-market funds and usually will offer somewhat less volatility than the stock market. You could consider bonds as a sort of halfway house for your money. That is to say, assume you have accumulated enough money in liquid cashlike accounts, so you can put your additional savings into stocks without losing sleep at night, and you are investing a regular amount of money each month in a broadly diversified or indexed stock mutual fund. You may then want to set aside perhaps 20 percent of the money you were targeting toward stocks and divert it into medium-term high-grade bonds. In a super-emergency, when you have already run through your cash resources, you run less risk of absorbing losses if you can choose between liquidating your bonds or some of your stocks.

For those with a more speculative appetite, long-term bonds, such as thirty-year treasuries, will offer very good capital appreciation opportunities in an environment of falling interest rates. But remember, such instruments are *extremely* volatile in the short term, and for the average investor they should never be more than a peripheral part of a portfolio.

Now what about junk bonds? Their name notwithstanding, there is nothing inherently wrong with good "junk." The modern junk bond market was pretty much the personal creation of Drexel Burnham's Michael Milken. Milken noticed that only the very largest companies had ready access to the corporate bond market. Smaller companies, which did not have "investment grade" ratings from the big rating agencies, had to pay a very high premium to raise money through bonds. The premium they paid, Milken calculated, was much higher than necessary to compensate investors for the actual risk of the borrower's default. Milken's great and lasting contribution to corporate finance was to create a virtually brand-new investment market where companies without "investment grade" ratings could borrow at reasonable rates. There are now about $200 billion worth of junk bonds outstanding.

The problem with financial markets, however, is that they are so prone to fads. Milken's junk bonds also turned out to be the ideal weapon for mounting hostile corporate takeovers. As takeovers became the magic elixir for lagging profits on Wall Street, takeover deals and the junk bonds associated with them became riskier and riskier. My own impression is that the great majority of takeover deals carried out between 1982 and, say, 1986, have worked out very well for the investors, including the junk bond holders. After 1986, almost all deals began to be overpriced, and the junk bonds associated with *them*, I believe, are very risky indeed. Not all of them, of course, but probably a majority.

The problem for the investor is that the risk in a portfolio of junk bonds will be very uneven. And unless you are a real expert in junk bonds, it is almost impossible to value one junk bond mutual fund over another. For the time being, at least, until the quality of information available to the average investor and the rating systems for junk bonds both improve dramatically, my advice is to stay away from them.

What about foreign stock funds? Over the past ten years or so, Asian funds in particular have shown spectacular growth. The danger for an American investor, of course—unless you have a chateau in the foothills of Mt. Fuji—is that you are piling *currency* risk on top of all the other risks we have been discussing. If your Japanese stock fund is up by 20 percent, for instance, a 20-percent appreciation of the dollar against the yen will wipe out all your gains. (At the end of the day, presumably, you will want dollars for your stock. When the dollar appreciates, it takes more yen to buy the same amount of dollars. In the example I gave, the extra cost of buying dollars will eat up all of your yen profits in the stock market.)

As investment markets continue to globalize throughout the 1990s, sooner or later the major trading nations will work out a smoother functioning system for maintaining stable currency relations than we have at present. But that day is still a good way off. For the time being, foreign stock funds, like long-term treasuries, or junk bonds, should be distinctly labeled "risky"—playthings for investors who have all of their other requirements taken care of and who can afford to indulge in a few rolls at the casino.

Finally, a word on real estate. I've discussed the prospects for real estate at length in Chapter 5. Think of your real estate as a place to live—that's all. Your home will probably hold its own with inflation (inflation will be low during the next decade anyway), but it will *not* offer a big opportunity for capital gains. So think of your monthly mortgage payment as rent. Above all, don't plunge over your head into an expensive house with the expectation that a rising real estate market will make you rich. That day is over for a long time.

The same, of course, applies to a second home. Buy a second home because you plan to *use* it, not as an investment. In general, you should already have saved your cash reserve and already be well on the way toward building a stock portfolio before you spend money on a second home. And the money you use should be *additional* money, not the money from your basic investment program.

You will not have to be a financial genius to make good returns in the coming decade. Over the longer term, stock markets will grow steadily, interest rates will trend gently down, and inflation should stay well under control. Sensible investing, good common sense, and a healthy skepticism of gimmicks can guarantee that you will reap the full fruits of the coming global boom.

A FINAL SUMMING UP

This is not a "feel-good" book. Some parts of the message are harsh. An investor who has plunged heavily into real estate, a stock trader facing obsolescence because of computerized trading programs, a factory worker whose company is changing too slowly to keep pace with a new foreign "transplant" factory, a middle manager in a vertically integrated conglomerate—all of these people will have reason to be concerned, even alarmed, by the changes that are afoot in the American and the world economies.

We are living amid a swirl of transition. For the last twenty years we've witnessed an exhausting cycle of oil crises, inflationary seizures, and sudden recessions. In America, our military and industrial pretensions have been cruelly undercut. Some of our proudest and oldest companies have been laid waste. New competitors from all over the world have invaded every market. Large sections of the industrial landscape have been virtually shut down—uprooting families, confusing children, and demoralizing parents.

The transitions are not over. Basic industries, such as steel and automobiles, have made enormous progress in stripping down to essentials, hacking away at the encrusted habits that are the residue from the years of complacent world dominance. But, as the continued struggle of the automobile companies shows, there is still a long way to go.

It is easy to dwell on the pain inflicted by major transitions. Few commentators, in fact, talk about much else. Preoccupied by the push and pull of daily events, we miss the significance of what we have been through and where the transition is taking us. But if we crane our necks just a bit, adopt a slightly broader perspective, the direction of the forces driving the world economy are strikingly clear. They are pointing to an end of the long period of dislocation and to much brighter days ahead.

In the industrial world, we are swiftly completing the transition to global markets for goods. Companies, large and small, are forming world-spanning strategic alliances, competing simultaneously in every major market. Global competition is speeding the diffusion of high-productivity manufacturing technology in every advanced country. As global companies spread their manufacturing and marketing operations around the world, they are breaking through the barriers that protect local inefficiencies, whether of labor or management, and are driving an inexorable convergence of manufacturing and service quality and productivity.

The technological convergence is mirrored by a convergence of consumer tastes and consumer demands for higher quality at the lowest price throughout the world. Global standards of quality and productivity are clamping a firm lid on inflation. Low inflation and high productivity will feed into a healthy cycle of growth and renewal.

The restructuring of world industries that has taken place on such an unprecedented scale over the past decade would, by itself, be a momentous event. But there is much more going on.

The United States is completing a major demographic transition. The generation that was born in the decade or so following World War II, 50 percent larger than the one that preceded it, is turning forty, entering the stage of life characteristically marked by high productivity, by thrift, by stability. As savings rise, and with the country's housing needs finally taken care of, the baby boomers will begin to carry their weight, pay back for their years of dependency, and provide the capital pools both for continued industrial expansion and to finance their own retirements.

Finally, governments in the industrialized countries as a whole are reducing their demands on their citizens. For the first time in many years, industrial country debt has begun to fall, measured against productive capacity. The sudden prospect of sharply reduced military spending adds impetus to the trend. The reduced drag of government will further ease the problem of capital formation. And the sudden prospect of dynamic new Eastern European economies, adding their markets and energies to the emerging global boom, is pure bonus.

None of these developments is hypothetical. Global markets and global companies are facts. The wave of strategic alliances and partnerships recasting the map of the industrial world is a fact. The sharp rise in manufacturing productivity over the past decade in every industrialized country is a fact. The convergence in quality and productivity in, say, the newest American and Japanese automobile factories or semiconductor foundries is a fact. The radical shift in the American age profile is taking place right now. So is the steady rundown in industrialized-country debt. Only the projected decline in military spending and the opening of the Eastern European economies are not quite yet facts, but the events that Mikhail Gorbachev has set in motion are rapidly approaching the point of no return.

These are all transcendent events. It is no wonder that mainstream economists pay so little attention to them. They are not neat linear developments, of the kind that can be captured easily by mathematical models. That is why Schumpeter's analytical framework fits current events so well. Schumpeter thought in terms of phase changes, of economies lurching through fundamental transitions—long periods of dislocation dominated by demographic changes, industrial restructuring, technological upheavals. The eras of dislocation are followed by periods of stability and progress, by extended economic golden ages, as all the rambunctious change gets sorted out and settled down.

We are emerging from just such a period of dislocation and are on the threshold of just such a "golden age," an extended global economic boom stretching at least through the decade of the 1990s and probably beyond.

Economic prosperity by itself will not solve problems of drug addiction or racial tensions, or perhaps even homelessness. An economic boom in the developed countries will not insure peace and prosperity for the miserable, and growing, populations in the world's most impoverished areas, such as sub-Saharan Africa. Economic prosperity, that is, will not mean an end to all of our problems. But for the first time in a long time, we should have spiritual and economic resources enough to solve them.

SOURCE NOTES

General: To avoid repetitious notes, all data on the U.S. economy, population, labor force, and output, unless specifically noted, come from the standard statistical services and publications of the U.S. Department of Commerce, the U.S. Bureau of Labor Statistics, and other federal agencies. I also omit detailed citations for recent news or business events that were extensively covered in the general or business press.

INTRODUCTION

For examples of the gloom hypothesis, see Ravi Batra, *Great Depression of 1990,* Venus Books, Dallas TX. 1985. Revised Ed. Simon & Schuster, 1987; Paul Erdman, *The Panic of 1989;* Doubleday, NY, 1987 and for the Marris/Bergsten view, see *The Economist,* July 2, 1988 and September 24, 1988. Yardeni quotations, unless otherwise noted, are from interviews. For Schumpeter, see Joseph Schumpeter, *Capitalism, Socialism & Democracy,* Harper & Brothers, NY, 1942 and *Business Cycles,* McGraw-Hill, NY, 1939. For sources for the material summarized in this section, see the notes to the main discussion below.

1

BIG BUSINESS GOES GLOBAL

For a summary of the relations between the automotive majors, see "How the World's Automakers Are Related, 1988–89 Edition," *Ward's Automotive International,* supplemented by various articles from the trade press—Wards *Automotive, Wards Communications,* Detroit, MI. and *Automotive Yearbook* and Chilton's *Automotive Industries,* Chilton Co. Radnor, PA. and interviews with Ward's analysts. The data on America's "industrial humiliation" are drawn, for the most part, from the Report of the MIT Commission on Industrial Productivity: Michael L. Dertouzas, Richard K. Lester, and Robert M. Solow, *Made in America,* MIT Press, Cambridge, MA. 1989, including particularly the two-volume supplement of working papers. (I should say that the book's well-publicized conclusions do not track well with its case studies, which exhibit far more recovery and restructuring than fits the editors' polemic. But the case studies themselves are invaluable.) All the data here were confirmed with U.S. Commerce Department industry analysts. The quote from David Hale (he is the chief economist of Kemper Financial Services) is from his unpublished paper "The Post-Chicago Era in American Economic Policy," November 1988, p. 2. I am grateful to him for sending it to me.

For a long list of industrial partnership examples, particularly ones including Japanese partners, see Kenichi Ohmae, "The Global Logic of Strategic Alliances," *Harvard Business Review,* March–April 1989, pp. 143–154, *Triad Power,* Free Press, NY. 1985 and *Beyond National Borders,* Dow-Jones-Irwin, Homewood, IL. 1987. The Becton-Dickinson story is from Marquise R. Cvar's "Case Studies in Global Competition: Patterns of Success and Failure" in *Competition in Global Industries,* Harvard Business School Press, Boston, MA. 1986, Michael E. Porter, ed., supplemented by material provided by the company. There are also good case studies, including detailed examinations of the Philips and Procter & Gamble strategies, in *Managing Across Borders: the Transnational Solution* (Boston, 1989), by Christopher Bartlett and Sumantra Ghoshal. The Takenaka, Schulhof, Altman, and Tarr quotes are from interviews.

Steven H. Nagourney's "Audacious Change," *Shearson Lehman Hutton,* January 17, 1989, is an excellent discussion, within a Schumpeterian framework, of many of the issues introduced in this chapter.

Profile: GE-FANUC

The statistical data on the machine-tool industry is drawn for the most part from the industry working-papers supplement to Dertouzos, *op. cit.* The market data in this profile were developed from a variety of analyst's reports. The material on the company comes from interviews and visits with the company.

2

The Third Industrial Revolution

Galbraith is quoted in Robert H. Hayes, Stephen C. Wheelwright, and Kim B. Clark, *Dynamic Manufacturing,* Free Press, NY 1988, p. 53. A capsule history of the Japanese quality movement is in David A. Garvin's *Managing Quality,* Free Press, NY 1988. The JEMCO/Plus example is from Hayes, *ibid.* pp. 175–76. IBM quality improvement was cited in a speech by Jack Kuehler, the company president, on September 21, 1989. The Toyota manual is *Kan-Ban, JIT at Toyota,* Productivity Press, Cambridge, MA. 1986. The Turner quotes are from Harvard Business School, "Note on the Motorcycle Industry—1975" (Note 578–210, 1978). Data on the Caterpillar factory investment program were furnished by the company. For Xerox's and Chaparall's "benchmarking" and related quotes see *The New York Times,* November 9, 1989. The wrong turns at General Motors are chronicled in Maryann Keller, *Rude Awakening,* Morrow, NY 1989. The international productivity comparisons in this chapter are calculated by the U.S. Department of Commerce. The best discussion of productivity and productivity comparisons available is William J. Baumol, Sue Anne Batey Blackman, and Edward N. Wolff, *Productivity & American Leadership;* MIT Press, Camb. MA 1989. It is absolutely essential reading for anyone seriously interested in the issue. Martin Neil Bailey and Alok K. Chakrabarti, *Innovation & the Productivity Crisis,* Brookings Institution, Washington, DC. 1988, also has a good discussion of the service measuring problem.

On implications of flexible manufacturing, see Stanley J. Feldman, "The Third Industrial Revolution and Prospects for Long-Term Growth," *Data Resources U.S. Long-Term Review* Fall, 1987. The Ted Levitt quotes are from his "The Pluralization of Consumption," *Harvard Business Review,* May–June 1988, pp. 7–8. The information on Allen-Bradley's contactor plant was provided by the company. For data on American applications of flexible manufacturing, see Ramchandran Jaikumar,

"Postindustrial Manufacturing," *Harvard Business Review,* November–December 1986, pp. 69–78, and Robert H. Hayes and Ramchandran Jaikumar, "Manufacturing's Crisis: New Technologies, Obsolete Organizations," *ibid.,* September–October 1988, pp. 77–85. And also see Dertouzas, *op. cit.,* working papers on the automotive industry. The quote on American automotive competitiveness is from *ibid.,* p. 187. Abbe's comments are from an interview. The data on color-television-set manufacture were provided by the U.S. Department of Commerce.

PROFILE: CUMMINS ENGINE

The market data in this profile were developed from a variety of analyst's reports. The material on the company comes from interviews and visits with the company.

3

GLOBAL "DIS-INTEGRATION"

For the early history of U.S. Steel and Standard Oil, see, e.g., Mathew Josephson, *The Robber Barons,* Harcourt Brace & Co., NY 1934 and Allen Nevins, *John D. Rockefeller,* Scribners, NY. 1940. Much of the material in this chapter on American and Japanese automotive industries is drawn from Davis Dyer, Malcolm S. Salter, and Alan M. Webber, *Changing Alliances,* Harvard Business School Press, Boston, MA. 1985, a comprehensive history through the mid-1980s, supplemented by the trade press. The Feiger and Wood quotes are from interviews. For the positive side of the recent corporate takeover boom, see Harvey H. Segal, *Corporate Makeover,* Viking, NY. 1989 and Michael C. Jensen, "Eclipse of the Public Corporation," *Harvard Business Review,* September–October 1989, pp. 61–75, an important article. Articles making the counter case are too numerous to mention. For the civil jet aircraft industry, see the industry working-papers supplement to Dertouzas *op. cit.* James Dykes's quotes are from a speech to the Semiconductor Industry Conference, January 1988. On the evolving supplier relationships in the automotive industry, and the Reuss quotation, see *The Economist,* July 29, 1989, p. 53.

PROFILE: INTERMET FOUNDRIES

The market data in this profile were developed from a variety of analysts' reports. The material on the company comes from interviews and visits with the company.

4

THE AGING "ARCHIPELAGO OF YOUTH"

For the impact of the baby boom generation, see Landon Jones, *Great Expectations,* Coward, McCann & Geohegan, NY 1980; Richard Easterlin, *Birth & Fortune,* Basic Books, NY 1980, *Baby Boom Generation,* Brookings Institution, Washington, DC. 1982; and Charles R. Morris, *A Time of Passion,* Harper & Row, NY. 1982. On the impact of the aging of the baby boomers, see Edward Yardeni and Amalia Quintana, "The Baby Boom Chart Book," *Prudential-Bache Securities Topical Study #16,* January 25, 1989; and Edward Yardeni and David Moss, "The New Wave Manifesto," *Prudential-Bache Securities Topical Study #15,* October 5, 1988. Margaret K. Ambry's *1990–1991 Almanac of Consumer Markets* is also very useful.

The fact that *gross* capital spending has been strong is usually obscured by focusing on the relatively anemic rate of *net* capital spending. It's a good example of how shaky statistics are at the root of so much of the current despair. Gross capital spending data are hard enough to collect by themselves and have wide margins of error. *Net* capital spending takes an already shaky data series and refines it by subtracting a hypothetical rate of depreciation from the investment data. Alan Meltzer of the Carnegie-Mellon Institute reports that the depreciation schedules are based on research done in 1939—the so-called Winfrey's Rules. When Meltzer attempted to apply more up-to-date depreciation schedules, much, but not all, of the apparent investment shortfall disappeared.

PROFILE: CLUB MED

Most of the material on the company comes from interviews and visits. There is also a helpful compilation of Club Med and competitive data in the Harvard Business School "Club Med" case study, 9-687-046, 1986, 1988, and related teaching notes.

5

THE COMING REAL ESTATE BUST AND WHY IT'S GOOD FOR AMERICA

Virtually all the data in this chapter were developed by Comstock Partners. For the impact of demographic change on housing markets, see also Louise B. Russell, *op. cit.,* 102–118. The quote from Adam Smith is from his *Paper Money,* Summit Books, NY 1981, p. 98, which contains an excellent discussion of housing inflation in the 1970s. The quote from Charles Clough is from an interview.

6

DISAPPEARING DEFICITS

For an exhaustive compilation of the empirical research on the effects of budget deficits, see U.S. Department of the Treasury, "The Effects of Deficits on Prices of Financial Assets: Theory and Evidence" (Washington, D.C., 1984); see also Paul Evans's "Do Budget Deficits Raise Nominal Interest Rates? Evidence from Six Countries," *Journal of Monetary Economics,* 20 (1987), pp. 281–300. In addition to the excellent Bernstein and Heilbroner book mentioned in the text, see Peter L. Bernstein, "All the things Deficits Really Don't Do," *Wall Street Journal,* November 10, 1988. And see Robert S. Barro, "The Ricardian Approach to Budget Deficits," Rochester Center for Economic Research, Working Paper No. 148; and *The Economist,* "Budgets and Mr. Barro," December 16, 1988; and also C. Carroll and L. H. Summers, "Why Have Private Savings Rates in the United States and Canada Diverged?" in *Journal of Monetary Economics,* 20 (1987), pp. 249–79. This section was immeasurably improved by an extended telephone conversation with Milton Friedman. For savings and loan debt treatment, see *Congressional Budget Office Staff Memorandum:* "The Savings and Loan Problem: A Discussion of the Issues," February 1989. For social security projections, see "The 1988 Annual Report of the Board of Trustees of the Federal Old Age and Survivors' Insurance and the Federal Disability Trust Funds" (Washington, D.C., 1988), Appendix G, p. 139.

Obie W. Whichard of the U.S. Department of Commerce has been quite helpful in advancing my understanding of the data on America's international debt. The

Department's *Survey of Current Business* contains a series of useful articles each June explicating the American–foreign asset position. See, in particular, Jack Bame, "A Note on the U.S. as a Net Debtor Nation," in the June 1985 issue, p. 28. Perhaps the best-known—in my view, the most egregious example—of the alarmist view of international debt is Benjamin M. Friedman's *Day of Reckoning,* Random House, NY 1988. For the potential shortage of government bonds, see Lenny Glynn, "The Great Government Bond Shortage," *Institutional Investor,* July 1989, pp. 213–16, and Roland Leuschel, "A Looming Shortage of Government Bonds," *Wall Street Journal,* January 17, 1989.

PROFILE: BEA ASSOCIATES

The material in this section is based on an interview with Mark Arnold and materials provided by BEA. Arnold's *Institutional Investor* quote is from Glynn, *op. cit.*

7
BARRIERS AND FORTRESS

The extensive trade data cited in this chapter are all from the standard U.S. Department of Commerce compilations, except for the value of Japanese overseas manufacturing, which was provided by the Bank of Japan. The analyses are my own. The Morita/Ishihara book is *The Japan That Can Say "No": The New U.S.-Japan Relations Card* Kobunsha, Kappa-Holmes, Tokyo, 1989. There is no official translation, but bootleg English translations have been widely circulated in the American business and government community. It consists of alternating chapters written by Morita and Ishihara.

PROFILE: CANADA BETS ON FREE TRADE

The Canadian material in this section relies on an extensive collection of company reports, news clippings, and other materials assembled by the research staff at Devonshire Partners. The material on the steel import quota fight was provided by Caterpillar. For the effects of the DRAM restraints, see *The Economist,* "Survey of Japanese Technology," December 2, 1989. The Semiconductor Industry Association points out, correctly, that similar import restraints on EPROMs did not have the same devastating effects, but appears to concede that the DRAM restraints were a disaster. (Interview with Gary Bonham, a member of the SIA Public Information Committee.)

8
MARX AND LENIN MEET ADAM SMITH

Gorokhov's LBO is reported in *The Economist,* September 22, 1989, p. 51. For the decline of the Soviet economy in recent years, see Seweryn Bialer's excellent *Soviet Paradox,* Knopf, NY 1986. In addition, for the current Soviet economic decline, American military spending and planning priorities, and the history of previous attempts to reduce arms spending, see Charles R. Morris, *Iron Destinies, Lost Opportunities,* Harper & Row, NY 1988. Robert B. Reich's criticisms of American technology policy is in his "The Quiet Path to Technological Preeminence," *Scientific American,* October 1989, pp. 41–47.

9

CAN AMERICA COMPETE?

David Hale's paper, *op. cit.,* includes an extensive statistical appendix and was a major source for data in this chapter. I appreciate his sending it to me. For Japanese worker output, see, e.g., *The Economist,* April 29, 1989, p. 61. For Peter F. Drucker, see his "Japan's Choices," *Foreign Affairs,* Summer 1987, pp. 923–941.

The market share data for the computer industry in this chapter was provided by Gary Bonham of LSI Logic and the SIA. A number of people at LSI Logic were very helpful in broadening my understanding of computer industry issues. The Prestowitz quote is from "Computers: Japan Comes On Strong," *Business Week,* October 23, 1989, p. 106. The same article is the source of the "MITI as Sugardaddy" quote later in the chapter (p. 112). George Gilder's argument is in his *Microcosm,* Simon & Schuster, NY. 1989. The Dataquest analyst quoted is Chris Willard in an interview.

For a generally hostile view of the Japanese system, and one that emphasizes the role of directive economic management from the government, see Chalmers Johnson, *MITI & Japanese Miracle,* Stanford University Press, Stanford, CA. 1982; Karl van Wolferen, *Enigma of Japanese Power,* A. A. Knopf, NY. 1989; and James Fallows, "Containing Japan," *The Atlantic Monthly,* May 1989, pp. 40–54. For the more hopeful view, see Bill Emmontt, *The Sun Also Sets,* Times Books, 1989 and his "The Limits to Japanese Power," *The Amex Bank Review Special Papers No. 16,* October 1988. I find Emmott's line of reasoning by far the more convincing and essentially follow it in this section. The Nissan advertisement was quoted in *The Economist,* October 27, 1989, p. 80. For demographic changes in Japan, see "Aging and Social Expenditure for the Major Industrial Countries, 1980–2025," *International Monetary Fund Occasional Paper No. 47,* November 1988. The indifferent success of recent Japanese forays into industrial policy is from Drucker, *op. cit.*

PROFILE: LSI LOGIC

The material on LSI Logic comes from interviews and visits with the company.

10

WHAT COULD GO WRONG?

The abbreviated version of my argument here is Charles R. Morris, "The Coming Global Boom," *The Atlantic Monthly,* October 1989, pp. 51–64. For a series of articles on the industrialized world's stake in the undeveloped countries, see the Summer 1989 issue of *International Security,* including Stephen M. Walt, "The Case for Finite Containment: Analyzing U.S. Grand Strategy," pp. 5–49; Steven R. David, "Why the Third World Matters," pp. 50–85; Michael C. Desch, "The Keys that Lock Up the World: Identifying American Interests in the Periphery," pp. 86–121; and Robert H. Johnson, "The Persian Gulf in U.S. Strategy: A Skeptical View," pp. 122–60. The energy reserve estimates are from *The New York Times,* October 15, 1989. For a summary of the science of the Greenhouse Effect, see Stephen H. Schneider, "The Changing Climate," *Scientific American,* September 1989, pp. 70–79. Mancur Olson's book is *Rise & Decline of Nations,* Yale University Press, New Haven, CT. 1982.

11

AN INVESTMENT STRATEGY FOR THE 1990S

A recent summary of long-term investment returns to various instruments is in *Fortune*, Fall 1989 Special Issue, p. 32. Data on performance of professional portfolio managers were provided by the Vanguard Group Inc., except for the 1989 data, which is from Lipper Analytics, as reported in *The New York Times*, December 31, 1989.

INDEX